Military System of the Mughals

Military System of the Mughals

Edited by

Dr. Raj Kumar

Commonwealth

Military System of the Mughals

First Published : 2004

ISBN 81-7169-858-1

Published by :

Ajay Verma
***for* COMMONWEALTH PUBLISHERS**
4831/24, Prahlad Street,
Ansari Road, Darya Ganj,
New Delhi - 110002
Ph. : 23272541, 23257835
Fax : 91- 011- 23257835
e-mail : campusbooks@hotmail.com

Laser Typesetting by :

Arjun Computers
Delhi - 110051

Printed at :
Roshan Offset Printers
Delhi

Preface

Military System of the Mughal was Turkish in its origins and retained the Turkish character and words to the end.

With their introduction of the two arms, cavalry and artillery, warfare entered a new stage in India. The two arms constituted a formidable instrument for the Mughuls to conquer and to hold their vast empire in India. But warfare remained a tumultuous and desultory affair as in the past. No effort was made to develop the art of war. Hence no military tradition developed under them.

In this work an attempt has been made to give an account of military system of the Mughuls. The work is expected to be of use to the general readers. All those who want to work on the military systems, students, teachers and policy makers will find it extremely helpful.

Acknowledgement

Authorities consulted on the subject namely William Irvine, Mohd. Habib, John Briggs, F. Bernier, Abdul Aziz, J.N. Sarkar and R.C. Butalia. We are indebted to them.

My friends and colleagues at the United Service Institute specially Gen. Y.M. Bummi has helped me in various ways. I am grateful to them.

The chief librarian of U.S.I., I.R. Kumar and his staff members have been very kind and extremely helpful. I am thankful to them.

Last but not the least B.R. Verma, my publishers, Ajay, Amit and their staff members have rendered me all possible help in preparing this work. They deserve love and kindness of my readers.

[illegible]

Acknowledgement

[illegible]

Contents

1
Introduction

Beginning with the invasions of Sultan Mohammad of Ghori, India remained the scene of constant warfare for a period of over one thousand years. Warfare during this period was between the invaders and the defenders of their hearths and homes, their national honour and integrity. . . in the first instance; between the successive invaders and the Muslim authority earlier established in the second, and finally between the invaders and the local rulers, who refused to accept the new authority until completely defeated in the field.

Despite the fact that the invaders were all Muslims, the period of their rule in India may only technically be called 'Muslim'. Throughout the period, there was a constant process of inter-mingling, inter-mixture and assimilation, which commenced immediately after the fall of Jayachandra and ultimately, triumphed under Akbar, the greatest of Mughal Emperors who was born in India and who adopted India as his own country.

Of all the countries in the world, India alone had the honour of accepting and accommodating in a truly national manner, the section of her people, who came to be known as Indian Muslims.

The first Muslim invasions of India were "Punitive expeditions". Gradually, however, they assumed the proportions of 'crusades' or 'Jehad' calculated to destroy the infidels and consign to oblivion, 'indolatory' which was not the genius of Islam. The so called 'Empire of Delhi, which the Muslim invaders sought to set up was, for a very long period, a province within hail and easy control of the capital, and it varied in extent with the range of ruler's power. The dynasty, which welded India into a gorgeous empire began with Babar and the man, who saw the dream, realized, was Akbar the Great. The armies under Akbar may, therefore, be taken as the highest mark of efficiency achieved by them, in the sphere of organization administration and field performance.

Babar

Babar, who has been recognized as a military genius in his own right (some of the military historians have gone to the extent of equating him with Changez Kahn and Taimur Lung), came to the throne of Franghana, a small principality on the eastern border of Persia, when he was only eleven years old. He had to face 'the shifting moods of capricious fortune' many a time until he was twenty-two. A prince of great humility, bold and adventurous, Babar was nurtured in the 'school of hardship'. His liberality bordered prodigality. A staunch believer in the Higher Power, he always thought that all issues in his life were fore-ordained and that Power manifested itself in all important events of his life. He lived in the age of great rulers... the age of Charles V, Francis I, Henry VIII and Suleman the magnificent ... The child of the central Asian steppes, some have regarded Babar 'in certain ways the greatest and most attractive of all'.

Babar's Invasions

Military historians are not agreed as to how many times Babar invaded India. They have, however, agreed that it was while Babar was in Kabul trying to bring about an ordered state of things, that the idea of invading the wide plains of Hindustan occurred to him. Conditions in India at that time were such as would definitely favour a bold adventurer like Babar. The old empire of Delhi was in name only. India was governed by the Lodhis in the Kingdom of Delhi, by Sultan Muzaffar in Gujrat, Nasrat Khan in Bengal, the Bahmani rulers in the Deccan, Maharana Sanga in Chittoor and the Raja of Vijayawada in South. There was no defensive alliance between them and there was not the remotest possibility of putting up combined resistance to any invader.

Babar's first invasion in January, 1505 was a mere raid, "a

grab and gallop affair", lasting for only four months after which he returned to his capital Kabul". His second invasion took place in the beginning of 1519, when he suddenly descended upon the territory known as Nilab and claimed Punjab, because the region, had once conquered and occupied by the house of Taimur. However, he returned to Kabul in March, the same year. About the end of 1519, Babar embarked upon his third invasion, and the objective this time was the reduction of Lahore. In 1520, he marched against India for the fourth time; but had to rush back, because the Arghuns of Kandhar had attacked Kabul. It was only after settling the affairs in Kabul that he found himself ready for decisive action against India. Babar campaigned in India for several years and ultimately his conquests comprised of the greater part of Rajputana, the Muslim Kingdoms in the north of Jumna and of the Ganga, as far as the western boundaries of Bengal.

Akbar the Great

Death of Babar removed for the scene the 'strong hand', so urgently needed to 'nurse the infant empire', which was not yet secure. The empire had been built by sword and could be retained by sword alone. Since the sword was virtually absent, separatist and fissiparous tendencies pushed themselves to the fore. The conditions deteriorated so much and so quick that under Humayun, who was given to indolent life as no monarch should, that when Akbar came to the throne on 14th February, it was nothing but a plain brick structure of 18 ft. long and 5 ft. high ...there was virtually no territory to claim. It must stand to the genius of Akbar that from scratch, he emerged as the wealthiest ruler in Asia and perhaps in Europe too. Prior to Akbar, his predecessors like Allauddin Khilji had, from time to time, conquered the major part of Northern India. But such conquests were in the nature of marauding campaigns. Akbar was the first Muslim ruler to conceive and achieve a consolidated empire in India, so bound together that the writ of his government ran throughout the dominions.

MUGHAL ARMED FORCES

The most significant feature of the Muslim rule in India was the constant process of assimilation by the Indians. Throughout the period, the invaders who crossed into the Indian territory, conquered and seduced whatever local chiefs they could and settle down in the country, giving up all their past association and attachment with their original homeland. Throughout the period, there was constant inter-mixture with the result that all branches of administration, not excluding the armed forces, were mixed in command and personnel. It is most significant to note that an Indian named Hemu, who was the Minister of Mohammed Shah Adil and the Commander of his forces, led a vast Afghan army contesting the title of Muslim prince to India's sovereignty. Strangely enough, it was Raja Man Singh, who was one of the ablest generals under Akbar, wielded the "sword of Islam" against Maharana Pratap. However, following were the outstanding characteristics of the Mughal armed forces.

Numerical Strength

It has not been possible to establish the exact numerical strength of the armed forces under the Mughal emperors. Military commentators are also not agreed on the number of armed forces committed to any particular battle. This is attributed to the peculiar system of recruitment, muster, training and discipline. Soldiers, it is said, were not entertained directly by the Emperor and they were not in the 'Service of the State' as in understood by the words today. For the most part they joined service with some chief or leader. These chiefs were ranked according to the number of men that they could raise. In this way, originated the system of 'Mansabs', first introduced by Akbar. This mode of recruiting the army through these chiefs or leaders, rendered it necessary to begin by a statement of the manner in which these officers themselves were appointed or graded. In Ain-i-Akbari, sixty-six grades of 'Mansabs' are mentioned. They begin with commanders of 10,000 and end at those set over ten men. The highest 'Mansab' that could be held by a subject not of the Royal House, was that of a commander of 7,000 men, though in later and more degenerated times, instances of promotion to 8,000 or even 9,000 men are found.

Discipline

According to European commentators, discipline in the Mughal armed forces was extremely lax, if not entirely absent. It seems to have been a very common practice with the chiefs to lend their men to each other to make up their respective strength when occasions required. It further appears that, very frequently, idlers from the bazar were mounted on the first baggage pony that came to hand and were caused to be counted with other on strength and efficient. There was no regimental organization. The only divisions known were those created by reason of each chief or noble having his own following of troops. The chiefs, for the most part constituted the command structure and conducted the battle with whatever inter-coordination could be possible under the circumstances. There definitely, was nothing like the centralized direction of war and the officer hierarchy.

As for the uniforms, the only sign of its originally was a red turban worn by all in the Imperial employ. For the great mass of the Army, there was usually no uniformity of dress. In a general way, however, each class of troops. Mughals, Persians, Hindustani Muslims, Rajputs, etc., dressed in a similar style. There seems to have been no drill for the soldiers and no training in combined movements of any sort. From time to time, nobles paraded their troops during public audiences when the state of horses and elephants were observed. These alone could be considered 'inspection parades' of a sort.

Branches of Service—Cavalry

According to William Irvine, 'Mughal army was essentially an army of horsemen.' Mughals from across the Oxus were accustomed to fight on horseback only. The foot soldier, they despised and in artillery they never became proficient. According to Orme, 'Under Mughals, the strain of all war rested upon the numbers of horsemen and goodness of the horses which were found in the army.' The Mughal bowmen were specially expert with their weapons. It is said that a Mughal horseman could shoot six times before a musketeer could fire twice.

Artillery

Commenting on this arm of service, William Irvine says : "It is doubtful if the Mughals knew much before they descended into the plains under Babar. What they knew was probably borrowed from the Turks and from Constantinople. Nor could the art and science of gunnery have been very advanced in India itself when the Mughals arrived. It their earlier period at any rate, the Mughal Emperors were dependent for artillery on the help and instructions of 'Rumis', Mohammadans from Constantinople or 'Feranghis' principally runaway sailors from Surat or, Portuguese half castes."

The general name for artillery under the Mughals was 'Topkhana'. It was generally divided into two categories : the heavy and the light artillery. The latter was given several names. More frequently used names in the Mughal military nomenclature were Topkhana-i-Rezah, or 'small artillery'. 'Topkhana-i-Jumbshi', or 'movable or mobile artillery', 'Topkhana-i-Jinisi', 'Miscellaneous artillery'. The various departments in the Service were : (1) Manufacturing Department. (2) Magazine or Ordnance Department. (3) Field Artillery in actual use. (4) Guns is use with the forts and fortresses. The Mughals seem to have been very fond of large pieces and they gave them very pompous names. According to Dr. Horn, 'Under Akbar, the artillery reached the highest point of efficiency which it ev r attained during the existence of the Mughal empire. According to William Irvine, however, 'artillery was much more perfect and numerous in Alamgir's reign that it was under his great-grandfather, Akbar.'

Infantry

This arm of service, held a very inferior position and was of little or no consideration. According to Orme, the infantry consisted of a multitude of people assembled without regard to rank or file; some with swords and targets, who could never stand the shock of a body of horse; some bearing matchlocks, which in the best of the order, could produce, but a very uncertain fire; some armed with lances, too long or too weak to be of any service even if ranged with the utmost regularity of discipline. The main service of the infantry under the Mughals seems to have been night watches and plunder of defenseless people. 'Their main *raison d'etre* in the armed forces were the chief or the nobles who received a fixed sum for every man and hired every man at a different and lesser price.'

Elephants

In his accounts of the Mughal armies, Dr. Horn includes the elephants. He, however, does not mention them as a separate department or arm of service. Most military commentators have agreed with the account of Dr. Horn because it is contended that with the introduction of fire-arms and the gradual extension of their use in wars, elephants ceased to be of much value in the fighting line of the battle. They also contend that long before the fall of the Mughal empire in decay, the elephants had become principally beasts of burden or means of display and their role in battle had become comparatively insignificant. Akbar seems to have made much use of elephants protected with armour, to carry into battle his musketeers, small cannons, generals, nobles and the women of the harem. The object of mounting generals and commanders on elephants seems to have been that they should be seen from a distance by all troops whose morale and battle efficiency was always so critically dependent upon the presence of the commander in their midst. Elephants, provided with large iron plates fixed on their foreheads, also seem to have been used to better-in the gates of fortified places.

Forts and Sieges

Ancient Indian practice of having walled and fortified cities and the science and art of siege warfare was not abandoned by the Mughals. Actually, it seems to have been carried many steps further. Some of the forts built by the Mughals in India are even today regarded as 'master achievements in the field of military architecture'. Forts and fortifications under the Mughals were not restricted to big cities only. On the contrary, even the remotest village was provided with some sort of defence of this nature. Military commentators are agreed that the Mughal armies, like all other armies in the Orient, were at their best when acting on the defensive. An army scarcely succeeded taking by storm and push, a place which offered fortified resistance. The place was generally reduced to term by the force laying around it. Mining had found its way to some but not to all parts of India. There are, however, very few instances of mining being practiced with success even in those parts where it was in use. Strongly fortified places were most commonly reduced by strict investment and starvation. There were few captures by *coup de main* (Sar-i-Suwari). The walls were rarely escaladed. Scaling ladders do not seem to be much known and, therefore, not very occasionally used. Elephants seem to have remained much as 'Live tanks and the means to batter-in-the iron protected wooden gates of the forts'.

Intelligence

The world-renowned 'horde' of Changez Khan was known for it effective 'spying system and intelligence service.' The intelligence organization of the Indian Mughals seems to have remained in operation, both in peace and war. Its excellence does not, however, seem to have been the same as in the Changez Khan horde.

Weapons

The generic names for arms and armour was Silah (Plural....Aslah). Weapons and armour of all kinds were much prized by the Mughals and much taste and ingenuity was expended on their adornment. Armour was worn by all horsemen who could afford it. Officers of a certain rank were required to produce their armour at the time of inspection. Failure to do so was very often subject to a fine. There was a sort of armour in use for the horses and elephants throughout the period. The use of armour does not seem to have been discontinued even when men of European descent entered service in the Mughal armed forces.

The cavalry, the main branch of services, had a variety of arms in use then. The most relied upon seem to have been those used in fighting at close quarters. They were called Kotahyaraq or short arms and they corresponded to the European 'arme blance'. Weapons of more distant attack were : (1) The Bow (Kaman) and arrow (Tir), (2) The Matchlock (Banduk or Tufung), and (3) Pistol. Rockets were also used, but they were under the charge of the artillery. Out of the vast wealth of weapons, it is not to be supposed the whole were carried by any man at one time; but a great number were so carried, and in a large army, all of them were to be found in use by some one or the other.

Armies on March

It appears, whenever a Mughal Emperor took the field, there were generally great difficulties and delays in making the start. Nothing was ever ready when wanted and then there were the astrologers to be consulted. No march ever began except at the lucky moment. These considerations almost invariably prevented the Mughal armies from taking the most obvious advantages of an enemy. The first service on march in the Mughal armies was always the artillery which formed the advance guard. This was followed by the baggage and the official records. Under the Mughals, the records, etc. were never separated from the Emperor. Following the baggage, etc. was the main army, composed principally of cavalry. after the cavalry came the Emperor followed by the seraglo. The near guard was swollen by the prodigious number of people always at the Court. The armies, it appears, always marched to the accompaniment of 'War Music'. Besides the marching songs, there was the practice of beating of drums, playing of cymbals and the blowing of trumpets at certain fixed intervals (naubat). The intention to make a march was generally announced by the beating of kettle-drums. The drums were also beaten at the opening of the battle and to announce victory.

Military Awards

The promise of honorary distinctions in all ages and in all countries had been one of the potential agencies to incite men to exertions in war. Mughal Emperors do not seem to have been less ingenious in arousing their soldiers to deeds of 'greater victories' by the means of honours and awards. The Mughal system of entitlature was very elaborate and included the creation of 'Khans', awards rolls of honour, gifts of money, grants of flags and ensigns, and kettle or drums, in recognition of gallantry in the field and outstanding services rendered to the State in other fields of activity. These awards and rewards were honour, wholly dependent upon caprice of the monarch, because by a quick turn of events a confident could become a criminal.

2
The Mughal Emperors

To understand the wars and military system of the Mughals, it is necessary to appreciate the character of each emperor that sat on the throne of Delhi. Unlike the modern age, the 14th Century was reflected the character and capabilities of the emperors who personally led their armies. In order, therefore, to understand the military achievements during the period 1525 to 1857, (strictly speaking only till 1707), it is necessary to study the life-history of each monarch that ruled from Delhi.

Most of the Mughal emperors, starting from Babar, were good administrators, soldiers and leaders of men. Some of them were also astute politicians who had a good knowledge of the country and its people, their manners and customs, with the result that they governed India with magnanimity, and with the co-operation and help of the people. The Mughal emperors thus ushered India into a period of military conquest with revolutionary weapons never seen before, of faith and goodwill, and of stability of organization and administration.

BABAR (1483-1530)

Babar is a curious mixture of the "daring and restlessness of the nomad Tartar" and the "culture and urbanity of the Persian." Born in the year 1483, he was the founder of the Mughal Empire in India in 1525.

It was by heredity that Babar was destined to be a conqueror. Prof. Rushbrook Williams has said : "Fate had joined forces with nature to make him a conqueror by environment, surrounded from his earliest infancy by an atmosphere of intrigue and ambition."[1]

Babar was groomed in the art of intrigue, diplomacy and fighting from his very birth. As he advanced in age, the factional strifes of his relatives in Farghana gave him sufficient scope to practise all the arts with which he was already conversant. He was more and more involved and took an active part to gain possession of the kingdom left behind by his father but claimed by many of his relatives, both from his father's and mother's sides. However, gradually by his strength of character, his ability to suffer hardships under all conditions, his attitude of firmness to the extent of ruthlessness combined with humanity, his astute sense of diplomacy and his extraordinary power of leadership, he consolidated his position on the throne, and thereafter began to think of India. To quote Prof. Rushbrook Williams : "But for all his love of action, it is perhaps in his patience and his endurance that he shows most plainly his greatness of mind."

Babar was born and bred up in the hard and unkind school of adversity. He was never cowed down by miseries that fate showered on him from time to time. On the contrary, they strengthened his determination and the will to fight against all odds. His persevering mind coupled with all the other qualities previously described, enabled him to carve an Empire for the Mughlas in India.

The ding-dong battles of his early life fought in Farghana and Samarakand, his adversity in exile and during flight, the conquest of Kabul, Herat and Kandahar, gave him enough experience in the conduct of siege warfare, employment of horsed cavalry, the assault and reduction of fortresses, and the use of artillery. They enabled him to achieve a swift and resounding success against all the enemies with whom he fought during his conquest of India.

The use and development of artillery, called "feringiha" by the Mughals, was the most notable feature during his age. The Memoirs of Babar contain an eloquent description of the casting of the cannon and his artillery officer, Ustad Ali Khan.

Time and again Babar had to deal with discontented soldiers who were at times keen to return to their homes in Kabul, and did not like the hardships of difficult campaigning in the hot climate of India. But again Babar showed his qualities as the leader of men when, by his speech, force of character, and toughness, he brought the mutinuous crowd under control and advanced for the conquest of India. Dr. Lane Poole describes the situation in these words : "The troops began to murmur. They longed for the cool air to Kabul, and even made ready to return. They looked upon India as a buccaneer looked on a galleon, the prize money secured, they wished to make sail. They had to deal with an obstinate man, however, and Babar summoned the chief officers together, and made them a speech. He recalled their past toil and labours together, the weary marches and grievous hardships, and reminded them that all these had been endured for the sake of the great reward which was now theirs."[2]

What sort of soldier was Babar? What soldierly qualities did he have? It is rather difficult to glean much data on this fact of his career, because they are so intermingled with the chronicles of his war. But to say that he had no equal in his age would not be an exaggeration. Alexander Dow has remarked : "He rendered the most dangerous enterprises easy, by his undaunted courage and perseverance, which rose above all difficulties, and made him much more the object of admiration in his adversity than in the height of his prosperity. Nor did he forget himself in the latter, but always behaved with that moderation and equanimity which characterises a great soul."[3]

At times he displayed certain inhuman qualities by ordering the wholesale massacre of the women and children after the capture of a city, but these were the very few occasions of his barbaric enthusiasm of genealogy, but "he was a prince of great humanity, and carried his generosity to such excess, that it bordered upon prodigality. With regard to the first, he so often pardoned ingratitude and treason, that he seemed to make a principle of rendering good for evil. He thus disarned vice, and made the wicked the worshippers of his virtue."[4]

In addition to the soldierly qualities, Babar was an excellent writer and composer of poems. He had a simple and lucid style of writing. His monumental work is his own Memoirs, which has been written in a simple, unaffected and pure style. Mr. Lane Poole has aptly said : "Hence his Memoirs are no rough soldier's chronicle of marches and counter-marches, escapes, mines, blinds, gabions, palisadoes, ravelins, half-moons and such trumpery; they contain the personal impressions and acute reflections of a cultivated man of the world, well read in Eastern literature, a close and curious observer, quick in perception, a discerning judge of persons, and a devoted lover of nature; one, moreover, who was well able to express his thoughts and observations in clear and vigorous language."[5]

Babar's Memoirs is an outstanding document throwing most of the light on his own self and the prevailing conditions in the then India. Mr. Beveridge paid a tribute in these words : "His autobiography is one of those priceless records which are for all times, and is fit to rank with the confessions of St. Augustine and Rousseau, and the memoirs of Gibbon and Newton. In Asia it stands almost alone."[6]

HUMAYUN (1508-1556)

Unlike his illustrious father, Humayun was a curious mixture of an astronomer and a soldier-politician. From the time of his ascendancy to the throne of Delhi in 1530, he had been facing plenty of family and other troubles from the far-flung empire. His brothers Kamran, Bahadur, king of Gujrat, and Sher Shah from Bihar, took up arms against him. Of these Sher Shah was only successful, and by trickery he defeated Humayun. He was thus forced to flee from one place to another, often living under very wretched conditions, and eventually fled to Persia where he designed the ways and means of re-conquering what he had lost in India.

Born in the year 1508, when his father Babar was deeply involved in consolidating his position, Humayun had a hard schooling in the art of warfare under the able guidance of his experienced father. From the age of 14, Humayun fought in battles, commanding his father's troops, and, in India, he fought wars which were for his dynasty, the Mughal empire, and the throne of Delhi.

Babar laid the foundation of the Mughal empire, but it

was not so securely laid when he died. It was left to his son to secure the loose ends of the empire which had been hurriedly secured for him by force of arms. But he had to face innumerable difficulties to keep his throne secure. Father Francis Catrou has rightly remarked : "The authority of Babar whilst he lived curbed the revolting spirit of the natives. But the commencement of a new reign, in a monarchy of such recent creation, furnished an opportunity for intrigue, and the setting up of various pretensions."[7]

After Babar's death, the Mughal dynasty in India degenerated. The wealth and wine of the country had made them slack, slovenly and pleasure loving. Father Catrou gives an illuminating description of the state of affairs : "They were no longer those gallant conquerors, of whom a small number had, under Babar, brought into subjection a great kingdom, and put to flight the largest armies. They were men already enervated by their residence in India, prone through the heat of the climate to indulgence, and the neglect of discipline."[8] No wonder Humayun also fell in line with the prevailing condition of his compatriots in the country. As a result, he lost the crucial battle in his struggle with Sher Shah, and lost his empire and the throne of Delhi.

What sort of man was Humayun who lost in a few years all that was gained by his illustrious father? Dr. Lane Poole makes some revealing remarks on the character of Humayun when he says : "The young prince was indeed a gallant and loveable fellow, courteous, witty and accomplished as his father, warm hearted and emotional, almost quixotic in his notion of honour and magnanimity, personally brave, as indeed were all the princes of his house and capable of great energy on occasions. But he lacked character and resolution. He was incapable of sustained effort, and after a moment of triumph would bury himself in his harem and dream away of precious hours in the opium eater's paradise, whilst his enemies were thundering at the gate.....His character attracts but never dominates. But as a king he was failure."[9] This is an admirable summing up of Humayun's character, and even though he was a perfect gentleman, he was no good as a king, soldier and administrator. At the time he came on the Indian scene, the king should have had a "firm grasp of the military situation and resolution to meet it." What was required was the quality of a soldier, and this quality Humayun lacked to a marked degree.

The political condition of the country was far from stable. George Dunbar describes the situation in these words : "But Humayun's position was insecure. Bengal was unconquered, Bahadur Shah, the powerful Afghan king of Gujarat and Malwa, was actively hostile, and Humayun's brothers were openly disloyal; while the intrigues of the Portuguese, now masters of the Western seaboard, created a disturbing influence." This state of affairs in the country needed a strong hand to quell the disturbances and hold together the disintegrating parts of the vast Empire. But Humayun was incapable of such an effort with the result that he had to flee and seek asylum in Persia.

However, eventually, Humayun staged a come-back at the head of an Army of 15,000 horsemen, and got back all that he had lost to Sher Shah.

Humayun was incompetent as a soldier. He did not grasp the military situation of the day, and time and again, when he had the enemy thoroughly beaten, he did not follow the retreating enemy, and thus gave them opportunity to reform and fight against him in subsequent battles. At times he showed a remarkable flair for surprise attacks and ruses when he "introduced armed men in women's litters" during the attack on the Rohtas forts. There is, however, one quality he lacked to a marked degree. His man-management was very poor. "His troops were demoralised by dissipation, disheartened by inaction, and reduced by sickness." The hardy Mongolian soldiers were "suffering the inevitable degeneration that overtakes a hardy race when exposed to the luxuries of wealth and the influence of an enervating climate."[10]

Humayun's handling of the military situation on various occasions was also defective. Dr. Lane Poole says—"But his worst enemy was himself. Instead of taking a statesmanlike view of the situation, meeting the most pressing danger first, and crushing one antagonist before he engaged another, he frittered away his army in divided commands, and deprived of its full strength; he left one enemy unsubdued behind him while he turned to meet another; and when victory by chance rewarded his courage rather than his tactics he reposed upon his laurels and made merry with his friends, whilst his foes used the precious time in gathering their forces for a fresh effort. Had he brought the whole of his strength to bear upon the enemy in turn, he might have been successful; for Babar's troops were still the men who had won Delhi and defeated Sanga, and Babar's generals were still in command of their divisions. But Humayun weakened their valour and destroyed their confidence by division and vacillation, neglected the counsels of the commanders, and displayed such indecision that it is a marvel that any still adhered to his falling fortunes."[11] Such were the deplorable military qualities of a king, who, more than any body should have possessed them to a very marked degree, to keep his throne secure in an age when such qualities only were respected.

After regaining the throne at Delhi, Humayun did not live long to enjoy the fruits of his labour. He died in 1556 leaving behind Akbar to complete the unfinished work. "His end was of a piece with his character. He tumbled through life, and he tumbled out of it."[12]

AKBAR (1542-1605)

Born in adversity in the year 1542, when Humayun was fleeing from place to place after losing his Empire at Delhi to Sher Shah, Akbar was the doyen of the Mughals who came both before and after him. Akbar had his baptism of soldiering at the early age of 14, when he took part in the battle of Sirhind under his father. Thereafter he had further experience in the conduct of military campaigns against Sikander.

All these campaigns early in age stood him in good stead when he gradually consolidated his empire during his life time. Akbar is known and termed 'Great' more for his statesmanlike qualities and as an administrator, than as a soldier. But he contributed more to the military science of his age than any other single individual.

At the time of his accession to the throne, Akbar was only 14 years old, and Bairam Khan was the regent and adviser. During the period of the regency, Akbar had to be guided by the regent in all his activities, and he did not relish this control as he had, at times, to do certain things which were not to his liking. Akbar's reign consists of three periods...the regency till 1560, the harem government till 1562, and lastly his own, when he fully established himself as the Emperor of India, till his death in 1605. What was lost by Humayun was regained by him. Gwalior, Ajmer and Jaunpur were annexed. Thereafter many more territories were added to his domain until it embraced the whole of India. Throughout his reign he pursued a systematic policy of military conquest combined with diplomacy. Gondwana was conquered in 1563; the rebellious Uzbegs were subdued in 1567; the Rajput war was successfully concluded in 1567; Gujrat was annexed in 1572, Bengal submitted to his prowess in 1576 after the battle of Rajmahal; Kashmir came under his sway in 1591; Orissa and Sind were subdued in 1590 and 1592 respectively, Buluchistan in 1594, and lastly the Deccan was added during closing years of his reign in 1596. The Hindu kingdoms of Bijapur and Golconda were spared his onslaught as he could not reach so far south. Thus in Akbar's reign the foundations were laid and secured for the emperorship of the Mughals over practically the whole of India.

Akbar was well educated by capable tutors during his childhood, and he continued his learning even after he had become emperor. As a boy he evinced a keen interest in poetry and art, and also for outdoor life. He was an "omnivorous listener" and had a "prodigious memory". He was born in the midst of hardship and brought up in captivity. His courage was exercised in his father's wars, and his prudence, called forth by the delicacy of the situation during the ascendancy of Bairam. He was engaging in his manners, well formed in his person, excelled in all exercises of strength and agility, and showed exuberance in his amusements, such as in taming of unbroken elephants, and in rash encounters with tigers and other wild beasts. Yet, with his disposition, and a passionate love of glory, he founded his hopes of fame at least as much on the wisdom and liberality of his Government as in military success. It required all his great qualities to maintain him in the situation in which he was placed.[13]

There is no doubt that Akbar's place in history has been secured by his statesmanlike qualities of bringing the various warring tribes into the common fold, his revenue system and other administrative measures, and lastly by his conquests. Akbar never forgot his Army which, it is estimated, was near about 4,400,000 soldiers of all types and departments. The conduct of the Army has been fully laid down in the 'Ayeni Akbari'.

In addition to his scholarly training, Akbar had a good grooming in practical soldiering. Sir George Dunbar says : "But with all this he was intensely practical, a master of detail, and uncommonly useful with his hands. One of his hobbies was to found cannon in his arsenal; and his active brain was continually busy with inventions from batteries which could be fired in salvos of seventeen guns with one match, to useful devices in elephant gear, and novel forms of travelling carriages."[14]

This was not all. Dr. Lane Poole says : "Akbar had mechanical genius. He devised a new method for making gun-barrels of spirally rolled iron, which could not burst, he invented a machine which cleaned sixteen barrels at once....There were many other things that he improved by his talent for mechanical invention."[15]

In war Akbar was indefatigable and unscrupulous. He never allowed much compassion for the defeated enemy, and allowed the common practice of trampling the prisoners under the elephants." He could be terribly stern, and was subject to paroxysms of rage, in one of the which he threw a servant from the battlements for falling asleep in the palace; but his natural inclination was ever towards mercy, and his forgiveness often cost him dear."[16]

Personally he was very courageous and resourceful. On many occasions during a battle he gave fight to the enemy without caring if he was strong enough to challenge the strength of his adversaries. "His character as a warrior was that of an intrepid partizan rather than a great general."[17]

Whatever it is, Akbar carved an empire out of chaos and anarchy. He gave the country for the first time a stable Government, a sense of unity and nationhood, and tolerance of thought and religion. He also gave India a sense of security against both internal and external aggression, and had a well organized army and cavalry, elephants and artillery.

The reign of Akbar was the golden age of Indian History. Sir George Dunbar rightly says : "A born leader of men and one of the mightest kings in history, Akbar transformed the Mughals from military adventurers into a great dynasty."[18]

JEHANGIR (1569-1627)

Jehangir was a complete misfit for the throne of Delhi. Father Catrou says : "He was a voluptous prince who passed the greater part of his life in the pleasures of the harem; and who abandoned himself to a species of sottishness, which was degrading to human nature."[19]

Such was the man who became emperor in 1605. It is an unpleasant truth that "sons dissipate what their father gained by the sweat of their brow; nor do all sons imitate the good qualities of their ancestors."[21] Jahangir was quite contented to dwell upon the fruits of his great father. He was a debauchee and fond of wine. He was generous and fond of pomp and splendour. He was liberal and approachable by any one. One of the other qualities which he displayed was his tolerant attitude to other religions, specially Christianity.

He was a curious mixture of cruelty and gentleness. At times he showed generosity even to the extent of humility, but yet revelled in barbaric pleasures. He was rather indiscreet in his dealings with his soldiers. Mr. Niccolao Manucci gives a very apt description of such beastly pleasures of Jehangir :

"When any soldier came into his presence with a

courageous look or with his turban cocked, he called him near and with one of the said lancets pierced his nose. If the soldier showed that it hurt him, he ordered the man to be ejected from the court with cuffs and buffeting, saying that a soldier who was afraid of such a little piece of iron as that, would never in war-time endure lance-thrusts and sword-cuts. On the contrary, if the soldier made believe to meet the lancet without fear, he would double the man's pay and his estimation at court. The king would say that such men deserved the name of soldier...they were veritable men of war."[19]

Jehangir fought no battle of note. Most of his wars were concerned with the subjugation of recalcitrant princes, rebellions of his gevernors and fratricidal wars with his sons and other favourites of the famous queen Nurjehan.

The fame and prosperity of the mughal Emperors rose to its zenith during the reign of Akbar but, unfortunately, love of wine and influence of women in the running of the Government made Jehangir's reign the beginning of the decline of the Mughal dynasty as well as of the empire.

To sum up the military qualities of Jehangir in the words of Mr. Alexander Dow : "In war he had no abilities, he was fond of peace and tranquillity; and rather a lover than an encourager of the arts of civil life."[20]

With his death in 1627 ended the most unproductive era from the point of view of military achievements.

SHAHJEHAN (1592-1666)

Shahjehan came to the throne through a bloody path of murders and assassinations. There were several claimants to the throne in his younger brother Shahryar, and Dawat Baksh, the son of Khusru. But he and his adherents made short work of his rivals and he ascended the uneasy throne of India. It was not all peace and tranquillity in India during this regime. Shahjehan had to fight the rebellions in Bundelkhand, Ahmednagar and Deccan, against the Portuguese in 1632, subjugate Bijapur and Golconda and other Deccan States, and lastly the unsuccessful campaigns in North-Western borders of India to regain the lost provinces of Kandahar, Balkh and Badakshan.

The deterioration in the empire and particularly in the army, which began during the reign of Jehangir, was well set in during this reign. Sir George Dunbar remarks : "The army of Akbar in spite of its usual encumbrance of an Imperial court was efficient. But by the reign of Shahjehan deterioration had already set in, and the policy of increasing the weight of the heavy artillery did nothing to counteract it."[21]

The emperor was a man of sound judgment and knowledge of the affairs of the State. But he was rather inclined to be intolerant of those who were non-Muslims and thus made religion over-ride statesmanship. He was a great builder and lover of art. Even to this day the buildings that were built during his reign bear eloquent testimony to the refined taste and grandeur of little use, when use of the sword was a necessity to hold the empire together. "The Emperor and the Court had reached a pitch of luxury that fostered effeminacy."

Shahjehan was intolerant and it was the persecution of the Hindus that contributed to his downfall. This activity was increased after the death of the beloved queen Mumtazmahal.

As far as dealing with his soldiers and generals was concerned, the Emperor was very considerate. He maintained a huge standing army of 1,44,500 horses, elephants, camels; the men were armed with bows and arrows, javelins, daggers, muskets and cannon and was a good fighting machine. He had a good command and control over his army, but at times they did not show either good fighting qualities or loyalty. But on the whole it was a better outfit than his father's and could be relied upon.

As Shahjehan grew old he passed the affairs of the state to his four sons, and thus sowed the seeds for a bitter civil was between them. "The three youngest, Suja, Aurangzeb and Morad grudged the eldest Dara, the succession which his father intended for him. They declared themselves independent in the governments which had been assigned to them and assumed the titles of kings. Shahjehan himself was conquered by their arms and ended his life as a prisoner."[22] The fratricidal war ended in the victory of Aurangzeb who ascended the throne in 1659 after liquid ating his rival brothers.

Shahjehan was kept in prison by his son and died full of years in 1666.

AURANGZEB (1659-1707)

For the first time in the history of the Mughals a bigoted Mussalman came to the throne of Delhi in 1659. He had an indomitable resolution and was a staunch upholder of the philosophy of his own religion. He was a puritan and nothing mattered in his life than to adhere to the principles and tenets of Islam as laid down in the Holy Bood. No sentiment of the courtiers, princes, ministers and soldiers bothered him, and swayed him from his already destined path. These traits of his character involved him in various religious wars, and even in his last days he was not destined to enjoy peace and tranquillity.

As Aurangzeb was a stickler in his food he was rather lean and thin and suffered from time to time various physical ailments which made him weak. But inspite of his physical handicaps he had a lion's courage. Dr. Lane Poole has rightly said : "His was no ordinary courage. That he was physically brave is only to say he was a Mughal prince of the old lion-hearted stock. But he was amongst the bravest men in their valiant rank. In the crisis of the campaign in Balkh, when the enemy 'like locusts and ants' hemmed him on every side, and steel was slashing all round him, the setting sun heralded the hour of evening prayer; Aurangzeb, unmoved amid the din of battle, dismounted and bowed himself on the bare ground in the complicated ritual of Islam, as composedly as if he had been performing the rite in the mosque at Agra."[23]

But with all these high qualities he was suspicious by nature and never delegated authority to his subordinates. On slightest suspicion he used to kill or imprison the ministers and even his own sons.

In spite of all the self renunciation he adhered to the pomp and splendour of the Mughal courts. He maintained almost all the Mughal customs of ceremonial, festivity and pomp and splendour. But in addition he had a glowing passion for the art of Government. Being educated by men of letters and of virtue in his father's court Aurangzeb showed the flair of his genius from his very childhood. His assiduity prevailed over the dullness of his tutor, and he made a progress far beyond his years."[24]

Schooled in the atmosphere of justice and fairplay in the court of Shahjehan, Aurangzeb showed qualities of uncommon sagacity and equity. He attended his father's court and at times gave his own views which were very much appreciated and also upheld by his father.

He had a thorough knowledge of the affairs of the state even to the extent of minutest details. He kept a strict watch over all his subordinates by spies so that they did not indulge in corrupt practices. He was also a good builder. Throughout the state good sarais were built and maintained at public expense, for the convenience of travellers. Universities were founded and men of letters were encouraged to conduct researches and write treatises." He called them to court; and, placed them, according to their abilities, in offices in the State; those who were versed in the commentaries on the Koran were raised to the dignity of Judges, in the different court of justices."[25]

Above all these he had remarkable soldierly qualities. He took keen interest in his troops and reviewed them regularly with pomp and grandeur; though physically frail he had remarkable strength of body and mind; he knew well the use of fire-arms and was a good shot. Mr. Alexander Dow has rightly summed his military qualities in the following words : "Aurangzeb was as experienced in war, as he was in the arts of peace. Though his personal courage was almost unparallelled, he always endeavoured to conquer more by stratagem than by force. To succeed by art threw honour upon himself; to subdue by power acquired to others fame. Such was his coolness in action, that, at the rising and setting sun, the times appointed for prayer, he never neglected to attend to that duty, though in the midst of a battle. Devout to excess, he never engaged in action without prayer; and for every victory, he ordered a day of thanks-giving and one of festivity and joy."[26]

To sum up, Aurangzeb's long reign from 1659 to 1707 was

the culminating point of the empire founded by Babar and consolidated by Akbar; It was also the start of its decay which had already set in during the reign of Shahjehan. He had enlarged the empire, seen the birth of two military Hindu nationalities in the Marat has and the Sikhs but the foundations were not strengthened. Immediately after his death Deccan, Oudh and Bengal threw off the Mughal yoke. His empire and conquests were held together both by statesmanship, diplomacy, treachery and also by military prowess. A fitting conclusion to Aurangzeb's life can be given in the words of Dr. Lane Poole : "Aurangzeb's life had been a vast failure indeed, but he had failed grandly. His glory is that he could not force his soul, that he dared not desert the colours of his faith. The great puritan of India was such stuff as win the martyr's crown."[27]

THE LATER MUGHALS

It is not of much interest to recount the exploits and deeds of the Mughals that came in succession after Aurangzeb. All the emperors that succeeded were weak, inefficient and fond of luxury and debauchery. Their reign was made miserable by the rise of the Marathas Sikhs, and foreigners like English, French and the Portuguese who originally came in as traders and finished up founding empires for themselves. Lastly, the invasion of Nadir Shah sounded the death knell of the already-tottering empire of the Mughals. The rebellious elements inside the country took full advantage of the disorganization started by the invasion, and eventually paved the way for the rise and consolidation of the British conquest of India.

The years 1757-1761 were fateful in Indian History. The destinies of India now lay in the hands of the British, who had, by now, through trade concession and force of arms, established themselves in the country. The battle of Panipat and the failure of the Marathas closed the Indian suzerainty of India.

Thus ended the Mughal rule after 350 years which gave India, among other things, a semblance of military organization and fighting technique of a revolutionary type.

REFERENCES

1. An Empire Builder of the 16th Century.
2. The Story of the Nations, Vol. 59.
3. The History of Hindustan.
4. The Story of the Nations, Vol. 59.
5. Babar.
6. Calcutta Review, 1897.
7. History of the Mughal Dynasty.
8. *Ibid.*
9. The Story of the Nations (Vol. 59).
10. *Ibid.*
11. *Ibid.*
12. *Ibid.*
13. Hindustan's History of the World.
14. A History of India.
15. The Story of the Nations (Vol. 59).
16. The History of Hindustan by Dow.
17. A History of India.
18. History of the Mughal Dynasty.
19. Storia do Mogor by Manucci.
20. A History of Hindoostan.
21. A History of India.
22. Historian's History of the World.
23. The Story of the Nations (Vol. 59).
24. The History of Hindustan by Alexander Dow.
25. The History of Hindustan
26. *Ibid.*
27. The Story of the Nations (Vol. 59).

3

The Advent of the Moghuls

Prior to the invasion of India in 1524 by Babar, a Chaghatal Turk, the Delhi Sultanate existed only in name, and India was at the time prey to the ambitions, disaffections, and rivalries of different nobles. Various reasons have been ascribed for the disintegration of the Sultanate of Delhi, one of which is that Muslim nobles excelled more in intrigue than in war and therefore they were not in touch with the development of the art of war in foreign countries. Babar, who had cherished the ambition of establishing an empire in India, was in fact encouraged in this and invited to India by some nobles who were either pretenders to the throne of Delhi or were dissatisfied with the ruler, Ibrahim Lodi. Babar made his first move towards India in 1524, when he entered Punjab and occupied Lahore, but his Indian confederates soon realised their mistake, turned against him and compelled him to retire to Kabul where he began to prepare for the final blow, knowing he could expect no more support from the nobles. In modern day military terminology, his first move into India can be termed a 'reconnaissance in force' by virtue of which he was able to gauge the composition and strength of the likely opposing forces.

The Battle of Panipat

Babar collected reinforcements and perfected his war machine before he decided to set foot in India for the second time. He had introduced guns in his army after coming in contact with the Persians. He had also secured the services of two Turks, Ustad Ali Quli and Mustafa, who were artillery experts. The Delhi Sultans were completely unaware of the new weapons then coming into use in Europe and Turkey. There is no doubt that at the time Babar possessed the most effective cannon east of the Suez but to say, as is generally stated, that he introduced artillery in India is not correct. Babar marched from Kabul in November 1525, occupied Punjab and then proceeded against Ibrahim Lodi, the nominal ruler of the shrivelled Afghan Empire, and met him on the historical field of Panipat on 21 April 1526. He had with him a large pack of artillery and about 12,000 men. Various estimates have been given by historians of the strength of the opposing forces but it is generally accepted that Ibrahim Lodi had 1,000,000 men, 1,000 elephants and no artillery at all, while Babar did not have more than 10,000 to 12,000 men. By superior strategy and generalship and use of artillery, Babar won a decisive victory and the mighty army of Ibrahim Lodi was defeated in half a day. This battle, known in Indian history as the First Battle of Panipat, is of great significance as politically it laid the foundation of the Moghul Empire in India, which was to last for three centuries till 1858. Militarily, it introduced artillery as the third fighting arm of an army (along with infantry and cavalry), something which was to influence the history of India for the next 400 years.

Employment of Artillery

The strength, composition and tactics employed by Babar in handling his army on that fateful day have been the subject of considerable discussion and controversy by historians and research scholars. One fact, however, has been agreed upon by all historians : that not with standing the superior generalship of Babar, and given the relative strength of the two forces, it was the artillery arm of Babar which tilted the balance in his favour. In carrying out this assessment it should, however, be conceded that Babar had the advantage of surprise as Ibrahim Lodhi's forces must have been totally shaken when faced by a weapon system which they did not know and which, apart from frightening troops and elephants with the noise of exploding shells and the discharge of guns, also had the battle-winning advantage of firing at longer range while keeping itself out of range of the weaponry of the Sultan. No wonder, therefore, that Babar wrote in his memoirs, "this difficult affair was made easy to me and that mighty army, in the space of half a day, was laid in the dust."

Not many historians have attempted to look in detail about the type, strength and tactics of the artillery in this battle. We do, however, know that Babar's defensive preparations consisted of the right wing resting on an outlying garden of the town. His centre was protected by a kind of stockade or field protection made up of guns chained together or rows of carts joined together with twisted bull hides or both. The following evidence is available from various known documents relating to the artillery :

(a) Babar had used artillery chained together (according to the custom of Rumi) with twisted bull hides. This arrangement was probably copied by him from the Rumi, or Osmali, order of battle. At the battle of Khaldiran in 1514, which was fought between the Osmalis and Persians, the former had not only chained the guns together but had also set up the breast work of baggage wagons.

(b) Babar appeared to have no light pieces.

(c) Babar had large cannon in his camp which fired huge stones. He also had several pieces which he styled "*feringis*" thus providing evidence of Europeans origin.

(d) Between every two gun carriages, there were six or seven "*tubras*" or moveable breast works. Matchlockmen stood behind these and discharged their matchlocks.

(e) Eight hundred gun carriages were prepared in one day.

(f) Babar ordered his men to bring as many "*arabah*" as they could and they collected 700. These were bound together with strips of hide, and in between palisades of some sort ("*turah*") were erected, the whole forming a kind of stockade or field protection.

(g) Babar linked his guns together with ropes of twisted leather.

(h) Babar used the word "*zarbzan*" for cannon which

literally means blow striker. Describing the battle, Budauni describes the cannon and swivel pieces which were upon carts.

(i) Babar seems to have used pieces of considerable size.

(j) The word "*arabah*" used by Babar means a cart.

However, Leydon and Erskine in their *Memoirs of Babar* (p. 304) and Elliot (p. 468) feel that "*arabah*" refers to the gun or gun carriage. A later Hindi Poet, Shridhar Murlidhar, wrote a poem (in 1712) describing the battle between Farrukhsiyar and Jahandar Shah in which he says, *kar kar, kara kar, sau arabe chhuten* which means, "a hundred *arabah* were fired with much explosive sound." Another poet of the 18th century, Lal, in his poem "*Chattar-prakash*", also used the word "*arabah*" saying *Goli gola chhute arabae* which means "*arabah* fired bullets and shells."

(k) The word *Rahkalah* has also been used in relation to guns and gun carriages. Literally, it means a cart,[17] but in historical works it means a field piece or small gun including a vehicle for its transport. Strictly speaking, *rahkalah* was a gun carriage as the following lines from *Akhbar-i-muhabbat* show :. *Har do dast dar zer-i-rahkalah burdah, top ra ba rahkalah to sinah bardasht* (Bringing both hands beneath the *rahkalah*, he lifted both gun and carriage as high as his chest).

(l) Fourteen years later, in A.D. 1540, at the battle of Kanauj, Humayun had 700 pieces (*zarbzan*), each drawn by four pair of bullocks (these guns fired balls of about 4 lb each). In addition, there were 21 guns, each of which required eight pair of oxen and which fired leaden balls ten times as heavy as the others. Whereas Erskine interprets this as 61 heavy guns, each drawn by 60 pairs of bullocks, Ross feels that there were 21 carriages, each drawn by eight pairs of bullocks. Assuming that the guns fired a ball of 40 lb (ten times as heavy as *zarbzan*, each of which required four pair of bullocks) it is more likely that the guns were very

heavy and could not be drawn by only four pairs of bullocks, given which the figure of 61 guns is likely to be more correct.

Type and Strength of Artillery

Before we attempt to evaluate the type and number of guns used by Babar at Panipat, we need to look at the light artillery weapons, which, when mounted on a cart, could be lifted by two hands along with the cart or which fired small or light rounds. The words used for these were *shatrunal, zamburak, shahin* and swivel guns. Swivel guns were light pieces carried on the backs of animals. A *shatrunal* is literally a 'camel gun barrel' and denotes that such guns were sometimes fired from a camel's back. According to Barnier, such guns were small pieces, the size of double muskets. Dr. Horn adds that a man seated behind such a gun on the camel could load and discharge the gun without dismounting. *Zamburaks* were long swivels firing one or two pound balls, two of them were carried fastened upon the saddle of a camel, and when they were brought into play, the camel had to kneel on the ground. Mundy adds that the camel gun was used differently : "the gun revolves on a swivel fixed on the pummel of the saddle and the bombardier, sitting astride behind it, loads and fires with wonderful quickness." *Zamburak* means a little wasp and *shahin* denotes a falcon. Both these were light guns which could also be fired from the ground by placing them on a rough wooden carriage.

Three well-known authorities of the period have given separate views on the artillery used by Babar in the Battle of Panipat. Elliot says that Babar had no light pieces and that he had guns only of a large size. This could imply that when Babar collected 700 *arabahs,* it meant carts only which were bound together with strips of hide-a kind of field protection. Dr. Horn, the well know French historian of the Moghul period, holds that it is improbable that Babar had 700 cannon of any sort. However, Irvine argues that taking into account the small size of these guns it would not have been difficult to collect 700 of them. He further adds that by *arabah,* Babar not only meant a cart but a cart with a small gun carried on it. His view can be reinforced by the interpretation of the word *rahkalah* were it is stated that using both hands beneath of *rahkalah*, he lifted both the gun and carriage as high as his chest. This implies a light cart or carriage with a light gun placed on it.

If the events of 1526 are read with the events of 1540, only 14 years later, where it is stated that Humayun had 700 pieces, each drawn by four pairs of bullocks, firing balls of four pounds each, and no mention is made of any light weapon placed on a cart, one tends to incline to the view that Babar did not in fact have any light guns on carts.

My own inclination is to go against the views of Dr. Horn and Irvine and support those of Elliot that apart from light field guns, Babar did not have any light pieces mounted on carts; certainly not as many as 700. The response is based on the strength of Babar's army which is authentically stated to have been between 10,000 and 12,000 something which no historian has taken into account when trying to evaluate the strength of the artillery. The figure of gun crew who only manned the guns (and this does not include other artillery personnel) during the Moghul period is assessed as follows :

(a) two men to each *shahin* or falconet.

(b) seven to sixteen men to each gun.

Now, if we accept the figure of 700 it would have required 1400 men to man these pieces. In addition, the field guns on wheels would require around 500 to 1000 gun crew depending on the number of guns used, for which no historical records are available. This means that out of an army of 12,000 men, around 2000-2500 soldiers would be manning the guns alone, which would have made Babar's army an ill-balanced one, as the strength of infantry and cavalry would then be reduced considerably. In actual reckoning, the artillery would have required many more soldiers over and above those manning the guns for other functions such as the supply of ammunition.

Further, when Babar asked his men to collect as many *arabahs* as they could, and they collected 700 of them, it could not have been his intention to collect them to mount only light guns. They were also to be used to form defence protection. Had he had 700 light guns which required 700 carts for mounting and his men could find, say, only 300, does that imply that he would have then used only 300 light guns ? The fact that these light guns could also be fired from the ground by placing them on a rough wooden carriage clearly proves that carts were not collected to mount guns. Babar was a good general and had come to India for a second time after making all preparations and it would not have been very good planning if he had mounted light guns on carts procured locally. He would have brought gun carriages or carts with light guns mounted on them.

The Battle of Panipat is a watershed in the history of India as it heralded the dawn of the Moghul Empire, a development which was to influence the course of Indian history for many centuries to come. Apart from Babar's good generalship, the major factor that influenced the battle was the use, by him, of artillery as a battle winning strategy as otherwise it would not have been possible for an army of 10,000 to 12,000 to defeat an army of over 1,00,000 men and 1,000 elephants in a few hours.

The Battle of Khanua

A year later in 1526, Babar employed his forces and artillery to great effect where he defeated the Rajputs in a decisive battle at Khanua. The result of this battle was more significant, in that he scored a victory over the powerful Rajput confederacy which was making a bid for Hindu hegemony in India because of the decay of the Delhi Sultanate. The leader of the confederacy was Rana Sanga, a more formidable rival then Ibrahim. He marched with an army of 120 chiefs, 80,000 horse and 500 war elephants and the rulers of Marwar, Amber, Gwalior, Ajmer and Chanderi. He was joined by Sultan Mahmud Lodi. Babar wrote in his memoirs :

> I advanced my wagons with all the apparatus and war engines that I had prepared and marched forward with my army in order of battle *i.e.* right wing, left wing and centre in three places. In front were wagons and gun carriages and in the rear came Ali Quli with a body of

matchlocks to maintain communications between the artillery and infantry behind them and enable them to advance

An Indian historian describes the battle.

He placed the guns and matchlocks in front. Ustad Ali Quli took position in front of the centre with his mortar and other wheeled guns, while the other artillery commander, Mustafa Khan, stood in front of centre of the right wing with his musketeers and swivel guns. Rana Sanga did not possess any of these hardwares which were absolutely unknown in Northern India. As earlier, in the first Battle of Panipat, he put his gun carriages so as to cover the front and chained them together at a distance of five paces. When the action started in the morning by a charge of Rajputs on horses on Babar's right, the artillery opened up and they were met by a hailstorm of burning slugs and stone chips spreading like grapeshot through their ranks. It came as a surprise as they had never experienced anything like it before. Failed in the attack on right wing, the Rajputs attempted an attack of left wing which was also repulsed. Babar then gave an unexpected order for his centre to advance. Guns were pulled forward with matchlocks following. Ustad Ali's cannon did fearful execution and the indomitable Rajputs were mown down. By sunset, Babar had overrun the Hindustani encampment. The Confederacy showed utmost gallantry but superior generalship of Babar and the guns decided the issue.

After this battle the Rajputs went into a decline, something which facilitated Babar's task and made possible the foundation of a new foreign rule.

Before studying the evolution of the Moghul artillery in the next 300 years, it is relevant to study two battles close to that period where the use of artillery influenced the outcome of history.

The Defeat of Bahadur Shah

In 1534, Bahadur Shah of Gujarat attempted to expand

eastwards : he knew Humayun lacked the determination of his late father, Babar. Knowing the power of the newly introduced artillery arm, he prepared himself and built up his artillery (under the well known Turkish gunner Rumi Khan), with Portuguese and European artillery men. He then stormed Chittor with his artillery and defeated the Rajputs. Thereafter, when Humayun advanced and laid siege to Bahadur Shah on the banks of Mandasor lake, the latter refused to attack on the advice of Rūmi Khan who wanted to batter the attacking forces of Humayun against his artillery, but the Moghuls cut off Bahadur Shah's communications, isolated his forces and defeated him.

The Second Battle of Panipat

In the second case, Hemu, the capable general and minister of Adil Shah Sur, came forward to oppose the Moghuls and met Akbar on the historic field of Panipat with a large army estimated at 1,00,000 men, 1,500 war elephants and a large pack of artillery. Akbar had 20,000 men as well as cavalry and artillery. The advance guard of Hemu met Akbar's forces on 5 November 1556. Hemu had placed most of his artillery forward in the battle, and the Moghuls under Ali Quli Khan captured the whole of Hemu's artillery leaving the latter under a severe handicap which led to a crushing defeat.

Why did Hemu place his artillery in his leading columns exposing them to capture well before the main battle was to be joined ? Was he so obsessed with the power of this weapon that he took this risk ? He was no ordinary general and had risen in the Afghan court by merit. He was asked to lead the Afghan army when there were other Muslim generals on their side. The answer is difficult to find. It is however pertinent to note that the Moghuls, invariably, when on the march, led their forces by artillery even as late as during Aurangzeb's time. The aspect of artillery in battle by the Moghuls will be examined in subsequent chapters and will throw some light on their philosophy of the use of this arm.

4

Equipment—Defensive Armour

The generic name for arms and armour was *silah*, plural *aslah* (Steingass, 693). Weapons and armour of all kinds were much prized in India, much taste and ingenuity being expended on their adornment. Every great man possessed a choice collection. The following extract describes that of the Nawab Wazir at Lakhnau, in 1785 :—"But beyond everything curious and excellent in the Nawab's possession are his arms and armour. The former consist of matchlocks, fuzees, rifles, fowling-pieces, sabres, pistols, scymitars, spears, syefs (long straight swords), daggers, poniards, battle-axes, and clubs, most of them fabricated in Indostan, of the purest steel, damasked or highly polished, and ornamented in relief or intaglio with a variety of figures or foliage of the most delicate pattern. Many of the figures are wrought in gold and silver, or in marquetry, with small gems. The hilts of the swords, etc., are agate, chrysolite, lapus-lazuli, chalcedony, blood-stone, and enamel, or steel inlaid with gold, called *tynashee*[1] or *koft* work. The armour is of two kinds, either of helmets and plates of steel to secure the head, back, breast, and arms, or of steel network, put on like a shirt, to which is attached a netted hood of the same metal to protect the head, neck, and face. Under the network are worn linen garments quilted thick enough to resist a sword. On the crown of the helmet are stars or other small device, with a sheath to receive a plume of feathers. The steel plates are handsomely decorated with gold wreaths and borders, and the network fancifully braided." ("Asiatic Miscellany," i, 393. Calcutta, 1795. 4[to]).

The fines for not producing at inspection a man's own armour and that of his elephant (*pakhar*) were as follows (B.M. 6,599, fol. 162a) :

Rank of Officer	*Amount of Fine for Non-Production of*				
	Headpiece (Khud)	*Body Armour (Baktar)*	*Elephant Armour (Pakhar)*	*Greaves (Ranak)*	*Harhai ?*[2]
	Rs. a p.	Rs. a. p.	Rs. a. p.	Rs. a. p.	Rs. a. p.
400	2 0 0	5 0 0	4 0 0	2 0 0	1 0 0
350	2 0 0	4 0 0	3 12 0	1 12 0	0 15 0
300	1 12 0	4 0 0	3 8 0	1 8 0	0 14 0
250	1 8 0	3 8 0	3 4 0	1 4 0	0 13 0
200	1 0 0	3 0 0	3 0 0	1 0 0	0 12 0

Armour was worn by all horsemen who could afford it; may, officers of a certain rank were required to produce it at the time of inspection, subject to a fine if it were not forthcoming. Its use was never discontinued : it was even worn by men of European descent when they entered the native service. For instance, James Skinner, writing of the year 1797, says, "as I was exercising my horse *in full armour*" (Fraser, "Memoirs," i. 125); and again, "I was only saved by my armour" (id. 127). George Thomas, the Irish adventurer, also wore armour (id. 229). Nor is the use of armour entirely discontinued even to this day, as those can testify who saw the troops of the Bundelkhand States paraded before the then Prince of Wales at Agrah in January, 1876.

The armour was worn as follows (W. Egerton, 112, note to no. 440) :—Depending from the cuirass was generally a skirt, which was at times of velvet embroidered with gold. Underneath the body armour was worn a *qabchah*,[3] or jacket quilted and slightly ornamented. Silken trousers and a pair of Kashmir shawls round the waist completed the costume of a nobleman of high rank. As to these quilted coats, we are told elsewhere (Seir, i, 624, note) that "common soldiers wore an ample upper garment, quilted thick with cotton, coming down as far as the knee. These coats would deaden the stroke of a sabre, stop the point of an arrow, and above all kept the body cool by intercepting the rays of the sun." Or as a still later writer tells us (Fitzclarence, "Journal," 143)[4] :—"The irregular cavalry throughout India are mostly dressed in quilted cotton jackets; though the best of these habiliments are not, as I supposed, stuffed with cotton, but are a number of cotton cloths quilted together. This serves as a defensive armour, and when their heads are swathed round, and under the chin, with linen to the thickness of several folds, it is almost hopeless with the sword to make an impression upon them. They also at times stuff their jackets with the rufuse silk of a cocoons, which they say will even turn a ball." This habit of swathing the body in protective armour till little beyond a man's eyes could be seen, gives the point to the scoffing remark of Daud Khan, Panni, at the battle against Husain 'Ali Khan, fought on the 8th Shaban, 1127 H. (6th Sept., 1715), that his assailant, one Mir Mushrif, "came out to meet him like a bride or a woman, with his face hidden" (Ghulam Ali Khan, *Muqaddamah-i-Shah Alam-namah,* fol. 22b).

I now proceed to describe each part of the armour, *seriatim,* beginning with the helmet.

Khud, Dabalqhah, or Top. This was a steel headpiece with a vizor or nose-guard. There are several specimens in the Indian Museum; and in W. Egerton, "Handbook," several of these are figured, Nos. 703 and 704 on plate xiii, No. 703 on p. 134, and another, No. 591, on p. 125. *Khud* is the more usual name, but *dabalghah* is the word used in the *Ain* (Blochmann, I, iii, No. 52, and plate xiii, No. 43). The latter is Chaghatae for a helmet; and Pavet de Courteille gives four forms, (p. 317), and (p. 322). I have only met with it once in an eighteenth-century writer (*Ahwal-ul-Khawaqin, c.* 1147 H., fol. 161b), and then under the form of *dobalghah. Top,* for a helmet, appears several times in Egerton; for instance, on p. 119 and p. 125. This is apparently an Indian word (Shakes, 73), which must be distinguished from the word *top,* a cannon, to which a Turkish origin is assigned. A helmet seems to have been called a *top* by the Mahrattas and in Maisur; but the word is not used by writers in Northern India. If we disregard the difference between and, then we can derive *top,* 'a helmet,' and *topi,* 'a hat,' as does the compiler of the "Madras Manual of Administration," iii, 915, from the ordinary Hindi word *topna,* 'to cover up.' But I hardly think this is legitimate.

Khoghi. The next name to the *dabalghah* on the *Ain* list, the *Khoghi,* No. 53, must be something worn on the head; but there is no figure of it, and I fail to identify the word in that form. From the spelling it is evidently of Hindi origin; and a note in the Persian text has *ghokhi* as an alternative reading. Has it anything to do with *ghoghi,* a pocket, a pouch, a wallet (Shakespear, 1756), or *ghunghi,* cloths folded and put on the head as a defence against the rain (Shakes., 1758) ? The latter may point to a solution : the *khoghi,* or, better, the *ghughi,* may have been folds of cloth adjusted on the head to protect it from a sword blow.

Mighfar is defined (Steingass, 1281) as mail, or a network of steel worn under the cap or hat, or worn in battle as a protection for the face, also a helmet. It is evidently the long piece of mail hanging down from the helmet over the neck and back, as shown in No. 45, plate xii, of the *Ain,* vol. i, and called there and on p. 111, No. 54, the *zirihkulah* (cap of mail). It was through the *mighfar* that, according to Ghulam Ali Khan's history, the arrow passed which wounded Abdullah Khan, Qutb-ul-Mulk, just before he was taken a prisoner at the battle of Hasanpur (13th Nov., 1720), and the following verse brings in the word, as also the *joshan* :

Chah yare kunad mighfar o joshan-am,
Chun Bari na kard akhtar roshan-am.
"What aid to me is vizor and coat of mail,
"When god has not made my star to shine."[5]

Baktar or Bagtar. This is the name for body armour in general, whether it were of the cuirass (*chahar-ainah*) or chain-mail (*zirih*) description. Steingass, 195, defines it as a cuirass, a coat of mail. See also the *Dastur-ul-Insha,* 228. The *bagtar* is No. 58 in the *Ain* list (i, 112), and is shown as No. 47 on plate xii. From the figure it may be inferred that, in a more specific sense, *baktar* was the name for fish-scale armour. *Bargustuwan,* as Mr. H. Beveridge has pointed out to me, is a general name for armour used in the *Tabaqat-i-Nasiri,* text 119 (Raverty, 466 and note); but that work belongs to a period long before the accession of the Moghuls. Steingass, 178, restricts *bargustuwan* to horse armour worn in battle : the *Ahwal-ul-Khawaqin,* fol. 218b, applies it to the armour worn by *elephants,* and I have found it in no other late writer.

Chahar-ainah. This is literally 'four mirrors' : it consisted of four pieces, a breast plate and a back plate, with two smaller pieces for the sides. All four were connected together with leather straps. Steingass, 403, has 'a kind of armour.' It is No. 50 in the *Ain,* i, 112, and figure No. 49 on plate xiii. It is also shown in Egerton, plate ix, and again on p. 144. The specimens in the Indian Museum are No. 364 (p. 103), 450, 452 (p. 112), 569, 570 (p. 119), 587 (p. 124), 707 (p. 135), 764 (p. 144).

Zirih. This was a coat of mail with mail sleeves, composed of steel links (*Dastur-ul-Insha,* 228). The coat reached to the knees (W. Egerton, 125, note to No. 591). It is No. 57 in the *Ain,* i, 112, and No. 46 on plate xiii of that volume. There are six examples in the Indian Museum—W.E. 361, 362 (p. 103), 453 (p. 112), 591, 591 T (p. 125), 706 (p. 135). Apparently, judging from the plate in the *Ain,* the *baktar* (fish scales) or the *chahar ainah* (cuirass) was worn *over* the *zirih.* W.H. Tone, "Maratta People," 61, note, gives a word *beata* as the Mahratta name for the chain-mail shirt that they wore. I cannot identify or trace this word.

Jaibah. Blochmann, *Ain,* i, 111, No. 56, and his note 4, says it was a general name for armour. He gives no figure of it. Erskine, "History," ii, 187, has *jaba.* Steingass, 356, says it is from the Arabic *jubbat,* and spells it *judah,* a coat of mail, a cuirass, any kind of iron armour. The word is used in the *Alamgirnamah,* 245, I. 7 :—"*Tan ba zeb-i-jabah o joshan pairastah*"— "body adorned with the decoration of *jabah* and *joshan.*" It is also used in *Ahwal-ul-Khawaqin* (*c.* 1147 H.), fol. 164a, in the form *jaibah.* Some variety of the *jaibah* is spoken of in the *Akbarnamah,* Daftar II, p. 249, line 4 (Lucknow edition), where we are told that a Rajput of distinction in the garrison of Chitor wore a *jaibah-i-hazar-mikhi.* Apparently it was covered with small studs or knobs (*mikh*).

Other items of body armour (*Dastur-ul-Insha,* 228) were the *Joshan,* the *Jihlam,* the *angarkhak* the *daghlah.* In other authorities we also meet with the *Jamah-i-fatali*, the *chihilqad, sadiqi*, the *kothi*, the *bhanja*, and the *salhqaba*. Of the last, the *salhqaba, Ain*, No. 66, we have no figure, and I am unable to identify it, as I have never seen the word elsewhere. Other words which have defied identification are *harhai*, as I read it (B.M. 6599, fol. 162a; B.M. 1641, fol. 37a), and three articles in the *Dastur-ul-Insha*, p. 228, which I read *subi*, *malk*, and *masari*. We have also the *kamal*, the *ghughwah*, the *kantha-sobha*. Finally, there were the *dast-wanah* or arm-pieces, the *ranak* or greaves, and the *mozah-i-aham*, a smaller pattern of leg-piece.

Joshan. This is No. 59 of the Ain, list, p. 112, and is figured as No. 48 on plate xiii. It appears to be a steel breastplate extending to the region of the stomach and bowels. Blochmann, p. xi, calls it an armour for chest and body; Steingass translates more vaguely 'a coat of mail.'

Jihlam. According to the dictionary (Shakes, 825), this is the Hindi for armour, coat of mail, vizor of helmet; but I do not know what was its special nature or form. Steingass, 405, has *chahlam*, a sort of armour; also *chihaltah*, a coat of mail. Kam Raj, 58b, has a passage—"Mir Mushrif came quickly and lifted his *jihlam* from his face." This makes the word equivalent to vizor. It is not in the *Ain*.

Angarkhah. Hindi for a coat, possibly identical with that sometimes called an *alkhaliq* (a tight-fitting coat). Probably this coat was wadded so as to turn a sword-cut. It is No. 63 of the *Ain*, i, 112, and figure No. 52 of plate xiv, where we see it a long, loose, wide coat worn *over* the armour.

Daghlan or Dagla. The second of these is the Hindi form of the word. It was a coat of quilted cloth.

Jamah-i-fatahi. This word is employed in the *Akbar-namah* (Lucknow edition), ii, 89, line 3. According to the editor's note it is "a robe which on the day of battle is put on beneath the coat of mail, and on it extracts from the Quran, such as *Anna fatahna*, are inscribed." Steingass, 351, defines it as "a fine silken robe." The coats worn by the Khalifah's men in the Sudan, and now at the United Service Institution, must be specimens, as they have words embroidered or sewn on to them.

Chihilqad. This is No. 67 of the *Ain*, 112, and is shown as figure No. 54 on plate xiv. Muhammed Qasim, *Ahwal-ul-Khawaqin*, 161b, spells it, chalqat. It was a doublet worn over the armour, and possibly identical with the *chilta* or *chihal-tah*, literally forty-folds (Shakespear, 884; Steingass, 398).

Sadiqi. *Ain*, 112, No. 62, and No. 51 on plate xiv, a coat of mail something like the *joshan* in shape, but with epaulettes.

Kothi. We have this in the *Ain*, 112. No. 61, and it appears on plate xiv, No. 50, as a long coat of mail worn under the breastplate and opening down the front.

Bhanju. This is No. 64 of the *Ain* list, i, 112, but I have never seen the word anywhere else; it must be a Hindi word, but it is not in Shakespear's Dictionary. The only figure is the one reproduced from Langles by Egerton, No. 9 on plate i, opposite p. 23. This might be almost anything; the nearest resemblance I can suggest is that of a sleeveless jacket.

Kamal. This word is literally 'a blanket,' and from it the corps known as the *kamal-posh* (blanket-wearers) derived its name. The word seems to have had the secondary meaning of a cuirass or wadded coat, possibly made of blanketing on the outside. There were wadded coats of quilted cotton, as well as of wool, which would stand the stroke of a sabre. Some stuffed with silk refuse were considered capable of withstanding a bullet (*Seir*, i, 143, note 105). This sort of protection was very common. "Almost every soldier in the service of a native power has his head secured by many folds of cotton cloth, which not only pass round but likewise over it and under the chin, and a protection for the back of the neck is provided of similar materials. The jacket is composed of cotton thickly quilted between cloths, and so substantial as almost to retain the shape of the body like stiff armour. To penetrate this covering with the edge of the sword was to be done only by the practice of cutting." (Valentine Blacker, "War," 302).

Ghughwah. This must, from its position in the *Ain* list, No. 55, be some kind of armour, but I cannot identify the word, which is of Hindi form. In plate xiii, No. 44, the *thing* is shown as a long coat and cowl of mail, all in one piece. In Egerton's plate (No. i, figure 4) it is something quite different, of a shape which it is difficult to describe, and for which it is still more difficult to suggest a use. The word seems to have some affinity to *khoghi* or *ghughi* (see *ante*). It represents the Eastern Hindi form of *ghogha*, following the usual rule of vowel modification, thus : H.H., *ghora*; E.H., *ghurwa*, 'a horse.' There being also a slight indication of the diminutive in this form, *ghughwa* would be a small *ghogha*. There is a chain epualette shown in one of the plates in Rockstuhl and Gille, which suggests the shape of the *ghughwa* figured by Egerton, and possibly that was its purpose.

Kantha-sobha. This is No. 70 in the list in the *Ain*, 112, and, as we can see from figure 7 on plate i of W. Egerton's catalogue, it was a neck-piece or gorget. No. 69 (*ranak)* and No. 71 (*mozah-i-ahani*) are both worn by the man and not the horse; then why does Blochmann, in his note, suggest that No. 70 (*kantha-sobha*) was attached to the *horse's* neck ? The derivation is from *kantha* (Shakes., 1616) a necklace, and *sobha*, *id.* 1338, ornament, dress, decoration.

Dastwanah. This was a gauntlet, or mailed glove, with steel arm-piece. It is No. 68 of the *Ain*, 112, and is shown as No. 55 on plate xiv. The specimens in the Indian Museum are Nos. 452, 453, 454, 455 (Egerton, p. 112), 568, 570 (id. 119), 587, 590 (id. 124), 745 (id. 139). Three of these are shown, two on plate xii, opposite p. 122, and one on plate xiv, opposite p. 136.

Ranak. In the *Ain* list, 112, No. 69, appears the word *rak* or *rag*, which is quite unmeaning. When we turn to No. 56 on Blochmann's plate xiv, we see that the thing itself is an iron leg piece or greave. Now, wherever there are lists of armour in the MS. *Dastur-ul-Aml*, I find a word, which is invariably shown with a fourth letter of some sort; it might be read *ratak*, *ralak*, *ranak*, but never *rak*. As *ran* means in Persian the 'thigh,' I propose to substitute for Blochmann's *rak* the reading *ranak*, the diminutive ending being used to denote relation or connection, a formation like *dastak* (little hand), a short written order, fit to be (as it were) carried in the hand. The word *ranak* is not in Steingass.

Mozah-i-ahani. This "iron-stocking" is No. 71 on page 112 of the *Ain,* and No. 56 on plate xiv. It is a smaller form of the *ranak.*

Patkah. I find in Ghulam Ali Khan, *Muqaddamah,* fol. 38b, an epithet, *patkah-poshan,* applied to both Sayyads and horse-breakers (*chabuk-suwaran*). It appears to refer to some part of military equipment, but what it is I do not know. It is evidently used in a depreciatory sense.

Having enumerated the man's defensive armour, we go on to that of the horse. The elephant armour I will leave till we come to the special heading devoted to those animals.

Kajim. This is in *Ain,* 112, No. 72 (*kajem*), and is shown as figure No. 57 on plate xiv. Erskine. "History," ii, 187, has the form *kichim.* It was a piece of armour for the hind-quarters of a horse, and was put on over a quilted cloth called *artak-i-kajim* (*Ain,* 112, No. 73).

The other pieces of armour for the horse were the frontlet (*qashqah* : *Ain,* 112, No. 74, and plate xiv, No. 60) and the neck-piece (*gardani* : *Ain,* 112, No. 75). Blochman's description of the latter (p. 112, note 3) does not seem very appropriate, as he makes it a thing which hangs down in front of the horse's chest. *Gardani,* however, is the name still applied to the head and neck-piece, the hood, of a set of horse-clothing. It is the neck-shaped piece in figure No. 58 of Blochmann's plate xiv, and is separately shown in Egerton's plate i, figure No. 3. *Qashqah* is the word used in Persian for the Hindu sect-mark or *tilak,* applied on the centre of the forehead. R.B. Shaw, J.A.S. Bengal for 1878, p. 144, gives *qashqah* as the Eastern Turki for an *animal's* forehead.

Horse trappings were often most richly adorned with silver or gold, embroidery or jewels. When so enriched they were styled *saz-i-tilae,* or *saz-i-marassa.* The names of the various articles are as follows (W. Egerton, 155) : *paltah* (headstall) and *inan* (reins), *zerband* (martingale), *dumchi* (crupper), *khogir* (saddle), *ustak* (shabracque), *balatang* (surcingle), *rikab* (stirrups), *shikarband* (ornamental tassels at corners of saddle). The bow or pommel of a saddle was either *qarbus* (Steingass,

963) or *qash* (id. 947). The former word is used by Shekh Ghulam Hasan, (Samin) Bilgrami, in his *Tazkirah* written in 1198 H. (1783); the second, by Rustam Ali, Bijnori, in his Urdu "History of the Rohelas," written about 1803, fol. 28a. Nizam-ud-din (Ishrat, Siyalkuti) in his *Nadir-namah,* fol. 50a, speaks of *yaltang-posh* as some sort of horse equipment. I have not been able to find out what this was. The list of stable requisites can be seen in *Ain,* i, 136.

REFERENCES

1. Probably for *tah-nishani,* inlaid with gold or studded with jems. *Koft* (beating) is gold or silver wire beaten into iron or steel.
2. Read *sari-asp* in B.M. 1641, fol. 37a, but to neither reading can I assign a meaning.
3. Apparently the diminutive of *qaba,* a close long gown or shirt (Steingass, 950).
4. Lieut. Col. Fitzclarence was created Earl of Munster in 1831, and he is the Lord Munster referred to by Dr. Horn on p. 8 as the author of a series of questions on Mahomedan military usages. His "Journal," the work of a close observer and graphic writer, proves that he was quite competent to write for himself, and not merely "schreiben zu hassen," the history that he had planned.
5. *Muqaddamah-i-Shah Alam-namah* by Ghulam Ali Khan, B.M. Add. 24,028, fol. 40a. The last line probably contains an allusion to Roshan Akhtar, the original name of Muhammad Shah, to whom Abdullah Khan succumbed.

5
Discipline, Drill and Exercises

According to our European notions discipline was extremely lax, if not entirely absent. Bernier, tells us that when once thrown into confusion, it was impossible to restore a Moghul army's discipline, while during the march they moved without order, with the irregularity of a herd of animals; and Europeans generally held the true cause of their dread of fire-arms, and particularly of artillery, to lie in the inexperience of their leading men, who never understood the advantage of discipline or the use of infantry.

Nobles while at headquarters were bound to appear twice a day, morning and evening, at the emperor's audience, and on this point they were strictly supervised. But there seems to have been no regular drill and no manoeuvres. From time to time they paraded their troops in the outer court during the time of public audience, and the state of the horses and elephants was then observed. Occasionally, but very rarely, there were special parades in the open;[1] these generally took place on the line of march, the emperor passing in review the troops of some particular commander, as he was making his march to his next camping ground. For instance, Daud Khan, Panni, thus paraded his troops before Bahadur Shah on the 26th Ramazan 1120 H. (8th Dec. 1708), *Danishmand Khan,* entry of that date.

Organization. There was no regimental organization; the only divisions known were those created by reason of each chief or noble having his own following of troops. Such words as *tuman* or *tumandar* have no strict or definite meaning. The first meant any body of soldiers, and the second the leader or head of such a body. *Jamahdar* is a word of the same signification and equally vague, though it may be taken as denoting a smaller man than a *tumandar*. *Qashim* is a word employed in the second half of the 18th century, having been borrowed from the Durrani system, but I do not think it had a much more definite sense than the above words. In the dictionary, Steingass 971, Qashun is defined as T., body, company, troop, army, soldier, military station.

As for uniform, the only sign of it originally was a red turban worn by all in the imperial employ. For the great mass of the army there was usually no uniformity of dress; but in a general way each class of troops dressed in a similar style, Persians in one way, Mughals in another, Hindustani Mahomedans could be distinguished from Rajputs, and so forth (Horn, 25). But such distinctions, though obvious at once to a practised eye, would take long to record, even if we knew sufficiently what they were. One Sabit Khan, at one time faujdar of Aligarh, was famed as the introducer of a king of attire for soldiers, which was called after him the *sabit-khani* dress. There were, however, some few regiments clothed in uniform. For example, as early as Farrukhsiyar's reign the "*Surkhposhan*" (the Red Regiment) is spoken of (*Ijad's Farrukhshah namah,* fol. 27, line 3). And it would seem from a passage in the *Sharaif-i-usmani,* p. 207, line 4, that in Muhammad Shah's time there were some regiments of body-guards clad alike, and known as the *surkhposh, zardposh* and *siyahposh,* from the colour of their coats, red, yellow or black. These men carried gold or silver clubs (*gathak*).

The Chaghatae origin of the ruling house and many of its officers was shown in the frequent occurrence of military terms from the language used in Central Asia. The emperor and many about the court spoke and understood the Chaghatae language so late as 1173 H. (1759-60), *Seir,* iii, 142; and Mustapha, id., iii, 400, note 63, tells us that up to the time he wrote (*c.* 1785), the word *atlan* (Be mounted) was "carried round to the horse guards when the emperor is going to mount his elephant". (P. de C., 5, from *atlanmaq,* to ride on horseback). Another instance of familiarity with Eastern Turkish is found in 1739, when Aghar

Khan of the Aghar tribe, whose family had been settled in India over a hundred years, talked to Nadir Shah in that language, and even composed some verses in it, Ashob, fol. 258a.

Punishments. For desertion to the enemy we read occasionally of men being blown from the mouth of a gun. In 1714 two Mina robbers were blown from guns by Husain 'Ali Khan, when on the march from Delhi to Ajmer. Again Haidar Quli Khan, when commanding at the siege of Agrah in 1131 H. (1719), had recourse to this punishment with good effect, *Siwanih-i-khizri* (my copy). In the year 1174 H. (1760) the Mahrattahs blew away from guns two Mahomedan leaders taken prisoners by them at Kunjpurah, "History of the Rohelas" by Rustam 'Ali, Bijnori, fol. 51a. And in 1175 H. (30th May 1762) the Mahrattah commander, Naru Pandit, blew two men from guns at Burhanpur, *Mirat-us-Saffa*, 116a. In the "Abrege Historique" prepared by Colonel Gentil in 1772, (E. Blochet, "Inventaireet description des miniatures des Mss. orientaux conserves a la Bibliotheque Nationale", p. 202, N. 219) there is a picture of a man tied to the mouth of a cannon. Horn deals with the subject of desertion on pp. 49 and 51, but both of his references to Babar's memoirs, *viz.,* P. de C. ii, (should be i) 325, and ii, 352, 353, seem to be cases of surrender. That to the *Badshahaamah* i, 334, is not a case of desertion at all. The garrison of Mansurgarh in Orissa (1049 H.) asked for quarter by holding blades of grass between their teeth. This is the well-known Indian custom of indicating submissiveness, see Elliot, "Supp. Gloss.", 252, s. v. *Dant-tinka (*teeth-straw), which is practised by villagers to this day. It is also said to have been resorted to by the Mahrattah horsemen at Dihli (Feb. 1719), when they were overpowered in a street riot, Mhd. Qasim, Lahori, *Ibratnamah* 244, my copy. Another instance is found in a book written *c.* 1147 H., *gah dar dandan giriftah (Ahwal-i-khawaqin,* fol. 217a).

Drill. There seems to have been no drill for soldiers, as such, and no training in combined movements of any sort. The individual, on the other hand, paid the minutest attention to the training of his body, and exercising himself with all his weapons. For this there were the series of movements practised daily, known as *kusarat.* In 1791 an English visitor to the Nizam's camp near Kadapah (Cuddapah) writes to the following effect, Ouseley, "Or. Coll", 1795, i, 21–32, "the traces of order, discipline, and science are so faint as to be scarcely discernible, except in the outward appearance of the men, the management of their horses, and their dexterity in the use of the spear and sabre, which individually gives a martial air". He adds that the men exercise at home with dumb bells or heavy pieces of wood; and he also describes the *kasarat* movements. There were in addition the clubs called *mugdar,* the chain bow or *lezam,* Egerton 147, 150-1, No. 808, and single-stick play. In this last, a stick covered with a loose sheath of leather was held in one hand and a small round buckler in the other, Egerton, 148, quoting from Mundy (3rd ed. 1858, p. 165, 191, 310, 322). The stick is called *gudka, gadka or gadga,* a little club, from *gada,* a club (Shakes. 1689). An account will be found in Briggs, "Ferishta", iii, 207, of *yak-ang-bazi,* play with one single-stick or sword, and *do-ang-bazi,* with sword and shield, or two swords, one held in each hand. There were also wrestling bouts, which usually took place in the rainy season. For mounted men there were tent pegging and shooting at bottles : and the archers had their daily shooting at an earthen mound or target.

Swordplay. The swordsmen were exceedingly skilful and active; their attack and defence being accompanied by the wildest gestures, the most extraordinary leaps, and elaborate feints of every sort. Something of this may still be seen at any Muharram festival, where the most complicated evolutions and sweeping circular cuts are made with the straight gauntlet sword or *patta.*

Burton, writing of Sindh in 1844, gives us a good picture of Indian single-stick and sword-play. The usual style of sword exercise in India is, he says, "*Life.*, i, 119, with a kind of single-stick, ribbonded with list cloth up to the top, and a small shield in the left hand. The swordsman begins by "renowning it", vapouring, waving his blade, and showing all the curious *fantasie* that distinguish a Spanish *espada.* Then, with the fiercest countenance, he begins to spring in the air, to jump from side to side, to crouch, and to rush forwards and backwards, with all the action of an excited baboon. They never thought of giving "point": throughout India the thrust is confined to the dagger. The cuts as a rule were only two, one on the shoulder and the other, in the vernacular called *qalam*,[2] at the lower legs. Nothing was easier than to guard these cuts and to administer a thrust that would have been fatal with steel. Colonel Blacker on the other hand, "War", 302, thought more highly of the native cutting stroke, it being the only one capable of penetrating the quilted jackets, or the many folds of cloth worn as turbans by Indians. The colonel held the opinion that the then Dragoon sword would not penetrate these, even by giving "point". He adds "the native practice not only requires a stiff wrist, but a stiff though not a straight elbow, for a cut that shall disable".

Fitzclarence, 102, thus describes the charge made on the Sitabaldi hill by the Nagpur Rajah's Arabs on the 26th Nov. 1817. "Their manner of advancing was exceedingly imposing. Being perfectly undisciplined, they advanced in a crowd; the bravest being in advance and taking high bounds and turning two or three times round in the air, they rushed forward to the sound of small drums, accompanied by the perpetual vociferation of the war-cry "Din! Din! Muhammad!" This sounds at a distance like 'ding, ding', which is often used instead of the correct expression". As this represents what was, no doubt, the long-established mode of fighting on foot, I give it, in spite of its referring to a period after the fall of Moghul rule.

Horsemanship. The cavalry had their horses trained to a sort of *manege*, where the horse was made to stand on its hind legs and then advance by bounds for a considerable distance. This manoeuvre was resorted to in Bundelkhand whenever a man on horse-back attacked any one on an elephant. Once, when Muhammad Khan, Bangash, invaded Bundelkhand in 1727, he was thus attacked. As he writes in his report to the emperor : "I drove my elephant straight into the thick of the enemy, where my men seemed to be struggling hopelessly against them. At this moment two of the enemy's horsemen, one after the other, rode their horses with the greatest boldness at my elephant, so that their forefeet were on the elephant. By God's aid they were, one after the other, dispatched by our arrows" (see the official report in Shakir Khan's *Gulshan-i-sadiq*, my copy). This caracolling is still adhered to by the cavalry in the Bundelkhand native states, as could be seen by those who witnessed the review of their troops at Agrah in 1876, in the presence of the then Prince of Wales.

The Persians in the Moghul service did not think much of Indian horsemanship, judging from the following passage of an anonymous memoir written about the middle of the 18th century. "As a rule the people of India do not know how to ride, and horsemanship is unknown in Hindustan. In addition, they use their utmost efforts to efface from horses all the qualities of the horse, and make it epileptic and mad. Their movements are not regulated by an intelligible principle, and it is impossible for them to be under the rider's control. I am a good rider and relying on my skill, I have often mounted Indian horses barebacked, in the belief that they would not be too much for me; and yet, when I have wanted to go east, they have carried me north, south, or west, and *vice versa*. If one wants to control the speed of the horse and make him travel at the speed one wishes, the beast either stands up on his hind legs or jibs, or hugs a wall till he crushes his rider or kills him in some other way. His paces are accompanied by jumps wholly unnatural" (*Tarikh-i-Farah Bakhsh*, trans. W. Hoey, i, App. p. 7).

In this connection the following passage, although written in 1844, is quite as applicable to the Indian Moghuls as if it had been written a century or two earlier. "All nations seem to despise one another's riding, and none seem to know how much they have to learn. The Indian style has the merit of holding the horse well in hand, making him bound off at a touch of the heel, stopping him dead at a hand gallop, and wheeling him round on a pivot. The Hindu (Indian?) will canter over a figure-of-eight, gradually diminishing the dimensions tell the animal leans over at an angle of 45^0, and throwing himself over the off side and hanging down to the earth by the heel, will pick up sword or pistol from the ground". (Burton, "Life", i, 135). This is as favorable as the preceding extract was unfavorable. When doctors disagree, who shall decide?

Mounting Guard. In time of peace the nobles took it in turn to mount guard with their troops at the palace gate. This was called *chauki* and the guard-house was the *chauki-khanah*.[3] The rules will be found in the *Ain*, i, 257. The duty lasted for twenty-four hours and recurred once a week. The relief took place every evening. There was also another division of the army into twelve parts, each of which mounted guard for one month. But I do not see how the two divisions, that into seven and that into twelve parts, are to be reconciled with each other.

Hunting. The nearest approach to army manoeuvres was when the army or a division was ordered out to take part in a royal hunt. This subject is touched on by Horn, 69. One branch of the army combined two functions; in peace they were huntsmen, in war, skirmishers. There were the *Qarawal*, with the *Qarawal Begi*, or Chief Huntsman, at their head.[4] Horn, 69, refers to two descriptions of a royal hunt, namely, Budauni, iii, 92, and Erskine, "History", ii, 286. I add another from Anand Ram, *Mirat-ul-Istilah*, for. 184a. *Shikar-i-qamrghah* (or *qamrgah*), also *shikar-i-jargah*, is called in Hindi *hata-jori*.[5] For this hunt a king gives orders, through his huntsmen (*qarawal*), to his governors and the zamindars and cultivators (ryots) to surround a wide space full of game. This was closed in on daily till the area was very small. Then the ruler and his friends arrived, entered the enclosed space, and hunted the game. As this was a privilege (*quruq*) of kings, no one else, not even a great noble, was allowed to practise it. This method was also followed in Iran; in India it was given up after the middle of 'Alamgir's reign.'

REFERENCES

1. These were the *Mahallah* already referred to see ante. p. 46. The phrase in Khurasan was *San didan*, see *Mujmil ut-tarikh bad Nadirigah*, p. 81, line 5.
2. Probably from *qalam kardan*, to lop or prune.

3. Steingass, 402, *chauki,* H. a raised seat, chair; a guard; a place for collecting customs; a watchhouse. J. Shakes. 507, *chauk,* a market, a city square; a courtyard.
4. Steingass, 962, a sentinel, watchman, spy, guard; the vanguard, a gamekeeper, a hunter.
5. *Kamrghah,* Steingass, 988, the hunting ring formed to enclose the game in the grand royal chase. Id, 360, *jargah,* a circle or ring of men or beasts. *Hatna,* H. to drive back, *jorna,* to collect, therefore *hata-jori,* a drive of *game.*

6
Battles

In the foregoing chapter I have given in brief the character sketch of each notable emperor with special reference to his soldierly qualities. This information is essential in order to assess the quality, quantity and organization of their armies. All the wars and campaigns fought in this age reflected the character and capabilities of their emperors, as they were the actual commanders both in peace and war, helped only by other generals as subordinates.

To understand the achievements of the Mughal Army, it is, therefore, necessary to have a knowledge of the various wars fought by the emperors during the period of their reigns. It will be rather difficult to put forward in detail each battle, war or campaign because their chroniclers, official or unofficial, did not leave the details on record for posterity. Most of the facts now available to the world are rather vague and based, at times, on certain inaccurate information. But it is the only material that is now available and we have to depend on them.

Even though detailed information may not be available, the general picture will give us some idea of the conduct of the wars during the Mughal times. In order to appreciate them it is necessary to have a brief idea of each important war.

Militarily, the reigns of Babar, Akbar and Aurangzeb were the most productive period in medieval India. During other reigns it was not so, as they were mostly local engagements in which not much was at stake. In others the facts of nations, kingdoms and personalities were involved.

Like all wars, the wars in medieval India were a continuation of the policy of the Government, and had the full backing of the emperor. These were fought with organized armies and the penalty of defeat was very severe. Hence the wars of the middle ages were fought with much fury and hatred. But the Indian wars were mostly religious wars, at times changing the complexion to a religious political struggle.

At places I have attempted to illustrate the battle formations employed during the battle by both the sides, but, in the absence of any detailed information on the subject, they may be open to comments. It will, however, give a rough idea of the various types of formations employed during the battles.

With the advent of the Mughals, warfare, as practised in India during the Muhammedan rulers, underwent considerable changes both in the use and type of weapons. It was the Muhammedans who introduced gunpowder in India, and this completely revolutionised the character of warfare, formerly fought with elephants, bows and arrows.

PANIPAT (1526)

The battle of Panipat again decided, for the third time, the mastership of India and this time the throne of India passed to the Mughals on April 21, 1526. "The decisive battle was fought on April 21, 1526, on the plam of Panipat—the historic site where the throne of India has been thrice won," says Dr. Lane Poole.[1]

After brushing aside all opposition on his march to Delhi, Babar advanced towards the capital and came to know that Ibrahim Lodi, the reigning emperor, was going to fight the Mughal's bid for the conquest of India. However, both the sides faced each other near the historic site of Panipat, and got busy with the preparation for the coming battle.

As the opposing armies faced each other, Babar took stock of the whole situation. He found that his army was much smaller numerically than the Indian emperor's and his only chance lay in out-fighting and out-generalling the Indian by his superior quality tactics. In his own Memoirs his thoughtful remarks on the situation are in these words : "Ibrahim was a young man of no experience. He was negligent in all his movements : he marched without order; retired or halted without plan and engaged in battle without foresight, ... and was too miserly to raise additional forces, or even to pay his troops in the field."[2]

On the eve of battle, Ibrahim had 100,000 men, and Babar had only 8,000. This numerical inferiority did not dismay Babar, as he was confident of the better fighting quality of the troops and his aggressive generalship. Actually these facts won Babar the battle.

As the preparations were going on, the troops, however, became restive as they were far away from their homes and also because their enemy was superior in numbers. All these facts dismayed the zeal to fight, and Babar realising this danger, attempted a surprise night attack on the Afghan position. This attack failed as his troops lost their way in the darkness and there was confusion all round. But this raid had one effect ... it forced Ibrahim to give battle to Babar earlier than expected as he became rather panicky.

Before forming his army in battle array, Babar made a short appreciation of the situation as he faced them. It will be recalled that even though Babar had only 8,000 troops, his effective strength during the battle of Panipat was still short. A considerable number of troops had been left behind in garrison duties, security of communications and wastage due to casualties. "If he were to triumph over the immensely superior forces of his adversary, it could only be by means of an effective combination, between his highly trained cavalry and his new firearms. Ustad Ali and Mustafa between them could do deadly work when they were confronted by a dense mass of enemy; but both cannoneers and matchlock men were liable to be ridden down and overwhelmed unless carefully protected by covering force of Infantry and cavalry."

"But how were these covering forces to be supplied from the tiny army? For, unless Babar could contrive to present a front equal in length to the effective front displayed by the enemy, his cavalry would be unable to employ the flanking tactics by which he hoped to roll up the Afghan wings upon the centre. Only by carrying out this manoeuvre, and by driving the enemy's forces into a huddled mass upon which Ustad Ali and Mustafa could direct their fire, would Babar be enabled to utilise his artillery to the best advantage," says Prof. Rushbrook Williams.[3]

After appreciating the problem posed above, Babar set upon fighting the enemy on his own chosen ground and in the desired manner. The two main problems to be solved were, firstly, holding the line against superior numbers and, secondly protection of the cannoneers and the matchlock men from being trampled by the charging cavalry.

This is how Babar found the answer to these problems. "Influenced probably by the example of Salim the Grim at Chaldiran in 1514, Babar determined to employ a line of wagons to stiffen his weak front."[3] This was not all. The wagons had to be securely fastened so that they did not give way before the rushing cavalry. This he achieved as follows : "He collected 700 gun-carts and formed a laager by linking them together with twisted bullhides, to break a cavalry charge."[4] What about the protection of the cannoneers? In order to give special shelter to the musketeers and artillery men, small breast-works, sufficiently large to protect one man were constructed in considerable numbers, and arranged six or seven between each wagon along the portion of the front which Ustad Ali and Mustafa were to occupy," says Prof. Rushbrook Williams."[4]

After completing the preparation of his position, Babar prepared to occupy it and dispose of his army in battle order. His troop dispositions were as follows : "His army was drawn up behind his laager in the usual order, right and left centre, right and left.

"Wing, advance guard, and reserve; but in addition he had placed flanking parties of Mughals on the extreme right and left, with orders to execute their famous national manoeuvre, the "tulghma" :—a rapid wheel charging the enemy's rear—of which Babar well knew the tremendous effect," describes Dr. Lane Poole Prof. Rushbrook Williams clarifies the detailed occupation in these words "... took up his ground with the town of Panipat sheltering his right wing. On the left, he strengthened position by digging a ditch and constructing an "abatis" of felled trees in such a manner as to render it impossible for the enemy to roll up his line from the left. Secure on both flanks, he now strengthened his centre with the line of breastworks and wagons which he had previously prepared. The line, however, was not continuous; for, at intervals of only bowshot apart, large gaps were left, wide enough for fifty or a hundred horsemen to charge through the abreast."[5]

After completing the preparations and is dispositions of his troops, Babar was ready to meet the Indian troops on the battlefield of Panipat. And the day came on 21st April 1526, when the fate of India was to be decided for the next three hundred years.

Babar was ready but what about Ibrahim? Unfortunately nothing much is known about Ibrahim's dispositions and preparations for the battle. All we see about the Afghan army is when it advanced against Babar. The battle is ably described by Dr. Lane Poole as follows : "The army of Delhi came straight on, at a quick march without halt from the start. They seemed to be aiming at Babar's right, and he sent up the reserves to its support. As the enemy came up to the ditches, abatis, and hurdles they hesitated, and the pressure of the troops behind threw them into some confusion. Taking advantage of this Babar sent out his Mughal flanking through the gaps in the laager, and they galloped round the enemy and poured their arrows into the rear. Part of the Emperor's left wing, advancing uncautiously, got into difficulties; but the general's eye was on them, and they were promptly supported from the centre. Meanwhile the right was also hard pressed and Babar sent forward his right centre to their assistance. The master gunner, Ustad Ali, made pretty practice with his "firengi" pieces, in front of the line and was admirably seconded by Mustafa, the Cannoneer on the left centre. The enemy was now engaged on all sides, front, flanks and rear, and their charges, which seemed ineffective to men who had stood up the Mughal's swoop, were easily repulsed and driven back upon their centre, which was already too crowded to be able to use its strength. In this jammed confusion they lay at the mercy of the hardy Turks and Mughals, who fell upon the strangled ranks with deadly effect."[6]

Thus the vast Afghan army was defeated and they suffered about 15,000 dead on the battlefield. The beaten remnants were hotly pursued by Babar's army till they surrendered. The flying columns of Babar did not give the defeated enemy any time or opportunity to rally and gather further strength. This column occupied Agra and then Delhi and thus brought a glorious victory to a fitting close.

Generally the battle of Panipat is not studied with the critical eye it deserves. It was more important than mere armed clash between the degenerated Pathans and the hardy Turks; the clash between the two opposing methods of warfare—the Ottoman and the Afghan methods and lastly between the two personalities—the energetic Turk and the degenerated tyrant. Alexander Dow rightly says : "But what contributed most to weigh down the scale of conquest was the degeneracy of the Pathans, effeminated by the luxury and wealth, and dead to all principles of virtue and honour, which their corrupt factions and civil discords had totally effaced; it being now no shame to fly, no infamy to betray, no breach of honour to murder, and no scandal to change parties. When, therefore, the fear of shame and the love of fame were gone, it was no wonder that a horde, without unanimity, order, or discipline, should fall into the hands of a few brave men."[7]

Militarily it was much more than this. The Mughal army brought new life into the decaying military institution of the Lodis. Not only tactics but a new look in generalship was also introduced. It will be recalled that when Babar disposed of his troops in battle array, he positioned himself centrally so that he could control the battle all round him. Thus personal touch and control in the field of battle by the commander came into vogue. "Babar's generalship, however, had much to do with the successful issue. His skilful disposition of his men behind a fortified laager, which checked the enemy's charges, above all their heavy elephants : his adoption of the Mughal flanking manoeuvre; and his alert support of each section of his line the instant he detected any wavering...these were among the causes of his victory. His men began the battle in no little alarm; it was their Emperor's cool science and watchful tactics that restored their confidence and gave them back their pluck," says Dr. Lane Poole.[8]

It is worth studying the reasons that prompted Babar to prepare, occupy and dispose of his troops in this manner at the battle of Panipat. Prof. Rushbrook Williams critically analyses the tactics of Babar in these words : "It has been the fashion to assume that Babar's wagon line was a movable fortress, behind which his small force might hope to escape annihilation; that it was an imitation of the methods employed by the Hussites of Bohemia when confronted by the heavy cavalry of the Empire. Neither of these suppositions will bear investigation. The wagon line was a stratagem of aggression rather than of defence; it was intended to hold the enemy along an extended front, so that his flank might be open to attacks. Certainly it provided shelter for the Artillerymen and Musketeers; but it was in no sense of the word a laager or a fortress. The proof of this is not far to seek. Men do not leave many wide gaps in a wall which is intended merely to protect them from attack; and had Babar designed to construct a "rampart" or a "movable fortress" he would surely have drawn up his wagons in a continues line, even if he had not surrounded himself on all sides with them. Nor is it correct to compare the wagon line of Panipat with the Hussite wagon units which were trained to manoeuvre and combine forming a real fortress of a movable type. In Bohemia conditions had been essentially different; infantry were compelled to meet cavalry in the open field, and the wagon laager was invented to shelter the infantrymen. But Babar was a cavalry leader; it was in his cavalry that his great strength lay, he had no need to cover behind a rampart to escape the shock of hostile horsemen. Even as his principal objective was to provoke, not to avoid, a combat, so was his wagon line a device to destroy the enemy, not a refuge in which his own forces might shun destruction."[9] Nothing is so truthful and clear as this statement about Babar's intentions. It will be noted from records that the area where the battle of Panipat was fought, was open and bare, and there was no natural landmark on which certain advantages could be taken when preparing for the battle. Hence, Babar's army being inferior in number, he had to secure one flank which was rested on the village of Panipat and also had to secure the personal safety of his gunners, who, obviously, had to fire from the open plains and thus were vulnerable to enemy cavalry. Thus Babar had to design a shield to parry the cavalry charge, hold the rushing enemy in the centre, and thus deliver the blow by flank attacks and artillery fire. This is what actually happened to the enemy: "Their front was badly cramped and although they seem to have brought their left wing to bear by adopting the expedient of inclining their line, they had not proper room to employ their strength. This superiority in numbers, so far from benefiting them, became the cause of their downfall.[10]

The battle of Panipat bears a striking resemblance to the battle of Canne during World War II. It may be that Field Marshal Montgomery had studied Babar's war in India.

The battle of Panipat was Canne to the Lodi dynasty. It was the end of their supremacy and their empire. It marked the end of one epoch and the beginning of another.

KANWAHA (1527)

The next formidable rival that Babar faced was the Rana Sanga of Chitor who was dominating the confederacy of the Rajputs. He was the biggest and strongest block that Babar had to fight, prior to his complete domination of India. Babar's supremacy over all his rivals and over India was decided in the battle of Kanwaha in 1527.

The trouble arose over Biana which both the sides claimed. As neither of the contesting parties was prepared to submit to the other, the result was to fight it out.

Both sides mustered formidable forces....the Rana had about 200,000 men and Babar had by this timeal so a large force. Both sides began preparations for the oncoming struggle.

Babar had to face a crisis on this occasion. His troops did not want to fight in this battle because they were concerned about their homes and families and primarily, because of the great fighting reputation of the Rajputs. But again, as before, Babar rallied all his men to his cause by fanatical speeches and vows.

After setting his house in order, he advanced to meet the redoubtable enemy. This is how he advanced : "I advanced my wagons (and guns) and tripods with all the apparatus and machines that I had prepared, and marched forward with my army in order of battle ... right wing, left wing, and centre in their places. In front were the wagons, gun-carriages, and tripods on wheels, and behind came Ustad Ali Kuli, with a body of his matchlock men, to prevent the communication being cut off between artillery and the infantry behind, and to enable them to advance and form into line. When the ranks were formed and every man in his place, I galloped along the line encouraging the Begs and men of the centre, right, and left, giving special directions to each division how to act, and to each man orders how to proceed and engage. Then, when all was arranged, I moved the army on in order of battle for a couple of miles, when we camped. The pagans, getting notice of our movements, were on the altert, and came close to our wagons and ditch. I did not intend fighting that day, but sent out a few skirmishers by way of taking an omen. They took a number of pagans and cut off their heads, which they brought in.....This raised the spirits of the army wonderfully and gave be them confidence."[11]

As before, Babar took great care to prepare his battle positions. Dr. Lane Poole describes it as follows : "As before at panipat he ranged the gun carriages, and probably the baggage wagons, so as to cover his front, and chained them together at a distance of five paces. Mustafa, from Turkey, ordered his artillery admirably in the Ottoman manner on the left wing, but Ustal Ali had a different method. Where there were no guns or wagons, a ditch was dug, backed up by portable wooden tripod on wheels, lashed together at a few paces apart."[12] He also had kept a larger reserve than before, and completely restored the confidence of the troops by all these preparations for battle.

Now came the crucial battle for the supremacy in India on 16th March, 1527. Here is the official account of the battle as given in the official despatch written by Shaikh Zainuddin : "The battle began about half past nine in the morning, by a desperate charge made by the Rajputs on Babar's right. Bodies of the reserve were pushed on to its assistance; and Mustafa Rumi, who commanded one portion of the artillery (and matchlocks) on the right of the centre, opened fire upon the assailants. Still, new bodies of the enemy poured on undauntedly, and new detachments from the reserve were sent to resist them. The battle was no less desperate on the left, to which also it was found necessary to despatch repeated parties from the reserve....When the battle had lasted several hours, and still continued to rage, Babar sent orders to the flanking columns to wheel round and charge; and he soon after ordered the guns to advance, and, by a simultaneous movement, the household troops and cavalry stationed behind the cannon were ordered to gallop out in right and left of the matchlock men in the centre, who also moved forward and continued their fire hastening to fling themselves with all their fury on the enemy's centre. When this was observed in the wings they also advanced. These unexpected movements, made at the same time, threw the enemy into confusion. Their centre was shaken; the men who were displaced by the attack made in flank on the wings and rear were forced upon the centre and crowded together. Still the gallant Rajputs were not appalled. They made repeated desperate attacks on the Emperor's centre, in hopes of recovering the day, but were bravely and steadily received, and swept away in great number. Ustad Ali's huge "balls" did fearful executions among the "heathen". Towards evening the confusion was complete, and the slaughter was consequently dreadful. The fate of the battle was decided. Nothing remained for the Rajputs but to force their way through the bodies of the enemy that were now in their rear, and to effect a retreat. The Emperor pursued them as far as their camp,...and detached a strong body of horse with orders to pursue the broken troops of the confederates without halting to cut up all they met, and prevent them from re-assembling.[13]

Babar had to fight a stubborn enemy, and the victory was not so easy. There were occasions during the fighting when the situation was very grave, and it was touch and go. The Rajputs fought most valiantly. The numerical superiority of the Rajputs put a terrible strain on the Mughals, and it was after a desperate charge that they finally won the day.

The battle of Kanwaha (Kanwaha (Kanna) had far-reaching effects. It crushed the confederacy of the Hindus in their bid for power; and finally it established Babar and his Mughal dynasty securely on the throne of Delhi for the next three centuries.

THE GUJRAT CAMPAIGN (1572-73)

Of all the wars fought during Akbar's reign (of which there were many) his expedition into Gujrat is the most famous and instructive military exploit.

All was not well with Gujrat. It was a scene of constant civil war between the various small districts controlled by the Muslim nobles, and anarchy and raids on the neighbouring countries were the order of the day. The people were oppressed by the tyrannical nobles who ruled over the small principalities (*e.g.*, Surat, Broach, Kaira, Ahmedabad, Baroda, Mahi Kantha and Rewa Kantha, Panch Mahas, Palanpur, Radhanpur, Baliana, Cambay, Khandesh and Kathiawar) and disorder and confusion reigned. In the circumstances Akbar decided to lead a military expedition to this part and clean up the disorder and anarchy that prevailed.

The Imperial army under Akbar set off for Gujrat on September 1572, with an advance guard of 10,000 horsemen. Very little opposition was met from the opponents during the advance till he reached Surat, a famous maritime fort. But the place was captured without much exertion.

Thus ended the first Gujrat expedition on 4th June, 1573 when Akbar returned to Agra after nine months. But he was not yet destined to have respite from the harassment of the Gujrat nobles. When Akbar left Gujrat he had thought that he had controlled and organized the place, but actually it was not so. No sooner had he left, than the unruly elements, who once had been the rulers, again raised their heads and embarked on the same policy which they had been previously carrying on. This unruly behaviors enraged Akbar and he despatched a second expedition to the place.

After a few marches, he reached Ahmedabad. There the enemy faced him with 20,000 men against his 3,000. As usual he organized the order of battle of his troops into three sections of brigades, centre, right and left.

The enemy, however, did not expect the arrival of the Imperial troops so fast and were taken by surprise. Stiff hand to hand fighting ensued and the enemy fought with great valour. Eventually the enemy was defeated and Akbar organized the Government on a sound basis. Dr. Vincent Smith says :

"Considering the distance traversed Akbar's second Gujrat expedition may be described safely as the quickest campaign on record."[14]

After successfully completing the Gujrat expedition in 43 days, Akbar returned home on 5th October, 1573.

THE MARATHA WAR (1689-1707)

Aurangzeb fought many notable battles during his time, but amidst all, Maratha War stands out as most bitter and in which both sides displayed super organizational ability and leadership.

Before we actually discuss the various fights it is essential to have a knowledge of the history of the growth of the Marathas as a nation. It will be recalled that they were a non-entity during the reign of Shahjehan. They gradually changed their status from ordinary tillers of the land to a mighty fighting nation through the able and farsighted guidance of the king of Bijapur. "Gradually they came to be employed in his army, first in garrison duty, and then in the light cavalry, a branch of the service for which they displayed extraordinary aptitude,"[15] says Dr. Lane Poole. It was one of these Marathas, Shivaji, who was the strongest opponent that Aurangzeb faced during his life time.

Shivaji gradually extended his area of activity towards the Mughal territory. He had, however, a surprising skill in harassing the Mughal and looting and plundering their territory. It eventually became difficult for the Mughal Emperor to control him. Efforts were made towards conciliation but the contemptuous behaviour of the Mughal Emperor kept him a sworn enemy for ever. The study of the Maratha Military System is itself a vast subject, and it is difficult to dwell on it at length, in this small volume, but I will attempt to give a brief idea of it to the readers.

The Marathas were mostly guerilla fighters who avoided pitched battles if their adversaries were numerically superior, surprise and swift attacks being the keynote; they adopted a scorched earth policy whenever the Mughals invaded their territory with their large army. A few incidents will illustrate these points. When the Mughals attacked Konkan, the Marathas laid waste the whole of the country so that there was no fodder left for the animals, they attacked from the rear when least expected, and after the attack they swiftly dispersed among the hills of the Ghats where they could not be followed or found. They also ambushed the stray parties of the Mughal army and ousted them off. Thus the elusive enemy struck terror in the heart of the mighty Mughal army.

Aurangzeb, therefore, planned to dam the source of funds of the Marathas, by exterminating the kingdom of Golkonda and Bijapur. So formidable was the power of the Marathas, that Aurangzeb had to spend 26 years in this part of the country to subdue them.

After prolonged and bitter fighting Bijapur was annexed in 1686 after a long siege. The fort of Golconda was captured in 1687, not by military force but by treachery. Thus Aurangzeb's conquest of the Deccan was completed after a terrible loss of men, money and prestige. Sir George Dunbar rightly remarks : "The war of Deccan so depleted the Imperial treasury that for the last ten years of the reign the pay of the troops was usually three years in arrears."[16]

In spite of this long unequal struggle, the Marathas were

not subdued by the Mughals. This is well illustrated by Sir George Dunbar : "The years of warfare with the Marathas from 1689 to 1707 proved a disheartening struggle for the Imperial armies. In the Western Ghats the forts offered obstinate resistance, and in the Deccan itself the Marathas plundered the country, cut off convoys and repeatedly defeated the Mughal columns."

"The camp was thirty miles in circumference, and held about a million people, the army consisting of 60,000 cavalry, 100,000 infantry, 3,000 elephants and 50,000 camels. This huge population ate up all the provisions for miles around, and whenever the lines of communications with the north were cut by the Marathas, Glagala ran considerable danger of starvation."[17] Most of the operations conducted in these parts were the reduction of the forts. But these forts were very strong and well manned : the fortresses were well stocked with ammunition and provisions; a horsed cavalry screen was put forward to keep the attackers at bay from the surrounding area of the fortresses; sustained fire was kept up day and night to deter the attackers from scaling the walls and other preparations for the attack; and a ditch was constructed round the forts to keep away men and guns. But in spite of this the Mughals filled the moats with earth, shelled the ramparts with their heavy guns and by means fair and foul (treachery and bribery) subdued these fortresses one by one.

Let us now analyse as to how the Marathas kept on winning such an unequal struggle, and why the Mughals fared so badly against their enemy. The reasons are not far to seek. Dr. Lane Poole had ably summed up the reasons in these words : "The explanation of this colossal failure is to be found partly in the contrast between the characters of the invaders and the defenders. Had the Mughals been the same hardy warriors that Babar led from the valleys of the Hindukush, or had the Rajputs been loyal protagonists who had so often courted destruction in their devoted service of earlier emperors, the Marathas would have been allowed but a short shrift. Aurangzeb had alienated the Rajputs for ever, and they would not risk their lives for him in exterminating a people who were after all Hindus...

As for the Mughals, three or four generations of court-life had ruined their ancient manliness. Babar would have scorned to command such officers as surrounded Aurangzeb—Instead of hardy swordsmen, they had become padded dandies...

The very rank and file grumbled if their tents were not furnished as comfortably as in quarters at Agra, and their requirements attracted an immense crowd of camp followers, twenty times as numerous as the effective strength. So vast a host, was like a plague of locusts in the country; it devoured everything and though at times it was richly provisioned, at others the Marathas cut off communications with the base of supplies in the north, and a famine speedily ensued."

"The Marathas, on the other hand, cared nothing for luxuries, a cake of millet sufficed them for a meal, with perhaps an onion for 'point'. They defended a fort to the last, and then defended another fort. They were pursued from place to place, but were never daunted, and they filled up the intervals of sieges by harassing the Mughal armies, stopping convoys of supplies, and laying waste the country in the path of the enemy. There was no bringing them to a decisive engagement. It was one long series of petty victories followed by larger losses. Nothing was gained that was worth the labour, the Marathas increasingly became objects of dread to the demoralised Mughal army, and the country, exasperated by the sufferings of a prolonged occupation by an alien and licentious soldiery, became more and more devoted to the cause of the intrepid bandits, which they identified as their own."[18]

Thus ended the long drawn out Maratha war during Aurangzeb's reign with a tactical victory, but a strategical loss.

REFERENCES

1. The Story of the Nations (Vol. 59).
2. Memoirs of Babar.
3. An Empire Builder of the 16th Century.
4. The Story of the Nations (Vol. 59).

5. *Ibid.*
6. *Ibid.*, and Babar by Lane Poole.
7. The History of Hindustan.
8. Babar.
9. An empire builder of the 16th Century.
10. *Ibid.*
11. Memoirs of Babar.
12. Babar.
13. Erskine's translation from the despatch.
14. The Story of the Nations (Vol. 59)
15. A History of India.
16. *Ibid.*
17. *Ibid.*
18. The Story of the Nations (Vol. 59).

7
Particular Battles, Stratagems, Losses

Dr. Horn devotes many pages (71-105) to reproducing detailed battle pieces. These comprise Babar's first battle at Panipat, 21st April 1526, Babar's battle against Rana Sanga, 16th March 1527, Akbar's battle at Panipat, 5th Nov. 1556, the battle at Korah between Shah Shuja and 'Alamgir, 3rd Jan. 1659 and the taking of a mountain pass near Ajmer. Most of these serve more as specimens of style than as plain and direct reports of what happened at these actions. All of them, except Babar's own description of the battle of the 21st April 1526, are written in that deplorably inflated, rhetorical style, of which Persian and Indian writers are so proud, where sense is drowned in sound and plain facts are buried under far-fetched metaphor. Such turgid stuff reduces the translator to despair and engenders disgust in the European reader. As will have been noticed, Dr. Horn brings his specimens no further down than the first year of Alamgir's reign. There was much fighting in the rest of that reign and in the following reigns, and from the later historians it would be possible to put together accounts of many other battles. I may instance those of Jajau (1707), Agrah (1712), Hasanpur (1720).

For the first of these recourse might be had to Niamat Khan (afterwards Danishmand Khan), poetically Ali. This well known poet and literary man, who died 30th Rabi i, 1122 H., 28th May 1710, was appointed historiographer by Bahadur Shah, and has left two descriptions of the battle at Jajau, in which his patron defeated a brother, Aram Shah, and obtained the throne. That in the *Bahadur Shah-namah* is the simpler; the other, a separate work known as the *Jang-namah*, is written in the florid, full-blown manner which was considered requisite for such show pieces. It is a very clever performance; an admirable specimen of a detestable *genre*. The proportion of bread to sack may be known from the fact that when, after transcribing the whole piece, I proceeded to make an excerpt of the bare facts, I found that they occupied only one-fifth of the original space.

Following Dr. Horn's example, I will give a description of the battle of Hasanpur, fought on the 13th Nov. 1720. On the 28th Sept. 1719, Muhammad Shah had been raised to the throne at Agrah by the two Sayyad brothers, Abdullah Khan and Husain Ali Khan. Shortly afterwards (8th Oct. 1720), with Muhammad Shah's tacit approval, the younger brother was assassinated. Abdullah Khan thereupon raised another scion of the royal house, Prince Ibrahim, to the throne, and marched from Delhi against Muhammad Shah, who was coming from the south-east. Just before the decisive battle, the emperor's head-quarters were at Hasanpur, those of Abdullah Khan about six miles further north, at Biluchpur. Both places are between Mathura and Delhi, on the right bank of the Jamnah, in parganah Palwal. The authorities on which the following description is founded are 1. Kanwar Khan, 2. Shiu Das, 3. Khafi Khan, 4. Mhd. Qasim, Lahori, 5. Mhd. Shafi, Warid, 6. Khwajah Abd-ul-Karim, Kashmiri, and 7. Mhd. Umr, son of Khizr Khan.

The Battle of Hasanpur. Early in the morning of Wednesday the 13th Muharram 1133 H. (13th Nov. 1720), before the sun rose, Muhammad Shah mounted his elephant, Padahah Pasand, and took his place in the centre. Haidar Quli Khan was sent on ahead with the strong artillery force under his commnad[1]; while Khan Dauran and Sabit Khan were ordered to follow and support him with the left wing. Muhammad Khan, Bangash, and Saadat Khan were sent towards the river and the rear. Round his Majesty's person were the new wazir, Muhammad Amin Khan, and his son, Qamr-ud-din Khan, Dil Daler Khan, Sher Afkan Khan, Hizbar Khan and others. Zafar Khan, Fakhr-ud-din Khan, his brother, Rajah Bahadur of Kishngarh, Nusrat Yar Khan, Jag Ram (Jai Singh's *diwan*) Aziz Khan, Mir Mushrif, and Rajah Gopal Singh, Bhadauriyah, were placed in charge of the main camp, which was at a distance of one kos from the position taken up by the emperor. The prisoner, Ratn Chand, diwan of Abdullah Khan, was now sent for. He was brought before the emperor on an elephant; he was there made to dismount, and was at once executed. The severed head was thrown before the emperor's elephant and trodden under foot.

Chura Jat, who was hovering near the army on the west, cut off many followers and penetrated into the camp. But the above-named Rajahs drove him out again. Next the Jats attacked on the south, whence they carried off some goods and part of the imperial property. Zafar Khan, Muzaffar Khan and Muhammad Khan, Bangash, once more repelled them. They then made a further attempt on the east side. Here Mir Mushrif and Alwi Khan, Tarin, of Lakhnau, met and defeated them. But the uproar was very great, and the camp followers and traders were so frightened, that they jumped into the Jamnah and tried to swim across it, many losing their lives in the attempt. By three o'clock the baggage camp was moved to a safer place, and the confusion continuing, it was again moved still farther off.

When Najm-ud-din Ali Khan at the head of the Sayyad vanguard, appeared in the distance from the direction of the river, Haidar Quli Khan, the imperial Mir Atash, moved out his heavy cannon into the open, and encountered the advancing enemy with a storm of balls from them and his field-pieces. The fire was so continuous and heavy that the artillery of the other side was silenced. After every volley Haidar Quli Khan urged on his men by lavish gifts of gold and silver. As the artillery advanced, the rest of the army followed and occupied the ground. Stimulated by their commander's liberality, the gunners worked zealously, and a second set of guns were loaded by the time the first were discharged. Khan Dauran's troops moved in support of the imperial artillery, Sanjar Khan and Dost Ali Khan, in command of that noble's guns, particularly distinguishing themselves. The latter was wounded in the foot. Sayyad Nusrat Yar Khan and Sabit Khan also took a leading part, while Saadat Khan and Muhammad Khan, Bangash, created a diversion on the left. During the day a rocket fell on Sayyad Abdullah Khan's powder-magazine, exploding it and causing much loss of life.

Throughout the day of the 13th, the battle was chiefly one of artillery. The brunt of the fighting on Abdullah Khan's side was borne by his brother, Najm-ud-din Ali Khan, who commanded his vanguard. Originally the Sayyads has intended to rely on a general onset. But Rajah Muhkam Singh, who had deserted from the imperialists, dissuaded them, pointing out that to charge down on such a powerful artillery as the other side possessed, would be to expose themselves to destruction. Their own small supply of guns ought, he said, to be entrenched in a good position on the edge of some ravine, and there they could await the favour of events. Although Muhkam Singh had acquired in the Dakhin the highest reputation as a soldier, his advice was not adopted. The Sayyads' artillery was placed on a high mound, under the shelter of some trees, near a deserted village, and it tried to reply to the other side's fire to the extent of its ability. In the field, the usual scattered fighting, charging and counter-charging, went on all day, and at one time it looked as if the imperialists would give way. But Khan Dauran, Sayyad Nusrat Yar Khan, Sabit Khan, Dost Ali Khan, Sayyad Hamid Khan and Asad Ali Khan by redoubled exertions prevented a catastrophe. In the end, some of the Sayyads' field pieces were taken and they were ejected from their sheltered position among the trees. Najm-ud-din Ali Khan was wounded by an arrow near the eye[2], and a ball from a swivel-gun struck him on the knee. Among the chiefs who lost their lives were Shekh Sibghatullah of Lakhnau, three sons, and seventy-five of his men, Abd-ul-Qadir Khan, Thathawi, (nephew of Qazi Mir, Bahadur Shahi), Abd-ul-Ghani Khan (son of Abd-ur-Rahim Khan, Alamgiri), Ghulam Muhi-ud-din Khan, and the son of Shuja Khan, Palwali. Many soldiers also were slain.

Abdullah Khan had decided to single out for attack the force under Sayyad Nusrat Yar Khan, who had command of the advanced guard near the emperor. Against this man the Sayyads had a special grudge, because he, one of their own clan and a relation, had sided against them. Having swept him on one side, Abdullah Khan hoped to be able to push on to

Muhammad Shah's centre (*qalb*). First of all, he tried to make his way to his objective from his own left, but found the river such an obstacle, that he changed his direction and moved across his front to the right of his own army. As soon as the movement was detected, reinforcements were sent for by Muhammad Shah, the centre having been left very weak. The generals who were thus summoned objected to quit their posts. The imperial artillery present with the emperor's division, was then despatched towards the river to bar the way, and part of the vanguard was also transferred to the same point.

Unfortunately the change in Abdullah Khan's line of advance resulted in his being drawn away from the river bank, and thus his main position was now some miles from the water side. The battle had continued till the afternoon, and so far Abdullah Khan showed no signs of discouragement. But his men, more especially the new levies, became uneasy, and soon lost their heads completely. On pretence of watering their horses and camels, they rode off towards the river, only to find their opponents in possession of the banks. Group after group, on the pretext of getting water, left the standard. These desertions continued until the night fell; and all night long, from the camp to Barahpulah just outside Dehli, the road was encumbered with fugitives. At night-fall there were not more than a few thousands left of the huge host that had set out from Delhi a few days before.

At first Abdullah Khan had ordered a small tent to be put up for the night where he stood, but countermanded it when he reflected that it would be a target for the enemy's fire. The night was a moonlight one, and the imperial artillery never ceased its fire. If any man stirred in the Sayyad position or showed himself, a gun was at once pointed in that direction and discharged; and from time to time the guns were dragged forward, the oxen being harnessed to the muzzle instead of, as usual, to the breach end of the gun. Among the guns in use were those named Ghazi Khan and Shah Pasand. These heavy guns were fired oftener than had ever been done before in the recollection of the oldest man. Haider Quli Khan kept up the energy of his men by continual gifts; Abdullah Khan's continued to make off in small parties. Muhammad Shah passed the night seated on his elephant so near the vanguard as to be under fire.

When day dawned on the 14th Muharram (14th Nov. 1720), Abdullah Khan found his army reduced to a few of his relations and his veteran troops. They were altogether not more than one thousand horsemen; with these he continued the fight to the best of his power. Najm-ud-din Ali Khan and Saif-ud-din Ali Khan, the wazir's younger brothers, Sayyad Afzal Khan, High Almoner (*Sadar-us-sadur*), Rae Tek Chand, a Bali Khatri, his chief officer, Ghazi-ud-din Khan (Ahmad Beg), Nawab Allahyar Khan, Shahjahani, and Ruhullah Khan were found among these faithful few, who had passed a sleepless night on their elephants, having seen neither food nor water for many hours. Access to the river-side was blocked by the Jats, who plundered impartially friend and foe. As dawn was drawing near, a ball struck the seat upon Muhkam Singh's elephant. The Rajah got down, mounted his horse, and galloped off; for many years it was not known whether he was alive or dead.

Early in the morning, returning to his plan of the previous day, Abdullah Khan, joined by Najm-ud-din Ali Khan and many Barhah chiefs, again delivered an attack, in the hope of reaching the emperor's centre. The imperial left opposed a stout resistance to this onset, and at length the Sayyads dismounted to continue the fight on foot at close quarters. Shahamat Khan and his son, Fath Muhammad Khan, Tahavvar Ali Khan (better known as Bahadur Ali Khan), and many others on the Sayyads' side were slain. Darvesh Ali Khan, head of Khan Dauran's artillery, was killed; Dost Ali Khan and Nusrat Yar Khan were severely wounded. Saadat Khan and Sher Afkan Khan were also prominent in this encounter. Abd-un-Nabi Khan and Mayah Ram, two of Haidar Quli Khan's officers, and Mhd. Jafar (grandson of Husain Khan) were the only other men of name who lost their lives on the imperial side.

After a time the men of Khan Dauran, Haidar Quli Khan, Saadat Khan and Muhammad Khan, Bangash, surrounded the ex-wazir, and an arrow struck him on the forehead, inflicting a skin wound. The soldiers then tried to make him a prisoner. But, clad although he was in chainmail, he leapt to the ground sword in hand, with the intention of fighting to the death. In spite of their knowing his practice of fighting on foot at the crisis of a battle, the ex-wazir's troops, when they saw his elephant without a rider, imagined that their leader must have fled, and each man began to think of his own safety. Then Tali Yar Khan charged at the head of his men, and cut down Shekh Nathu, commanding Abdullah Khan's artillery; the Rajputs, coming up, took possession of the Shekh's body, and carried it to the imperial camp. Najm-ud-din Ali Khan and Ghazi-ud-din Khan did their best to rally their men, but no one paid them any heed. Shuja-at-ullah Khan, Zulfiqar Ali Khan, and Abdullah Khan, Tarin, fled. Even Saif-ud-din Ali Khan, the ex-wazir's brother, thought the day was lost, and left the field along with two or three hundred men, taking with him Prince Ibrahim, who abandoned his elephant and mounted a horse. His elephant and imperial umbrella were afterwards found, and taken by Muhammad Shah's men. The feebleness of the defence would be fully proved, if we believe, as Warid tells us, that after two days' fighting, only forty men were left dead on the field.

Najm-ud-din Ali Khan, a drawn sword in his hand, rode on to enqire after and search for his brother. He found Abdullah Khan standing on the ground quite alone, and although wounded in the hand, still fighting like a lion, while on every side the crowd of assailants grew greater every minute. Still not one of them had the courage to lay hands upon him; one of Khan Dauran's men had wounded him on a finger of the right hand, but the Nawab returned the blow by a cut, which struck the man's leg and his horse's shoulder. Najm-ud-din Ali Khan dismounted from his elephant and joined his brother. Abdullah Khan called out to him "Behold the inconstancy of Fortune, and the end of all earthly greatness!", adding a verse of Sadi, Shirazi, fitting to the occasion.[3] Haidar Quli Khan, who had noticed that the howdah of Abdullah Khan's elephant was empty, made enquiries, and was informed by one of his soldiers that the Nawab was on foot and wounded. Coming up at once with a led elephant, Haidar Quli khan addressed the Sayyad, in the humblest manner, with words of praise and flattery. "Was he not a well-wisher, and was not his life one with his? Except to set forth for the presence of the emperor, what course was there left?" Najm-ud-din Ali Khan made a movement to cut the speaker down, but Abdullah Khan held his brother back. Then, with a haughty and dignified air, he took Najm-ud-din Ali Khan's hand and mounted the elephant. Haidar Quli Khan followed on his own elephant, and conducted his prisoners to the emperor, Muhammad Shah.

His hands bound together by Haidar Quli Khan's shawl, Abdullah Khan was brought before Muhammad Shah. Saluting him with a "Peace be upon you", the emperor said "Sayyad! you have yourself brought your affairs to this extremity". Overcome with the disgrace, Abdullah Khan answered only "It is God's will". Muhammad Amin Khan, unable to contain himself, leapt from the ground with joy, and exclaimed "Let this traitor to his salt be confided to this ancient servitor". But Khan Dauran, in respectful terms, intervened. "Never! never! Make not the Sayyad over to Muhammad Amin Khan, for he will at once slay him in an ignominious manner, and such a deed is inadvisable. What did Farrukhsiyar gain by the murder of Zulfiqar Khan? Let him remain with Haidar Quli Khan, or be made over to the emperor's own servants". The prisoner was accordingly made over to Haidar Quli Khan, along with Najm-ud-din Ali Khan, his brother, whose wounds were so severe that he was not expected to recover. Hamid Khan, Turani, was also taken a prisoner and brought, bare-headed and bare-footed, before his cousin, Muhammad Amin Khan, and Khan Dauran. The wazir calmed his fears and assured him of being tenderly dealt with. There were many other prisoners, among them the chief being Sayyad Ali Khan, (brother of Abul Muhsin Khan, Bakhshi) and Abd-un-nabi Khan.

On the Sayyads side the entrenchments were held and the fight maintained by Ghazi-ud-din Khan and others for nearly an hour after the capture of Abdullah Khan. When at length they were satisfied that the day was lost, they desisted. Ghazi-ud-din Khan with such baggage as could be saved, followed by Allahyar Khan and many others, moved off and marched straight for Delhi; while the Barhah Sayyads endeavoured to cross the Jamnah, in order to make their way to their homes. Saif-ud-din Ali Khan had brought Prince Ibrahim off the field of battle, but owing to the entire absence of carriage, was obliged to leave him in the orchard of Qutb-ud-din Khan close to the village of Nekpur. Saif-ud-din Ali Khan went home to Jansath, sending Baqir Ali Khan and Khizr Khan to Delhi to bring away the Sayyad women and dependents. These messengers reached the capital before the emperor, and carried off the ladies and children to the Sayyads' country.

To return to the field of battle. The Moghul soldiery, as their custom was, took to plundering, and appropriated to themselves whatever horses, camels, mules, and cattle fell into their hands. Churaman Jat followed suit, and plundering both sides with strict impartiality, made off with his booty to his own country. Among his spoils were over one thousand baggage oxen and camels, which had been left negligently on a high sandy mound close to the river, several camel-loads of goods meant for charitable distribution, and the records of the Grand Almoner's department.

Reports of Battles. Somewhat in the same way that after a battle a modern general sends off a despatch to his superiors, a Moghul commander prepared and submitted a report (*arzah-dasht*) to the emperor. Often he also drew up a separate description of the fight for distribution to his friends and equals. These latter papers were styled *tumar*, or roll, (a word which had another technical signification in the finance department). If the emperor was especially satisfied with any general, he gave orders that the victory should be recorded in the imperial diary of proceedings (the *waqiah*), equivalent to our gazette. Many specimens of battle reports sent in from Bundelkhand by Muhammad Khan, Bangash, will be found in Sahib Rae's *Khujistah Kalam;* and the same work contains a *tumar* circulated by Nizam-ul-mulk after his victory over Sayyad Dilawar Ali Khan, Rajah Bhim Singh, Hada, and others.

Stratagems of War. Dr. Horn, 70, states that deceit and stratagem did not play a leading part in Moghul warfare. This may be so, still they were not unknown. Of a character similar to the pretended desertion, in order to obtain information of the enemy's plans and strength, which was employed by Rumi Khan at Chunar in 1538 (Horn, 71, quoting Erskine, ii, 140, note), is a plot put into execution once by Nizam-ul-mulk. In the middle of 1720, when about to fight for supremacy in the Dakhin against Sayyad Alim Ali Khan, governor of Aurangabad, he arranged with one of his principal officers that a fictitious dispute about pay should be raised, that the officer should behave disrespectfully, and after receiving his money, should desert to Alim Ali Khan's camp. So said, so done. After an altercation, Nizam-ul-mulk paid the man and let him go. When he reached the Sayyad's camp, this officer was received with honour and taken into the Sayyad's service. But on the day of battle, as secretly agreed on with Nizam-ul-mulk, the deserter turned his men traitorously on Alim Ali Khan's rear, and bringing him under two fires contributed materially to his defeat (Shiu Das, fol. 42b).

Ambush (*ba kamin-gah nishistan*) was not an uncommon stratagem. Matchlockmen were hidden in high crops, or on the edge of a ravine, at a spot where the opposite leaders would most probably pass. At the proper moment a volley would be discharged, and occasionally with deadly effect. It was in this manner that Qaim Khan, Nawab of Farrukhabad, and many of his chief officers lost their lives on the 12th Zul Hijjah, 1162 H. (22nd Nov. 1749), see J.A.S.B. for 1878, p. 881. An ambush was not infrequently supplemented by pretended flight, so arranged as to draw the pursuers on and bring them under fire. We have an instance of this in Nizam-ul-mulk's fight with Sayyad Dilawar Ali Khan in Barar on the 19th June 1720.

Between the two forces there were deep ravines, where a large army could have been effectually concealed. Nizam-ul-mulk sent out his guns and placed them in position, so as to command from both sides the only road across this ravine. His advanced guard was concealed in the hollows on each side. Then two or three men, closely resembling the Nawab in beard and features and age were dressed up, placed on elephants, and sent out to represent Nizam-ul-mulk at the head of his main body, which showed itself in front of the entrance to the ravine. Dilawar Ali Khan's men came straight at their foe, and were drawn on and on by a simulated retreat. Anxious to slay or capture the opposite leader, who as they believed was in command, they pursued steadily, disposing on their way of several pretended Nizam-ul-mulks. When Sayyad Sher Khan at length brought his elephant close to that of Iwaz Khan, the Moghul by a sign caused his elephant to kneel, and by this trick, escaped with his life. When the ravine was reached, the guns did their work; and their leaders being killed, the rest of Dilawar Ali Khan's army dispersed (Shiu Das, 37b, M. Qasim Lahori, 314, *Tarikh-i-muzaffari,* fol. 183).

This device of having "six Richmonds in the field" was not unusual, it having been put in practice against us in our own early fighting in the Dakhin (R.O. Cambridge, "War", Introd. xi). It was also resorted to earlier in the century by Saadat Khan, Burhan-ul-mulk, founder of the Audh family. The Khichar zamindars of parganah Ghazipur in *sirkar* Korah, *subah* Allahabad, had long given trouble to the imperial officers, although several ineffectual attempts had been made to reduce them to order. At length, the *Sirkar* was made over to Burhan-ul-mulk; and on the 10th Jamadi ii, 1148 H. (27th Oct. 1735) that noble while on his way from Audh to Delhi, undertook to eject the then zamindar, Bhagwant Singh, son of Udaru. When the contending parties came face to face, a servant, clad in rich robes belonging to the Nawab, was placed upon the Nawab's elephant. Burhan-ul-mulk took his seat upon another. Several fierce attacks on the suppositious Nawab were repelled successfully. Finally, the Rajput chief gathered together some seven hundred men, and fully resolved on death or victory, made his way to the centre of the Mahomedan army, which he reached at the head of only forty to fifty men. Then, with not more than seven or eight men left, he arrived close to the leader's elephant. Bhagwant Singh knew the Nawab's attire, and thought he was in presence of Burhan-ul-mulk himself. Before the Mahomedans could attempt a rescue, he pulled the supposed leader out of his high-sided seat (*imari*) and slew him, with rejoicings at having successfully carried out his enterprize. But Burhan-ul-mulk, who had stood aloof, now ordered one of his officers to advance with five hundred men, and in a few moments Bhagwant Singh was slain. The body was skinned and the skin filled with straw : then, with its head and that of the rebel's son, it was sent to Delhi; where in Shaban of the same year Rustam Ali, Shahabadi, saw them hanging in the main street, near the chief police office (*Nadir-uz-zamani*, B.M. Or. 1844, fol. 152a, 152b, and Rustam Ali, fol. 268b).

When a leader took to flight on his elephant, it was not unusual for him to change places wth the driver in order to escape molestation in case of pursuit and capture (Fitzclarence, 133).

Night surprizes (*shab-khan,* night-blood, or *shab-gir,* nightseizing) were also a form of stratagem not unfrequently employed. It was in this way that Ahmad Khan, Bangash, on the 1st August 1750, attacked and overcame the superior force of Naval Rae on the bank of the Kali-nadi river near Khudaganj (13 miles east of Farrukhabad). The Pathans started during heavy rain at three hours after sunset, and avoiding by a long detour the front of Naval Rae's position, they got round to his rear near the river. An hour and a half before sunrise, when it was so dark that you could not tell friend from foe, the attack was delivered. Naval Rae's guns were fired at random and did no execution, he was killed, and his troops dispersed.

Statistics of Losses. Dr. Horn devotes one section of his work (xiii, pp. 113-115) to the subject of losses in battle. Here again, as in the question of the total number present, or the strength of particular divisions, I agree with him that to obtain any idea of the numbers of killed or wounded is exceedingly difficult, historians either omitting to mention them, or if they do so, contradicting each other irreconcilably. After a battle no attempts were made to ascertain the losses or count the slain. An statements that we may meet with are thus mere guesses, and we may be quite certain that they are much exaggerated for the defeated, and much diminished for the victorious army. From these causes such statements are quite worthless, and can form no basis for the calculation of percentages, or such-like strict arithmetical treatment. Incidentally, we learn from passing allusions the severity of the losses in a battle, or the number of the slain in some special group of those who were present. Thus, after the battle of Jajau, fought on the 18th June 1707, we are told that the defeated fugitives made off towards Gwaliyar "and so many lost their lives on the way at the hands of Jat plunderers and the Rohelahs of Dholpur, that the ravines leading to the Chambal were encumbered with decaying bodies" (Kamwar Khan). Another writer, Khushhal Chand, fol. 373a, tells us that the loss on both sides in this battle is said to have amounted to ten thousand men. As to losses among a particular group, or of men from one town, we have an instance in the *Tabsirat-un-nazirin* of Sayyad Muhammad, Bilgrami, who informs us, under the year 1163 H., that thirty seven men from Bilgram lost their lives on Naval Rae's side, when he was attacked by Ahmad Khan, Bangash, near Khudaganj. Scattered notices of this sort might be collected. But of what value would they be? They might enable us to say whether the fighting had been severe or not. But as we do not know the total strength and have only vague accounts of the losses, how can any minute calculations be made? The figures, such as they are, for nine battles in the time of Babar and Akbar will be found collected in a table on p. 115 of Dr. Horn's essay. De la Flotte, i, 258, who knew something of the south of India between 1758 and 1760, is of opinion that battles were much less bloody than in Europe.

Slain and wounded. Plundering of the slain and wounded seems to have been universal; the camp followers were those chiefly concerned, but the fighting men were not above lending a hand. In reading the memoir of Colonel Skinner's life, a man half Indian by blood and wholly so by education, one is struck with his exultation over a piece of valuable plunder, and his obvious belief that it was a legitimate source of income. The dead bodies left on a field of battle do not seem to have been usually buried they were left to lie as they fell; but once or twice we are told of their being collected in great pits, which were styled *ganj-i-shakid,* or martyr store-houses. For an instance, see Rustam Ali, *Tarikh-i-Hindi,* fol. 217b. The wounded seem to have been left mostly to their fate; there was no organization for their succour, nor any attempt to heal their wounds; this was left to their relations or friends.

REFERENCES

1. If we are to interpret Khushhal Chand literally, Berlin Ms. 495, fol. 1014b, Haidar Quli Khan used a telescope to make out the enemy's position. He says H.Q.K. at a distance of one *farsakh* (3 miles) saw the enemy's army by the eye of a durbin (telescope). Or is it only his "farseeing eye" (*chashm-i-durbin*)? A late writer (*c.* 1790) Rustam Ali, Bijnori, in his "History of the Rohelahs", fol. 52b, states that at the battle of Panipat in January 1761, Ahmad Shah, Durrani, used a telescope (*dur-bin*) to watch the movements of the Mahrattahs. As he was writing thirty years after the event, I do not know whether he is to be relied on for such a detail. Also in the *Husain Shahi* of Imam-ud-din Chisti, fol. 65b, we have mention of the field telescope as used by Taimur Shah, son of Ahmad Shah, Abdali : "The king mounted his elephant and slowly inspected the army. From time to time he raised his telescope to his eye" (*qarib-i-chasm-i-mubarik guzasht*). This telescope produced unexpected results for some of the commanders : they received a severe beating from the sticks of the *nasaqchis* sent to them. A learned man standing by the king, puzzled by this infliction of punishment, asked what it meant. Taimur Shah replied : "Through my telescope I saw that these commanders were seated under the shade of their horses, while the men of their regiments were exposed to the full heat of the sun. Tomorrow I will give them robes of honour to console them."
2. He lost his eye from this wound, and the glass ball by which he replaced it was a subject of wonder to the common people for the rest of his life, (*Maasir-ul-umara,* ii, 508).
3. Khizr Khan, who took part in the battle as one of the Sayyad army, was near enough to know that Abdullah Khan called out, but from the uproar could not hear his words. Some years afterwards (1138 H.) he met at Mathura, Najm-ud-din Ali Khan, then on his way to Ahmadabad, and obtained from him the details in the text. Khafi Khan, ii, 933, on the contrary, makes out that A.K. claimed *aman* (safety for life) by announcing himself as a Sayyad.

8
On The March

When an army of the emperor first took the field, there were generally great difficulties and delays in making a start. Nothing was ever ready when wanted; and if a great noble was put in command, he had always some further petition to urge or objection to make before he could be persuaded to start. Then there were the astrologers to be consulted. No march began until the lucky moment (*saat-i-said*) had been fixed by reading the stars. If it were not possible to make a real departure on the proper day or at the proper time, the advance tents would be sent out and a pretended start would be made in the hope of cheating the Fates (*Seir*, i, 309, note 248). In all cases, however, the first march out was a very short one, in order that stragglers might have time to join and anything left behind might be sent for. This regard for lucky and unlucky days was a great obstacle to the Moguls' success in war, as it often prevented them from taking the most obvious advantages of an enemy (Cambridge, "War", Introd. xi).

Emperor's taking the field in person. The emperor was not supposed to take the personal command unless the army was large and the campaign important (Horn, 46 relying on the *Tuzuk-i-Taimuri*). Thus, when Bahadur Shah in 1710 headed the army sent against the Sikh, Bandah, he was blamed for meeting an antagonist unworthy of him. On the way it was usual to pay visits to holy men of repute in order to obtain their blessing; and the shrines of any noted saints situated near the line of march were perambulated and the saint's help implored. Thus Shah Alam Bahadur Shah when on his way to fight his brother, offered up prayers at the tombs of Qutb-ud-din and Nizam-ud-din Auliys at Delhi. In the same way Farrukhsiyar, marching up from Patnah to Agrah, prayed at the tombs of Taki-ud-din ut Jhusi, of Badi-ud-din at Korah, and of Shah Madar at Makhanpur. Another curious practice is described by Yahya Khan, 129b. He says that when in 1721, Prince Muhammad Ibrahim was raised to the throne and was about to start against Muhammad Shah, he was taken, in accordance with an old custom, to Qutb-ud-din's shrine, to have his turban wound round his head there, and a sword attached to his waist. Then a bow with its string loosened ought to have been placed near the tomb. If the string of itself resumed its place, this would be held a sign of victory. On this occasion, such was the uproar and confusion, the order to bring the bow was not carried out.

Description of an army on the march. Catrou, 12mo ed. 1715, iv, 49 – 57, or 4to edition p. 126, gives us the following picture of a march of the emperor Aurangzeb. The heavy artillery went first and formed asit were the advance guard. The baggage followed in good order. First came the camels bearing the imperial treasure, one hundred loaded with gold and two hundred with silver coin. The load of each did not exceed 500 lbs. The treasure was succeeded by the hunting establishment. There were a great many dogs used for coursing deer and numerous "taureaux"[1] for hunting tigers. Next came the official records. It is the practice of the Moghul empire for these never to be separated from the emperor. The accounts and other archives of the empire were carried on eighty camels, thirty elephants and twenty carts. Immediately behind these came fifty camels carrying water for the court and the princes. This is a necessary precaution in Indian travelling, you are often in a waterless country or the water, speaking generally, is stagnant and unwholesome. Behind these camels came the imperial kitchen and fifty camels with the provisions for the day. There were fifty cows to give milk, as Aurangzeb chiefly lived on milk. One hundred kitchen servants riding on horses followed. Each man prepared one particular sort of stew....Next was the wardrobe of the emperor and the harem, and for this fifty camels and one hundred carts sufficed. Thirty elephants bore the harem jewels and the store of swords and daggers, from which the emperor makes presents to his generals. In front of the baggage train and the artillery two thousand pioneers marched with spades ready to smooth the ground. There were other thousand who followed to repair any holes made by the camels or elephants.

The army came after the baggage. It was composed almost entirely of cavalry. As for the infantry it is made up in case of need from the numerous sutlers, traders, and servants that follow the army. These are armed only with the sword, spear and shield. After the cavalry came the emperor, followed by his seraglio. Ordinarily he rode an elephant. On the back of this great animal, they had built a room with glass windows, in which was a couch and a bed. By the see of the elephant were palankins all ready for use should the emperor wish to change his mode of conveyance. His elephant was followed by led horses. Aurangzeb was fond of riding and at a considerably advanced age he was still the best rider in his empire. Some camels preceded the emperor bearing some large cooking-pots always steaming, perfuming the air as they went by. Forming the two wings on the two sides of the emperor's elephants, marched in good order the whole of the imperial guard. The queens, princesses, and ladies of the harem followed the emperor. They were carried, as he was, on elephants, but the room which contained them was surrounded with wooden blinds (*jalousies)* covered over with loose, thin muslin. They saw all and could breathe the air without being seen. The other women who worked in the harem were on horseback, wrapped in long mantles covering their faces and reaching to their feet. The line of march was brought up by the light artillery, each field piece on its carriage being drawn by horses.

The rear guard was swollen by the prodigious number of people always at the Court, and the innumerable multitude of servants leading elephants, camels, horses, and those carrying the tents and baggage of the lords of the court and the generals of the army. All moved in order and without confusion. This rear guard had its place allotted as exactly as the disciplined troops.

Standards. The flag of the noble or sovereign was carried on an elephant during the march (De la Flotte, i, 258 Fitsclarence, 138). These was a special officer entrusted with the insignia and standards. Of these some account has been given under the head of *Mansabdars.* Collectively they were called the *qur,* an Indian usage of the Turkish word which is not given among the definitions in P. de Courteille, "Dict." 425. The officer's title was *Qurbegi,* lord of the *Qur,* and the men under him carried a supply of weapons for the emperor's use. The details, as they stood under Akbar, will be seen in the *Ain,* i, 109, 110. Bernier 871, speaks of the *qur* (or as he spells it, *cours*) preceding the emperor on the march : these standards and emblems were surrounded by a large number of players on cymbals and trumpets.

The following graphic description of an emperor on the march with music playing and standards displayed is found in a Hindi poem by Shridhar Murlidhar of Allahabad, lines 355–376.

Phaiir Shahanshah sajeu,
Sakal brind gayand gajeu,
Baji naubate gahgahi tab,
Bhai naubat rawari ab,
Ghor dhaunsa dhuni dhankarat,
"Phateh, phateh", manu pukarat,
"Ho-hu-ho" karanai bajat,
Shahanshah-hi sagun sajat,
Sagun son suranai baji,
Siddhi ram kariju saji.
"Jharu-jharun" jhanjh jhankat,
Khanan lagi-hi ghant "khanakh-kat",
Phil war nishan jhaharat,
Man-hu aga phatuh phaharat,
At part anup rajat,
Indr syon prabhu tabi rajat,
Jhalari muku tasu lachhak,
Man-hu rakhshak sang dini ar,
Tog sundar maha mahi,
Sagun ki manu det gwahi.

Next morning the King of Kings started,
The throng of elephants roared,
The royal march was beaten loudly,
Then played the music of His Majesty,
The big drums shook with mutterings and growlings,
Men shouted 'Victory! Victory!'
The trumpets brayed 'ho-hu-ho'.
The King of Kings' good omens appeared,
The hautboys sounded happy augury,
Rama and the sages joined the throng.
'Clash, clash' clanged the cymbals,
Jingling bells began their 'tinkle, tinkle',
The elephant riders displayed their standards,
In front ran men shouting 'Victory'!
Everywhere incomparable brightness reigns,
The splendour is that of Indra's heaven,
Fringes hang over their faces,
Guardians of stars and umbrellas,
Sun screens waving in their hands,
Hearts full of joy, they shout for the Faith,
Yaktails, *sundar,* the fish dignity,
Give evidence of happy augury.

Military Music and the Naubat. The beating of drums, accompanied by the playing of cymbals and the blowing of trumpets, at certain fixed intervals (*naubat),* was one of the attributes of sovereignty. The place where the instruments were stationed, generally at or over a gateway, was the *naubat* or *naqqar khanah,* the latter name coming from *naqqarah,* one kind of drum used. Details will be seem in the *Ain,* i, 51. As I read that passage, there would seem to have been nine *naubat* in the twenty four hours, but generally they are spoken of as recurring at the end of each of the eight watches (*pahr*) into which that period was divided. The number is differently stated by different writers. Haji Mustapha. *Seir,* i, 3 note 31, after saying that in its origin this music was a mark of sovereignty, though later usurped by all provincial governors, goes on, "It played four times by day and once by night, and also to announce good news". Others speak of only three *naubat.*

Fitzclarence, 192, writes "the continual beating of the *naubat*, or great drums, is one of the highest signs of rank and power; over the gate of every palace is a gallery or balcony where this noisy instrument is beaten at certain hours in the day and night. One of them (*i.e.* a drum) is always carried on an elephant before the commander of a native army. At Murshidabad, when I was there, the Nawab had them continually beaten. Four gates to his place had each a *naubat*, and each of them sounded a quarter of each hour and made the most horrid din imaginable". As to the beating of kettle drums on the march there is a passage to the same effect in Captain J. Williamson "Oriental Field Sports", p. 79.

In addition to the fixed periods at which the imperial drums were beaten and the music played, it would seem that music and drum beating accompanied the march of the emperor (Fitzclarence, 138). The intention to make a march was announced by the beating of kettle drums, as was done for instance by Prince Ala Gohar in 1171 H., *Tarikh-i-Alamgir Sani*, fol. 155b. Or as Manucci asserts, ii, 68, a trumpet was sounded for the same purpose. If the emperor were not present, the commander, if entitled to this high honour, caused his own drums to be beaten, and as Horn, 17, remarks, the sound of these drums was a sing that some great noble was in command and that probably the army under him was a large one. The drums were also beaten at the opening of a battle. We are told by one writer of the year 1169 H. (1756), *Tarikh-i-Alamgir Sani*, fol. 49a, that a horn was blown at night in the emperor's camp to indicate a halt for the next day. We read of one noble who kept in his service one hundred horn-blowers (*karranai)*, so that when a fight was trembling in the balance, they should all blow together and inspire the other side with dread. (*Ma asir-ul-umara*, i, 514). After a battle the drums and trumpets were also employed by the victors to announce their victory; and even on ordinary occasions a noble was preceded by music. In 1757 Anquetil Duperron, *Zend Avesta*, i, xliv, after being presented to Siraj-ud-daulah, speaks of the Nawab coming out to visit the mint, and "nous entendimes un bruit affreux de tymbales, de trompettes, entremele de coups de fusils et de cailletoques." This picture taken on the spot must represent, as I take it, the usual practice.

The kettle drums (*naqqarah)* were made of iron hoops, and they were twice as big as those used by cavalry in Europe (Seir, i, 24, note 31). One of the drums used was called *Dankah*, a small wooden drum, no doubt identical with ढका, Shak. 1129, a bass kettledrum, in size between the *naqqarah* and the *lakora*, or as *Qanoone Islam*, App. p. Iv, has it, the bass end of the small kettle-drum. De la Flotte, 211, compares the sound of their trumpets (*trompettes*), ten or twelve feet long, to that of a French cowherd's goathorn, ony louder; and G. Careri iii, 182, speaks of seeing a man walking in front of the camp Provost Marshal (*kotwal*), blowing a copper horn 8 "palmes" in length, the sound of which made him laugh, "il ressemble tout a fait a celui que les porchers font en Italie lorsqu'ils veulent rassembler leurs cochons egares".

Patrolling and Watching. At night time some troops were sent out to march round the camp and protect it. The name of these detachments was *tilayah* (*Mirat-ul-Istilah*, fol. 202b, Steingass, 817). In 1151 H. (1738) when Muhammad Shah marched out to Karnal to oppose the advance of Nadir Shah, these night rounds or patrols were apparently still carried out; Ashob, fol. 182b calls them *shah-gard,* which seems the correct technical name, Steingass 732. He uses *taliah*, fol. 182a, for advanced posts or pickets, which seems the more exact meaning of that word, Steingass 819. The same form, *taliah*, is used *c.* 1169 H. (1755-6) by Muhammad Ali, Burhanpuri, in his *Mirat-us-safa*, fol. 99a. As for the care of the interior of the camp, Bernier, 369, describes the system of watch and ward then prevailing. His watchmen with their cries of *khabardar* (Take care), the guards at their watch fires every five hundred paces round the camp, and the *kotwal* with his armed men and their trumpet, were better fitted to prevent thieves and robbers entering the camp than to act as military precautions against surprize. In later times even these imperfect precautions seem to have been abandoned. In the 18th century it was found that, often as native troops had been surprized in the night by

Europeans, they could never be brought to establish order and vigilance in their camp. When they acted as allies of the English, the most earnest entreaty could never prevail upon them to be upon their guard, or quit their ground in the morning to take part in a surprize. The men ate a heavy meal just after night fall, many indulged also in drugs, and about midnight a whole army would be in a dead sleep (Cambridge, "War", Introd. xiii). In the police of the camp the provost-marshal, or *kotwal*, was aided by a censor, or *muhtasib*, whose special duty (usually very imperfectly performed) was to suppress gambling, drinking, and other breaches of the Mahomedan law.

Escort. The name used for this duty was *badraqah* (Steingass, 163).

Emperor's conveyance and usages on his passing by. Shah Alam Bahadur Shah (1707-1712) generally travelled his stages on a moving throne *(takht-i-rawan)*. It is described by Bernier, 370. Another account, *Seir*, ii, 171, note 95, tells us it was a chair resting on two straight bambus or poles and carried on the shoulders of eight men. Two or three persons could find place in it, and it had not only a canopy over it, but an awning in front to intercept the glare of the sun. Preceding the moving throne were the *yasawals* (Steingass, 1531), whose business it was to preserve order (*Malumat-ul-afaq*, fol. 79b). Sometimes Bahadur Shah mounted a horse, but he does not seem to have ridden on an elephant exempt in the battle field.

Whenever the emperor passed, it was the etiquette for princes, nobles, and chiefs to come out to the edge of their camp and present a gold coin or other offering. There are numerous instances of the practice in the historians such as Danishmand Khan and Kamwar Khan; and Bernier, 382, also speaks of it. The custom was observed by Herr Kotelar, the Dutch envoy, when he was in Bahadur Shah's camp at Lahor in 1712. The practice spoken of by Bernier of entering the camp sometimes on one side, sometimes on another, was the *taghaiyur-i-rah dahan* (*Mirat-ul-Istilah*, fol. 80), a custom either founded on superstition or devised as a precaution against assassination.

Crossing Rivers. On this subject Horn. 25, quotes P. de

Courteille, "Memoires", ii, 336, the occasion being Babar's boat bridge across the Ganges near Kanauj. The practice was exceedingly common. Any river, if unfordable, was crossed by a temporary bridge of boats, such as are still to be seen in the present day. Horn, referring to Elliot, vi, 363, somewhat emphasizes the fact that elephants could cross such bridges, but this is a matter of every day experience. A special officer, dignified with the name of Mir Bahr, Lord of the Sea, was charged with the construction of these bridges and the provision of boats. The description of one of these bridges in Bernier, 380, can hardly be improved upon. "The army crossed by means of two bridges of boats constructed with tolerable skill, and placed between two and three hundred paces apart. Earth and straw mingled are thrown upon the planking forming the foot way, to prevent the cattle from slipping. The greatest confusion and danger occur at the extremities; for not only does the crowd and pressure occur most there, but when the approaches to the bridge are composed of soft moving earth, they become so broken up and full of pits, that horses and laden oxen tumble upon one another into them, and the people pass over the struggling animals in the utmost disorder. The evil would be much increased if the army were under the necessity of crossing in one day; but the king generally fixes his camp about half a league from the bridges of boats and suffers a day or two to elapse ere he passes to the opposite side of the river; when, pitching his tents within half a league from the bank, he again delays his departure so as to allow the army three days and nights at least to effect the passage". The practice referred to in the last sentence could be illustrated by more than one instance of river-crossing in the reign of Bahadur Shah (1707-1712).

It seems that there was one defect in the purely native system of making a boat-bridge. They did not make use of grapnels. Instead of these, they followed the tedions mode of driving stakes into the river bed. The result was a bridge less secure; and what might have been ready in one day took eight or ten days to complete (Remarks by Major R.E. Roberts, "Asiatic Miscell." i, 419).

In Ashob's *Shahadat-i-Farrukhsiyar,* for. 112b, I have come across a curious device by the Mahrattas to mark the fordable part of a river. In 1148 H. (1735) Pilaji Jadon crossed the Jamna to attack Saadat Khan, Burhan-ul-mulk. At the place of crossing he caused bamboo poles to be planted in the water, to show the line of shallow water in case they had to retire. His forethought was, however, of no avail; they were badly beaten, fled in haste, and missed the ford, those that were not drowned being taken prisoners.

Marching through Passes. The passage through a hilly country of such a huge assemblage as a Moghul army, consisting as it mainly did of undisciplined men, was, it need hardly be said, a matter of extreme difficulty, and in the presence of an active enemy likely to end disastrously. Of this difficulty Bahadur Shah had ample experience while governor of Kabul during the last ten years of his father's life. It was with the greatest difficulty, and more by guile than force, that he was able to pass yearly from his winter quarters at Peshawar to his summer residence at Kabul, and back again (Raverty, "Notes", 84, foot note, 86, 90, foot note, 372). Warned by what had happened to him in Kabul, we find Bahadur Shah adopting special precautions whenever he came to any narrow defile. On his return from the Dakhin, when he arrived at the Fardapur pass between Aurangabad and Burhanpur on the 23rd Shawwal 1121 H. (25th Dec. 1709), he sent ahead his eldest son, Jahandar Shah, with orders on reaching the other end to occupy in force a position in the open plain beyond (Kamwar Khan, entry of above date). Shortly afterwards he came with his army to the Mukand *darrah,* or pass, and the three great Rajput chieftains of Udipur, Jodhpur, and Jaipur being in open revolt, there was every reason to take precaution against a sudden onfall. This narrow valley in the Kotah state has a melancholy interest in Anglo-Indian history as the scene of Colonel Monson's disastrous retreat before Jaswant Rao, Hulkar, in July 1804 (Thornton, "Gaz." 624, Thorn, "War", 358–363, Wellesley "Despatches", iv, 178).[2] Bahadur Shah took very great precautions. A plan of the pass was prepared a week before they came to it : the road was reported to be only 4½ *dirah* wide (about 12½ feet). Accordingly on the 25th Muharram 1122 H. (25th March 1710), the eldest prince, Jahandar Shah, was again deputed to march through in advance of the main army, and occupy the exit from the narrow valley. It seems to have taken the main body eight days to get clear, as it was not until the 6th Safar (5th April) that the emperor quitted his camp on the hill side, at the top of the pass, a position which had been occupied by him since the 29th March (Kamwar Khan, entry of above date).

Scouts and Spies. The intelligence department was always in active operation, both in peace and war. Reports of all sorts, descending even to idle gossip and scandal, were always welcome. Danishmand Khan, entry of 11th Ramazan 1120 H., tells us that there were in all four thousand spies (*harkarah*) in the imperial service scattered throughout the kingdom. There was a head spy (*daroghah-i-harkarah,* who was a man of influence and much feared : his establishment formed a branch of the postal department, managed by a high court official called the *Daroghah-i-dak,* or superintendent of the Post. When in the field, these spies were sent out in all directions. Their name, *harkarah* (literally "for every work"), arose in the Dakhin but was adopted by the Moghuls (Danishmand Khan, l.c.). In modern usage it has been transferred to the runners carrying the mail bags. Despatches and orders were either sent through the ordinary post, manned by foot runners, or by special messengers on camels. If the recipient was to be specially honoured or the matter was very important, one of the imperial mace-bearers carried the message or letter to its destination.

Negociations. These were carried on as a rule through holy men (*darvesh)* or through eunuchs, the sacred character of the one and the peculiar position of the other class making their persons more likely to be respected. Connected with this subject is the case in Erskine "History", ii, 248, quoted by Horn, 51, where during Humayun's flight through Sind in 1542, Mal Deo, the son of Rae Landaran of Jaisalmir, when he came to remonstrate about plundering, bore a white flag. Another instance is found in Ashob, fol. 256b. He tells us that during the general slaughter of 1739 in Delhi, the Shah's men were opposed in superior force by the Wazir's troops stationed round the latter's mansion. It became necessary to communicate with the Wazir and send him a letter. The messenger displayed a white sheet "that is to say, the signal of peace and negociation", and then advanced to state his purpose. The only other instance that I have met with of a flag of truce being used, was at the siege of malligam in 1818, where Lake, 127, says "the garrison hung out a flag of truce, that we might carry away our dead and wounded."

REFERENCES

1. This must surely be a mistake; perhaps leopards (*chitah*) are meant or buffaloes for fighting with tigers. But the original Portuguese text of Manucci, Berlin Ma, Phillipps 1945, p. 47, says nothing about bulls. The sentence reads : "One hundred and fifty camels loaded with nets (*redes*) for hunting tigers, of which sport I have already spoken." For the use these nets, see Constable's Bernier, p. 378.
2. The best account of this retreat is perhaps that in Fraser's "Skinner", ii, 7–15, 31–35.

9
Length of Marches

Rennell, 317, speaking from his experience, says the length of a day's journey in Hindustan was 11 to 12 *kos* or about 22 miles, for an ordinary traveller; but that of a courier may be reckoned at 30 or 33 miles; and on occasions of emergency they could travel even more, and that for a continuance of fifteen or twenty days. But these figures must not be taken as any standard for army marching. These was an official rate of progress laid down for single officers or small parties travelling to or from Court. At times there were, however, forced marches which much exceeded the ordinary length; on the other hand, the rate of advance of a large army was very much less than the official rate of marching, for "slowness of motion and the smallness of the stages are in the idea of the Indians a part of the state that must attend a great man" (*Seir*, i, 187, note 131). Bernier, 358, alludes to this when he writes, "this is indeed slow and solemn marching, what we here call *a la mogole*".

In detailed histories where events are recorded day by day, such as Danishmand Khan's *Bahadur Shah nantak* and Kamwar Khan's *Tazkirah-i-salatin-i-chaghataiyah*, the length of each day's march is stated with great precision in *Jaribi* or measured *kos*. This precision is accounted for, no doubt, by a statement found in Firishtah, *Maqalah* ii, p . 212, line 1. He tells us that a *tanab-i-paimaish* followed the army, and by it the distance traversed was measured. The introduction of the practice into India was attributed to Babar. One hundred *tanab* made one *tanab* (the word is *kos*, in the quotation of the passage to be found on fol. 38a of B.M. Or. 2005, *Tarikh-i-Ahmad Shahi c.* 1167 H.). Each *tanab* was of 40 yards (*gaz*) and each *gaz* was of nine average fists (*musht*). This would make a *kos* of 4000, instead of 5000 *gaz*, as the later reckoning was. It was apparently Akbar who lengthened the *tanab* from 40 to 50 *gaz* (*Ain* (Jarrett) ii, 414).

Niccalao Manucci saw these measurements actually being made when Alamgir left Delhi in 1663, Berlin Ms. Phillips 1945, fol. 48, and he gives a detailed account of the process. "Other men on foot march with a rope to measure the road, as follows. They begin at the royal tent when the king starts. The first man, who holds the rope in his hand, makes a mark in the ground, and when the man behind comes up to it, he calls out "One". Then the other man makes another mark and counts two : and thus they continue for the whole march, counting "Three", "Four" and so on, the other peon also keeping count. Should the king ask how far he has gone, they calculate the number of ropes making up a league, and answer accordingly".

Dr. Horn, 115, states that his researches have not yielded him material for an exhaustive treatment of this section. Without any pretence to be exhaustive, I hope to he able to throw some further light upon the subject.

The official day's march. If a man was summoned to court, the time for his arrival was calculated in the following way (B.M. 1641, fol. 40b):

(1) For the order to reach him by the postrunners, 30 measured (*jaribi*) *kos* (78 miles) a day.

(2) For preparation to march, one week.

(3) For the march, 7 measured *kos* (18.2 miles) a day.

The imperial measured *kos* was 200 *jaribs* of 25 *dirah* each, that is, 5000 *dirah* (B.M. 1641, fol. 51a). The following doggrel lines afford a *memoria technical* of this fact :

Panj alaf amad zi gaz miqdar-i-mil,
In manabazat bar in bashad dalil.

"Five thousand will yield in yards the mile's length. This specification affords the proof thereof."

(Khushhal Chand, *Nadir-uz-Zamani,* B.M. Or. 1844, fol. 159b).

The *dirah* may be safely assumed to be the same as the

gaz-i-ilahi, which has been found to be, as nearly as could be ascertained, 33 inches in length (Elliot, "Supp. Gloss." 480, under "Ilahi Guz", and 229, under "Coss", see also Prinsep, "Useful Tables", Calcutta, 1834, p. 88, 889). Thus the length of one *jaribi* kos would be 4583 1 1/3 yards or 2.6 miles; and 7 kos equals 18.2 miles. The reputed (*rasami*) *kos* was shorter, one *jaribi* equalled 1.71 *rasami* kos, and the *rasami* kos was thus 1.52 miles in length. But his latter kos varies greatly in different parts of the country.

We can prove the ordinary rate of a day's journey from other sources. For instance, Khushhal Chand *Nadir-uz-Zamani,* B.M. 24,027, for. 247b, tells us that from Delhi to within twelve kos of Kabul the distance was 306 *jaribi* kos, or 535 ½ *rasami* kos, and that it was one and a half month's journey. Taking thirty days to a month, or forty five days in all, we find that this brings out a rate of 6 4/5 *jaribi* and 11 2/3 *rasami* kos travelled each day, or almost exactly the same as the distance fixed in the official manual.

Then Mirza Muhammad, Harisi, gives in his Memoirs details of several journeys that he made. After Bahadur Ṣhah's death he came from Lahor to Delhi in twenty three marches, via Nakodar, Phalur, Ambalah, and Karnal. The reputed distance was 107 kos, measured on the map it comes to about 288 miles, or at the rate of 2.6 miles to the kos to 278 miles. This give only 4.65 kos or 12.09 miles a day. But then we must recollect that for most of the time he travelled in the company of Bahadur Shah's widows, who were bringing that emperor's body for burial at Delhi. Under these circumstances they may be supposed to have travelled less quickly than was usual. Again in 1130 H. (1718) the same Mirza Muhammad went from Delhi to Jalalabad in the Muzaffarnagar district in five marches; the distances he gives, when added up, come to 53 kos, an average of over 10 kos (27 miles) a day. He also returned to Delhi in five marches. The next year, 1131 H. (1719) the same man went as an Amil to parganah Rahun in the Jalandhar *duabah.* He reached the place in twelve marches. Measured on the map the distance is roughly about 200 miles, which gives an average of 16 2/3 miles as his daily march. Again in 1126 H.

it took Abd-ul-jalil, Bilgrami, four months to march from Bhakkar to Delhi, a distance of about 850 miles (Oriental Miscellany, pp. 133 – 295, Letter No. 6) by the usual route via Lahor. This yields an average of a little over seven miles a day; but then we do not know what halts he made.

Forced marches. The *ilghar*, or forced march, is mentioned by Horn, 21. Some remarkable feats of this nature were performed by Akbar; notably his advance on Gujarat in 1573 (Elphinstone, 443). Such activity was not displayed in later times, and the Moghuls were habitually outmarched and out-manoeuvered by the Mahrattas. It is true that late instances of forced marches by Maisur troops are on record, but these can hardly be taken as applicable to the Moghul organization. Haidar and Tipu Sultan kept their troops in exceptional order, and what they did could not be done by other native armies. In 1781 Haidar marched one hundred miles in two days and a half, and in November 1790 Tipu's entire army marched sixty three miles in two days. In our early days in India our own troops performed feats quite as wonderful. In 1805 General Smith's cavalry followed Amir Khan 700 miles in 43 days (Blacker, 281). Lord Lake also made some wonderful marches in 1803 and 1804.

Army Marching. We possess several detailed accounts of long marches undertaken by the later emperors at the head of large armies. When Alamgir died two of his sons fought together for the crown. But at the time of their father's death, one was at Jamrud, a little west of Peshawar, and the other was in the imperial camp at Ahmadnagar in the Dakhin. There were thus about 1200 miles between them; they at once commenced to march towards each other, and finally met in battle in June 1707 between Agrah and Dholpur.

The eldest son, Prince Muazzam, Shah Alam, reached Agrah in sixty-two days. The route was covered thus; Jamrud to the Indus, 8 days, the Indus to Lahor, 19 days, Lahor to Delhi, 25 days, Delhi to Agrah, 10 days. The distance measured on the map, with an addition of one eighth for the windings of the road,[1] is about 690 miles. The average distance covered is thus about 11.1 miles (including halts).

Starting from the other direction, Prince Azam Shah, the second son, was ninety two days on the march. From Ahmadnagar to Aurangabad took him 15 days, Aurangabad to Burhanpur, 22 days, Burhanpur to Sironj, 20 days, Sironj to Gwaliyar, 29 days, Gwaliyar to Dholpur, 6 days. The total number of days being ninety two and the distance on the map about 505 miles, the average rate of progress was about 5.48 miles (including halts). Some farther details may be noted. Aurangabad to Burhanpur was, we are told, 56 ½ kos done in 18 marches and 4 halts; the actual marching thus averaged here 3 ¼ kos (8.16 miles) a day. Burhanpur to Sironj, given as over 114 kos (296.8 miles), was done in 17 actual marches, or a daily average of 6.7 kos (17.42 miles). By the map I make it 242 miles, which yields an average of 14.2 miles

The two marches above described were made under the strongest possible pressure of haste, and must represent the utmost that a Moghul army was able to do in the way of continuous marching. In ordinary times the usual march of an army never exceeded 4 ½ kos (11.7 miles) and was sometimes as little as 1 ¼ kos (3.25 miles). When Bahadur Shah marched from Agrah to the Dakhin, and then back via Ajmer to Lahor, the historians record the length of 340 separate marches. Most of them were of 3 to 3 ½ kos each (7.8 to 9.1 miles). This monarch always halted on Friday, and there was generally a long halt in the month of Ramazan on account of the fast. Some of the facts may be tabulated as follows :

The whole period occupied, namely from the 12th Nov. 1707 to the 11th Aug. 1711, comprises 1369 days, of which 1190 days are shown above. The remaining 179 days were spent at some of the principal places named in the first column.

Another instance is when Dara Shukoh was sent to recover Qandahar. He reached that place in thirty three marches from Multan (Raverty, "Notes", 22). Assuming that his route was by the Bolan pass, the distance may be estimated as 608 miles. This gives an average daily march of 18.4 miles.

We have also some other accounts, which are sufficiently specific to afford as information of the usual rate at which an

Name of Place		Number of Marches	Number of Halts	Total Number of Days	Total Distance Marched (Approximate)	Average Daily March (Excluding Days Halted)
From	To					
					miles	miles
Agrah	Jaipur	20	50	70	155	7.75
Jaipur	Mairtha	16	12	28	140	8.75
Mairtha	Ajmer	14	17	31	45	3.21
Ajmer	Burhanpur	40	39	79	427	10.67
Burhanpur	Haidarabad	61	144	205	360	5.9
Haidarabad	Aurangabad	44	87	131	315	7.15
Aurangabad	Burhanpur	15	38	53	135	9.0
Burhanpur	Narbada bank	11	17	28	72	6.54
Narbada bank	Ajmer	50	130	180	355	7.1
Ajmer	Sonpat	21	97	118	318	15.14
Sonpat	Thanesar	8	11	19	68	8.5
Thanesar	Beyond Sadhaurah	7	8	15	48	6.85
Sadhaurah	Lahor	33	200	233	220	6.66
	Total	340	850	1190	2658	7.81

Stages		*Number of Marches*	*Number of Halts*	*Total Number of Days*	*Total Distance Marches (Approximate)*	*Average Daily March (Excluding Days Halted)*
From	*To*					
					miles	miles
Patnah	Banaras	19	23	42	180	9.47
Banaras	Allahabad	5	6	11	90	18.0
Allahabad	Makhanpur	17	11	28	180	10.58
Makhanpur	Agrah	17	8	25	157	9.23
Agrah	Khizrabad (outside Delhi)	12	8	20	130	10.83
	Total	70	56	126	737	10.51

Stages		*Number of Marches*	*Number of Halts*	*Total Number of Days*	*Total Distance Marches (Approximate)*	*Average Daily March*
From	*To*					
					miles	miles
Lahor	Delhi	(not known)		44	288	6.54 (with halts)
Delhi	Agrah	16	5	22	135	8.43 (without halts)

army marched. For example, we have the advance of Farrukhsiyar from Patnah to encounter his uncle, Jahandar Shah, in the neighbourhood of Agrah. The prince left Patnah on the 22rd Sept. 1712 and reached Sarae Begam, opposite Samugarh, east of Agrah, on the 4th January 1713. The distance from Patnah to Agrah was commonly reckoned as 300 *kos* (780 miles), Khushhal Chand, B.M. Add. 24,027, fol. 220a. I make it no more, however, than 585 miles on the map (allowing 1/8th for the windings of the road); and as Farrukhsiyar did not keep to the usual route, but deviated a good deal to the right, in order to visit the shrine of Shah Madar at Makhanpur, I should estimate the distance actually travelled at about 610 miles. The stages (including the final advance to Delhi) were :

We have the record of two long marches of Jahandar Shah, first from Lahor to Delhi shortly after his accession, secondly, from Delhi to Agrah to oppose Farrukhsiyar.

Again the march of Sayyad Husain Ali Khan from the Dakhin, a march undertaken under circumstances of extreme urgency, should afford an excellent test of the rate at which a Moghul army could march. He left Aurangabad about the 11th Nov. 1718, and reached a suburb of Delhi on the 16th Feb. 1719. His march thus occupied 98 days, and his route by way of Burhanpur, Ujjain, and Agrah, measures about 695 miles on the map, allowing 1/8th for the windings of the road. His average daily rate of marching (including any days on which he halted) was thus 7.1 miles.

The last instance I shall refer to is the march of Muhammad Shah in 1719 from Agrah past Fathepur Sikri to Todah Bhim in the direction of Jaipur. I make out the distance to be about 90 miles; it took the army twenty seven days to reach Todah Bhim; but hey marched on twelve days only and halted on fifteen days. The average daily march made was thus about 7½ miles.

REFERENCE

1. Rennell's rule, "Memoir", 7, is "Break the horizontal distance into portions of 100 or 150 miles, and add one eighth to get the road distance."

10
Sieges

In India the art of fortification remained in the same state as it was in Europe before the introduction of the regular systems. The Indians placed their reliance more on a strong profile than on a judicious plan; and they never realised the importance of the maxim that every work of a fortress should be flanked by some other (Lake, 11). Blacker holds that nothing proved more forcibly their ignorance of the attack and defence of fortified places than their manifest superiority when acting on the defensive. A native army scarcely ever succeeded in taking a place which attempted resistance; it was generally reduced to terms through the distress caused by the force lying around it. On the contrary, some very vigorous defences had been made, prolonged by determined defence of the breach and by bold sallies to the trenches. Mining had found its way to some but not to all parts of India; but there were few instances of its being practised with effect (Blacker, "War", 23). In the *Mujmil-ut-tarikh bad Nadiriyah,* p. 78, line 7, it is stated that the Afghans had a practise before commencing a siege of killing a dog and throwing it in the direction of the fortress. I have never seen this mentioned elsewhere, and one does not quite see what was symbolized by the act.

Strong places were most commonly reduced by strict investment and starving out (Fitzclarence, 245). There were few captures by a *coup de main* (*sar-i-suwari*), the walls were not often breached, and rarely escalated. Trenchery within the walls was as frequent a cause of surrender as any other thing. In sitting down before a fortress, a Moghul army tried to surround it completely so as to prevent any ingress or egress. As Grant Duff, 165, expresses himself, "they never considered an army capable of undertaking a regular siege unless sufficiently large to surround the place invested and completely obstruct communications". Earth works (*murchal*) were thrown up, in which the siege guns were placed. The system of digging approaches and laying mines (*naqb*) was known and practised, at any rate in Northern India. No doubt, Lake, 14, holds the contrary view; he says "the natives appear to be utterly ignorant of the art of conducting approaches by sap : and generally they are also unacquainted with Mining". But this opinion must be understood as applicable to the Dakhin only.

There was also a plan, to which recourse was sometimes had, of building high towers with the branches of trees, and when these were of a height to command the interior of the place, guns were mounted on them. These were called *siba*. Scaling ladders (*narduban*) were not unknown, and were occasionally brought into use. Elephants were frequently brought up to batter in the wooden gates of a fort. The *Seir* translator, iii, 182, note 45, says the gates, being always covered by some work, could not be broken in except by grenades (of which the natives knew nothing), or by pushing against them elephants, protected by iron, or by setting fire to them. It was as a protection against elephants that the gates were studded with iron spikes; to meet which it was the practice to furnish the elephant with an iron frontlet (Fitzclarence, 137). For instance, we read in the *Siyar-ul-mutakharin* (translation, iii, 181), with reference to an assault by the Mahrattas in 1173 H. (1759), that the Khizri gate of the Delhi citadel "was covered with sheets of brass and set thick with iron nails jutting out twelve inches, and an inch square at the bottom". Often the gateway was bricked up when a siege was imminent, and this device rendered it impossible to blow it in. At Cuttack in 1803, the gate was partially built up in this way, and we had considerable difficulty in entering (Lake, 211, note).

These general remarks are borne out by a passage in Lake's "Sieges of the Madras Army", 14 : "when one of their armies sits down before a place, the object appears rather to be to harrass the besieged and weary them out by a strict blockade, than to effect an entrance by breaching the walls : for although guns are used, they are placed at such a distance from the town, out of musket shot, and not always in battery, that their effect is uncertain, and even this desultory fire is only kept up at intervals during the day; for at night, to guard against the consequences of a sally, the guns are always withdrawn to the camp; and this ridiculous process is continued till the besieged are tired out, and a compromise is entered into".

Fitzclarence, "Journal", 245, also enters at some length into the question. " The investment of an eastern fortress did not in general consist of anything beyond a blockade; and it will be seen by a reference to Indian history, that the surrender of these forts has been caused more by treachery and scarcity than by any other means, and that the length of some sieges in this country equal those of Troy, Ostend, and Mantua. The food of the Indians being almost entirely rice,[1] which is the least perishable of any article of subsistence, the defence of such places may be the longer protracted. Though the natives did not understand the advantage of a glacis, still they saw the necessity of covering the foot of the wall from the enemy's fire when exposed to it, and formed a defence similar to a faussebraye, which they call *rainee* (see back, p. 265). They are very partial to loopholes to fire through, ... Each of these narrow and confined [entrance] lanes is generally enfiladed with guns and loopholed on every side, so that should the enemy force the outer gate, they find themselves exposed to a continuation of fresh dangers from an invisible garrison at every turn. I am not, however, a good judge of native fortresses, having only seen those of Chunar on the Ganges, of Alighur, of Agra, and Delhi. The gates at Agra, Alighur and Chunar are examples of this difficulty of entrance".[2]

"The Indians, in the defence of their forts, behave with the greatest gallantry and courage, and in this differ from the Europeans, who often fancy that, when a practicable breach is made in their walls, surrender becomes justifiable. But here all feel desirous of fighting man to man, and look upon the contest in the breach as the fittest occasion for meeting their enemies with sword and dagger. They use large heavy wall pieces called gingalls" (see *ante,* p. 109), "which send a ball of two or more ounces to a very considerable distance. Having no shells or handgrenades, they cast bags of gunpowder into the ditch, which exploding by fire thrown on them, scorch the assailants; and at times they have recourse to thick earthen-ware pots with fuses and full of powder, the pieces of which wound dreadfully. They have been known to line the sides of the ditch with straw thatches, and by throwing other lighted thatch on their enemies, envelop them in flames. Our success against Hatras by bombardment has been a wonderful encouragement to taking all the native forts by similar means; and from their having no casements, shells are the most effective means for reducing them" (id. 246).

Approach by sap and mine. The word used for the galleries of approach seems to have been *sabat.* This is defined by the Lucknow editor of the *Akbarnamah* (Vol. ii, p. 245, note 7) as a roof (*saqaf*) between two walls, which is also called "the path of safety" (*kuchah-i-salamat*); *sabat* is, he says, the name of a town in Transoxiana. Steingass, 638, explains it as a covered passage connecting two houses. The ordinary Hindi word for a mine is *surang* (Platts, 656) and *surang urana* is to spring a mine. This mode of attack was known and practised. For instance Sher Shah in 952 H. (1545-46) at the siege of Kalinjar advanced galleries (*sabat*) to the foot of the wall, and then prepared *naqb,* which appears to mean here mines, and not the mere digging through of a wall (Budaoni, Text, i, 371, Ranking, 482). Again at a siege of Budaon in 963 H. (1555-56), the besiegers resorted to mining, and the commander of the garrison thwarted them by counter-mining, having detected the direction of their approach by putting his ear to the ground and listening, just as our engineers did at Lucknow in 1857, Budaoni, Text, i, 465 (Ranking, 599), and McLeod Innes' "Siege of Lucknow". And again, at the siege of Gurdaspur in 1715, Abd-us-samad Khan made covered ways or aproaches (*sabat*), Yahya Khan, 123a. Once more, at Allahabad in 1719 the imperialists worked their way close to the walls of the fort "and began to mine under the walls", and Girdhar Bahadur, believing that the day was lost, made overtures through

Muhammad Khan, Bangash, (*Siwanih-i-Khizri,* 13). So also at the siege of Agrah (July, August 1719) Haidar Quli Khan, who had under his command many Europeans whom he had brought from Surat, drove several saps towards the walls (*id.*).

Sabat. According to the dictionary this is "a covered passage connecting two houses"; and as a military term it means a trench or approach made in besieging a fortress. According to Briggs, "Firishtah", ii, 230 (siege of Chitor) the *sabat* were constructed in the following manner. "The zigzags, commencing at gunshot distance from the fort, consist of a double wall, and by means of blinds or stuffed gabions covered with leather, the besiegers continue their approaches till they arrive near to the walls of the place to be attacked". There is another passage to the same effect with reference to the year 1595 and the siege of Ahmadnagar.

The text of Firishtah is even more explicit as to the siege of Chitor (Lucknow edition, Maqalah ii, p. 257, beginning at line 22). A body of five hundred carpenters, stone-cutters, blacksmiths, excavators, earthworkers, and shovelmen were set to work to construct *sabat,* "which are peculiar to India". These men laboured at making sabat and digging mines (*naqb*). "*Sabat* is the name for two walls which are made at the distance of a musketshot; and under the shelter of planks and baskets which are held together by skins, the said walls are carried close to the fort. Then the matchlock men and the mine-diggers (*naqqab*) come in safety, through the wide way between those walls, to the foot of the fort, and there they dig a mine and fill it with gunpowder. When the fort has been breached (*rakknah shud*), the rest of the army reaches the spot by way of the *sabat,* and effects an entry into the fort".

We have the story of the same siege told by Nizam-ud-din in the *Tabaqat-i-Akbar Shahi,* fol. 209a, line 17, (under the 12th Ilahi year, the beginning of Ramazan 974 H., 1566 A.D.). It is practically the same as Firishtah, sometimes word for word the same. He says work was begun in two places. They prepared something like a lane (or narrow street) up to the wall of the fort. "The *sabat* which began from the emperor's entrenchment was so wide, that ten horsemen could ride abreast along the bottom of it and so deep[3] that a man seated on an elephant, holding a spear in his hand, could go along it". In spite of the shields of ox-hide, a hundred men a day were killed by shots from the garrison. The bodies were built into the walls.

There was in addition a place upon which Akbar sat and picked off men appearing on the fortress walls. "His Majesty sat upon the top of a building (*khanah*) prepared for his reception upon the *sabat* of his entrenchment (*murchal*). He sat there matchlock in hand". Budaoni, ii, 103, (Lowe 106), here copies and abridges Nizam-ud-din : and in describing the siege of Kalinjar in 952 H. (1545), he uses the word *sabat* as if he meant by it a sap or trench, and not a tower.

Allowing for a certain amount of obscurity and vagueness in the native historians, we may, I think, assert that, so far, the meaning of *sabat* is tolerably plain. It was a trench begun at some distance from a fortress, deep and wide enough to conceal the wokers, the excavated earth being thrown up on each side to increase the protection. In rocky soil it may have been necessary to form the protecting wall of material, such as planks, trees, or earth, brought from elsewhere; but in most instances the obvious and easy method was to dig a trench in the ground, and use the earth from it to heighten the sides. But a *sabat* was not a tower or erection, built up from the surface of the ground. If Abul Fazl had not thrown the subject into confusion by his use of the word *sabat* in the *Akbarnamah,* the meaning of the word would be clear enough. But he persists in using it as the name for a temporary tower, or a battering ram, as he explicitly says in ii, 261, last line, (Lucknow edition), describing the siege of Ranthambhur in the 14th year, 22nd Ramazan 976 H. The besiegers of Ranthambur came to the conclusion that the fort could not be taken without recourse to *sabat, kih sarkob-i-gardan-kashan bashad.* As to this siege Nizam-ud-din fol. 212a, also uses the word *sabat,* but enters into no details. Budaoni, ii, 107 (Lowe, 111), follows Nizam-ud-din very closely.

Abul Fazl persists in using *sabat* in a different sense from everybody else. To begin with the siege of Chunar, Abul Fazl

(Lucknow edition), Book i, 114, line 6, says Rumi Khan, *ba kishtihae tartib-i-sabat sakhtah.* The passage is translated by Mr. Beveridge, i, 331, "Rumi Khan, ... constructed a covered way (*sabat*) upon boats, and arranged such a roof (*sataha*) . . . .". But if we go to Jauhar, Aftabchi, my Ms. fol. 16b, or to Nizam-ud-din, *Tabaqat,* fol. 151b, we find that Rumi Khan took three boats and built on them a battering ram (*muqabil-kol*). The passages are rendered to the same effect in Stewart, *Tezkereh-al-Vakiat,* p. 20, lines 11-25, Erskine, "Babar and Humayun", ii, 140, Budaoni, Ranking, i, 456, and Elliot, "Mahomedan Historians", v, 199. In none of them is there a word about a *sabat,* nor did they ever dream of calling this high erection built on boats, a *sabat.*

It is the same with Abul Fazl's long account of the siege of Chitor, (Lucknow edition) ii, from line 11 of p. 245, although in one place he says they made *diwar-i-gitin-i-ariz-i-marpech,* "serpentine, wide, earthen walls"; but he writes elsewhere that Akbar sat aloft upon a *sabat,* which commanded the walls, and from thence he shot. How could a serpentine wall be a tower, from which a man shot; or a battering ram, as he elsewhere defines a *sabat* to be? Abul Fazl has misled Count von Noer "Kaiser Akbar", i, 234-240, French edition, i, 165 (Horn 121) into asserting that a *sabat* should "if possible command the walls", that from "the top of the *sabat,* cannon breach the walls of the fortess". Then he speaks of the rolling of movable shields. Dr. Horn seems here, by a reference to the *tarah* (see ante p. 142) to identify it with the *sabat.* But I think the text of the *Akbarnamah* ii, 243-254, Lucknow edition, leads to the conclusion that three things were employed by Akbar at Chitor, 1) a long and deep trench (*sabat*), 2) movable shields to protect the workmen (*turah*), and 3) a high erection commanding the walls (*siba*).

Apparently open trenches were resorted to by the Mahrattahs so far back as 1670 at the siege of Karnala, for Grant Duff, 110, quoting the Bombay Records, says "the advanced by throwing up breastworks of earth".

Sandbags. In order to facilitate and attack, the ditch of a fort was at times filled up with sacks (*juwal,* Steingass, 376), filled with earth. This was done at Alamgir's siege of Gulkhandah in 1097 H. (1685-86), Khafi Khan, ii, 356, line 1. We find these bags mentioned as part of the Sikh equipment when they advanced in 1710 against the town of Rahun in the Jalandhar *duabah,* Khafi Khan, ii, 658, line 9, *o Juwalah-hae pur az reg, barae murchal bastan,* "and bags full of sand to make batteries".

Movable shields. In 1710 the Sikhs, when attacking the town of Jalalabad in the Ganges *Duabah,* adopted the plan of using movable wooden screens, or mantlets, mounted on ordinary cart-wheels. These they brought close to the walls, and from their shelter showered bullets and arrows on the besieged (Khafi Khan, ii, 656). Mantlets in general have been described, ante p. 142, under the word *Turah,* when dealing with Light Artillery.

Shatur. In Budaoni, Text, i, 382, we find this word, and it would seem from the context to refer to some article made of the trunks of trees, something connected with a siege. Colonel G. Ranking, 494, note 7, not finding it in any dictionary, suggests the Turkish *satu,* the roof of a house, meaning a shelther under which to approach the walls, something like the Roman *vinea,* a roof of planks and wicker work supported on poles eight feet long, and carried by the men as they advanced. May not the correct word be *shahtir* a beam?

Malchar. This is an obscure word used by Abd-ul-hamid twice, *Badshahnamah,* i, Part 2, p. 107, 1, 15, and p. 108, 1, 18. Both passages belong to the year 1044 H., 1634-35, and the first refers to the siege of Urchhah, the second to that of Dhamoni, fortresses in Bundelkhand. The wording in the second instance leads one to infer that the *malchar* was something in the nature of an approach by trenches.

Temporary Wall. Another device was to surround a fortress with a temporary wall, leaving a few openings at which strong guards were posted, and no one was allowed to enter or come out without a pass. This was done by Alamgir at Gulkhandah in 1098 H. (1686-87), *Maasir-i-Alamgiri,* 296. The materials employed were trunks of trees and clay. A somewhat similar plan was resorted to be Abd-us-samad Khan, when he invested Bandah, the Sikh, in Gurdaspur.

Towers (Siba). In connection with this siege of Gurdaspur, we are told of the building of high wooden towers, on which guns were mounted, the inside of the fortified place being thereby commanded, so as to make it untenable. The following passage gives a description of these towers by a contemporary, who was present. "At a distance of two arrows' flight, batteries were erected of a size sufficient to allow of the guns being worked. They were about three cubits (4½ feet) in height and in shape like bastions. A constant fire was kept up on both sides. Whenever a gunner shewed his head above the top of the earthwork, he would be fired at by one of the Sikhs concealed behind the battlements. In the same way a head showing above the wall was immediately fired at. The Sikhs answered shot for shot, and the imperialists were unable to move out to an attack in the open. Then, at the battery of Arif Khan, Abd-us-samad Khan prepared a tower over-topping the fort wall, and mounted his guns upon it. This device disconcerted the besieged, as the interior of the fort was now commanded and their movements thereby hampered. Similar towers were raised on two other sides of the attack, where Zakariyah Khan and Qamr-ud-din Khan, fol. 37a.

Ijad, fol. 23a, with respect to the same operations, uses a word which I read *chob-sibae,* and I suppose it applies to these towers. "The besiegers threw up *chob-sibae,* and drove subterannean passages towards each corner of the fort". But I am doubtful of this interpretation, as he had just spoken of "mounds of earth raised on the trunks of trees and placed from distance to distance round the fort" *i.e.* in other words, "towers" Why then should he refer again to the same thing by another name (*chob-sibae*) in the next sentence?

Siba is defined by Steingass, 714, as from the Turkish, "a place surrounded by walls"; but Horn, 103, quoting the *Alamgirnamah,* 313, translates *siba* "aus den Befestigungen sich erhebender Bastionen", or in other words what was called in

Europe, a *cavalier.* This latter meaning would apply equally to Abd-us-samad Khan's towers, although they were independent structures, and not part of a fortress.

It was evidently a *siba* that was built by Dara Shukoh when besieging Qandahar in 1063 H. (1653). "He mounted a battery on a high and solid mound of earth" (Elphinstone, "History", 513). We also find the word used in the *Mirat-us-safa,* fol. 99b, when in 1169 H. (July 1756)[4] the French under Bussy were invested in the Chahar Mahal at Haidarabad. The assailants erected *sibah.* Something of the same sort was had recourse to by the native besiegers of Arcot in 1751 (Orme "Mil. Trans." i, 191). They filled up a house with earth, and on this as a base they raised a square mound, which commanded the gate and every part within the fort. The same kind of thing is referred to by Orme, "Hist. Frag.", 153, on the authority of Manucci (Catrou, 4th edition of 1715, 3rd part, p. 177), as having been used at the siege of Gulkhandah in 1687. A vast mound of earth was raised to a level with the wall and the artillery mounted on it. Wilks, ii, 360, was told by Sir Barry Close, one of the garrison, that when Tellicherry (Malabar District) was besieged in 1782, Sirdar Khan employed what was evidently a *siba,* though the name is not used. "An immense extent of base served as the foundation for several successive stories, constructed of the trunks of trees in successive layers, crossing each other and compacted by earth rammed between the intervals; the contrivances in the rear for raising the guns were removed when the erection was complete; successive stories were raised as the besieged covered themselves from each in turn". Lake, 221, calls these erections "cavaliers", and compares them to the great mounds raised by the ancients in their sieges. (For "Cavalier", see Voyle, 69).

Storming. With the inefficient artillery of those days, a breach was very rarely effected, and we hear of very few forts being actually stormed. Entrance was oftener secured through breaking in the gate, and for this purpose elephants, as already stated on p. 177, were employed.

Scaling ladders. The name for scaling ladders was

narduban, Steingass, 1395. Babar mentions them more than once. Their use in the reign of Humayun, 963 H., 1555-56 is proved by a passage in Budaoni, text, i, 465, Ranking 600. The words employed there are *zinah-pae,* the round of a ladder or step of a stair, and *kamand,* which Ranking translates literally "noose", though from the context "ropeladder" would be better. Again they were used in Shahjahan's reign, (1044 H. 1634-35), at the siege of Urchhah, *Badshahnamah,* i, part 2, p. 107, line 15. From time to time we hear of their being used at a much later period. For instance, at the end of 1719, when Girdhar Bahadur was besieged in Allahabad fort by Haidar Quli Khan and other imperial officers, we read that a general attack in two directions was ordered. One of these was headed by Sher Afgan Khan, Daud Khan, an officer under Muhammad Khan, Bangash, and others. They drove the besieged back to the very foot of the wall, then "Daud Khan, Bangash, brought up the scaling ladders, hoping to make an entry, but after much struggle and effort, he was obliged to abandon the attempt", *Siwanih-i-khisri.* In 1710 the Sikhs had scaling ladders with them when they tried to take Jalalabad in the upper Ganges *Duabah,* Khafi Khan, ii, 657.

Modes of repelling assault, Burning oil, Powder Bags &c. In a quotation already given on p. 273, from Fitzclarence, reference has been made to the throwing down from the walls of bags of gunpowder and burning thatch. I have also referred on p. 131 to the *huqqah-i-atash* used for a similar purpose. Other missiles are named by Horn, 123, quoting Von Noer i, 254 ("French trans.", i, 161), who says that at the siege of Chitor the Rajputs brought sacks of cotton cloth and fascines steeped in oil, which they endeavoured to set fire to while the breach was being stormed. As to the throwing of skins full of gunpowder with a match attached, we read of this being done by the defenders of a fort in the Dakhin in the fourth year of Shahjahan (1631 A.D.). Horn, 132, quotes the passage from the *Badshah-namah,* i, 376, sixth line from end, *az darun-i-hisar ban o tufang o huqqah o sang o mashk-hae barut ra atash zadah mi andakhtand,* "From inside the fort they threw rockets and bullets and grenades and stones and lighted powder-skins".

A somewhat later instance of the use of the *huqqah* or hand-grenade and the *handi* or firepot, was at the siege of the Ghasahri fort (Aligarh district) by Suraj Mal, Jat, in the year 1753. In the *Sujan Charitr,* Canto v, stanza 24, we have :

> *Uththan maru ghani padau, saththi mukh mode;*
> *Handi hukke aggi de, gadh-walaun chhode.*
>
> "There he fierce fighting fell, his men turned back;
> The defenders threw lighted *handis* and *huqqahs.*"

Quite at the end of the Moghul period, we find these means of defending a breach resorted to by George Thomas' officers, in resisting the Mahratta assault on Hansi (3rd Dec. 1802) : "Burning *choppers* (*i.e.* thatch from the roofs of houses), powder-pots, and everything he could get hold of, were showered upon us; but our greatest loss was from the powder-pots, which greatly disheartened the men" ("Military Memoirs of Lt. Col. James Skinner, C.B." i, 228). Again, at the siege of Bhartpur in 1805, we find in use similar means of repelling an assault. Thorn, "War", 457, says "the people on the walls continually threw down upon their heads ponderous pieces of timber and flaming packs of cotton previously dipped in oil, followed by pots filled with gunpowder and other combustibles, the explosion of which had a terrible effect". See also a case, which occurred in 1781, quoted by Lake, "Sieges", 212.

Stones. Where the fort was on an eminence and stones were available, these latter were stored, and rolled down the hill upon any besieger (Blacker, "War", 318). In 1044 H., 1634-35, when Dhamoni in Bundelkhand was besieged, the defenders rolled stones down on their assailants. *Badshahnamah,* i, part 2, p. 108. This was also done at a fort in the Dakhin in 1674, when it was attacked by Shivaji (R. Orme, "Hist. Frag.", 47). And it is only a year or two ago that we found the same mode of defence still resorted to at Hanza in the Himalayas.

This use of stones was the principal cause of our failure at the first storming of Chunar on the Ganges, Nov. 29th 1764, (Carraccioli, "Clive", i, 64). "Large stones, which the enemy rolled out of the breach and on each side of it, threw our men so often down and rolled them back again by twenties at a time ..... Our people were at last so fatigued that they were obliged to give it up". Here Captain Dow (the historian) had his skull fractured by a stone, for which he was obliged to be trepanned. Khair-ud-din, *Ibrat-namah*, 75, tells us that *sang-asiya* were thrown from the walls of Patnah when it was attacked in 1173 H. (1759); the dictionary, St. 701, says these are whetstones, possibly the stones of hand-mills are intended by the author. We were also repulsed twice, in 1789 and again in 1791, at Kistnagarhi (Salem District) "simply by (the garrison) rolling down stones and large masses of granite on the assailants", Lake, 207, note. Again, at Trimbak, in Khandesh, our assault on the 24th April 1818 was chiefly repulsed by the garrison rolling down large stones on their assailants (Lake, 105); and great damage was done in the same way at Gopadrug on the 13th May 1819 (id. 201).

Evacuation after a repulsed assault. Lake, 150, remarks, as among the many inconsistencies of the Indian character, that while they surrendered impregnable fortresses without a blow, they would not only defend a mere walled town, but stand an assault after a practicable breach had been made. Another curious habit connected with these defences is pointed out by Blacker, 346. It frequently happened that a garrison would repulse an assault in the most dauntless manner and with severe loss. Yet during the following night they would silently evacuate the place they had defended so well. Naturally Europeans wondered and sought for a cause. The object did not seem to be to divert the attacking force from some enterprize of greater danger to the general cause. The effort was nearly always isolated and desperate. Why not abandon the place at once, or ask for terms? It seemed that it must be a point of honour with them to try their strength, and having proved their valour, they then withdrew.

Reduction by Starvation. Many instances of this cause of surrender might be adduced. This was, for example, the principal reason of the surrender of Agrah in 1131 H. (Aug. 1719), when Nekusiyar, after laying claim to the throne, was invested in that fort by Husain Ali Khan. "After a month, provisions began to be scarce. Many of those who had joined from the country round began to desert, getting over the walls at night, only to be seized by the Nawab's sentries. These fugitives informed Husain Ali Khan of the disheartened and suffering condition of the garrison. All the good grain had been used up, and nothing was left but inferior pulses, and even these had been stored over seven years and smelt so strong, that even the fourfooted beasts would not eat them with avidity. Attempts were made to bring in small supplies of flour, which were dragged up by ropes let down from the battlements. Some of the artillery of the besieging force took part in this traffic. After this was found out, the strictness of watch was redoubled, anything moving in the river at night was fired upon, and expert swimmers were kept ready to pursue and seize any one who attempted to escape by way of the river", Mhd. Qasim, Lahori, 286, 287. Negociations commenced, and the fort was surrendered on the 12th Aug. 1719, after an investment of nearly three months.

Gurdaspur. The reduction of Gurdaspur and the consequent surrender of Bandah, the Sikh leader, is another instance of the starving out of a garrison. Abd-us-samad Khan appeared before the place in April 1715, but it was not taken before the 17th Dec. of that year. Some time before this happened, the provisions had come to an end, not a grain being left in the storehouses. The garrison obtained a little food from the common soldiers outside, for which they paid at the rate of two or three shillings a pound; they also slaughtered oxen and other animals, and having no firewood, ate the flesh raw. Then they picked up and ate whatever they found on the road. They gathered the leaves from the trees; when these were gone, they stripped the bark and gathered the smaller shoots, and grinding these down, used them as a substitute for flour. The bones of animals were also ground down and used in the same way. It is said that some of the Sikhs even cut flesh from their own thighs, roasted it, and eat it.

Thun (First Siege). In another instance the attempt to take a place by starvation was not successful. Thun was a fort built by the ancestors of the Jat rajahs of Bhartpur, and it was their chief place of strength before they removed to Bhartpur. It was situated somewhere between Dig and Gobardhan, to the west of Mathura. In 1716 the cup of Churaman's transgressions being full, it was resolved to proceed against him, and the duty was confided to Rajah Jai Singh Sawae of Amber. Thun having been completely invested, the siege began on the 19th Nov. 1716. The fortress was provided with lofty walls and a deep ditch filled from springs, and round it spread a thick and thorny jungle "through which a bird could hardly make its way". Supplies were abundant; indeed (though this is probably an exaggeration) there were, it was said, grain, salt, ghi, tobacco, cloth and firewood sufficient for twenty years. When the siege was imminent, Churaman had forced all merchants and traders with their families to quit the place, leaving their goods behind them. He made himself personally responsible for compensation, if he gained the day, and as the property could not be removed, the owners gave their consent without much demur. Churaman's son, Muhkam Singh, and his nephew, Rupa, issued from the fort and gave battle in the open. In his report of the 21st Dec. 1716, the Rajah claimed a victory. He next cut down the trees round the fort, and erected a large number of small guard-houses, in which he placed his men. A large cannon was sent to him from Delhi, while three hundred *mans* of gunpowder, one hundred and fifty *mans* of lead, and five hundred rockets were supplied from the arsenal at Agrah. The siege dragged on for twenty months, and even in the end Thun was not taken. The rains of 1717 were very late in coming, prices rose very high, and great expense fell on the Rajah in bringing supplies from his own country of Amber. In January 1718 the Rajah reported that he had had many encounters with the Jats, in which he had overcome them, but owing to support at Court, they were not willing to yield. Soon after this Sayyad Khan Jahan, Barhah, a near relation of the wazir, negociated a peace over Jai Singh's head, and Churaman was allowed to settle matters by offering a tribute of thirty lakhs of rupees to the government, and a present of twenty lakhs for the minister himself. Rajah Jai Singh was then recalled.

Thun (Second Siege). On a second occasion, in the year 1722, Rajah Jai Singh was more successful, and Thun was then razed to the ground. He reached Thun a few days before the 25th Oct. 1722; the fort was then held by the sons of Churaman, and at first there were daily fights. On the 31st a report came from the Rajah stating that he had taken three small forts from Muhkama (who was the son of Churaman), and he expected that Thun would soon fall. He asked for a large cannon, one hundred *rahkalahs*, five hundred *mans* of lead and powder, and three hundred rockets. The capture of the fort was reported to the emperor on the 20th Nov. 1722. Churaman's sons had fled. This speedy and apparently brilliant victory was, however, the result of treachery and not of hard fighting. Badan Singh, who was on bad terms with his cousin, Muhkam Singh, had been persuaded to betray the fort, on a promise that he would be appointed to the chieftainship.

Communication between Besiegers and Besieged. In Fraser, "Mil. Mem. of Lt. Col. J. Skinner", i, 231, we read that at Hansi the Mahrattas rolled letters upon arrows and shot them into the fort from the trenches, and received answers from George Thomas' men in the same way, agreeing to give their leader up. In 918 H. (1512) at Gazhdawan, Babar is said to have communicated in this way with the Uzbak garrison (Budaoni, i, 444). Another case is at the siege of Qandahar in 1545 : "The dwellers in the fort wrote daily accounts of Mirza Askari, and shot them down from the walls, twisted round an arrow", *Akbarnamah* (Beveridge) i, 466, line 4. The same mode of communicating, Manucci tells us, Philipps Ms. 1945, Part i, p. 251, was employed by the besiegers of Bhakkar in Sind (1658); one of these arrows struck Manucci on the shoulder, and he took it just as it was to the eunuch commanding the garrison.

Keys of Fortresses. Horn, 133, quoting Elliot, v, 176, says that the fortresses had gold or silver keys; in this particular passage the place referred to is Ranthambhur. An instance of this practice in *Persia* is found in *Mujmil-ut-Tarikh-i-bad-nadiriyah* (ed . Oskar Mann) 85, line 21. We are told here that the keys of Naishapur were delivered to Ahmad Shah, Durranti, when peace was made. Again, we have a somewhat earlier instance. In 1119 (1707) when Mir Waïs, Ghilzai, killed Gurgin Khan, Gurji (Georgian), governor on behalf of Sultan Husain Mirza, Safawi and took possession of Qandahar, he sent his submission to Shah 'Alam Bahadur Shah, together with a golden key (*M-ul-u.*, iii, 702). Another Central Asian practice is to be found in *Mujmil-ut-larikh bad Nadiriyah*, p. 88, line 2, the planting of a flag on the bastion of a fort as soon as it was taken. I have found no mention of this in India. As showing the importance attached in India to the keys of a fortress, we may instance the trouble taken by Aurangzeb 'Alamgir to make his father, Shahjahan, surrender those of Agrah, sending his eldest son, Sultan Muhammad, to demand them (Bernier, 63). In 1707, Mhd. Yar Khan, the qilahdar of Delhi, sent his son with the keys of the fort of Bahadur Shah in token of submission (Khafi Khan, ii, 577). And we read in Ghulam Ali Khan's *Muqaddamah-i-Shah Alam-namah,* fol. 61b, that during Nadir Shah's invasion (1738), Burhan-ul-mulk and Tahmas, Jalair, were sent ahead from Karnal with a note from Muhammad Shah addressed to Lutfullah Khan, Sadiq (*subahdar* of the province), directing him to give up the keys of the fortress at Delhi to the Shah's agent, which was done accordingly. Then, when Najaf Khan took Agrah from the Jats in 1773, the mesenger conveying the news to Delhi "carried with him the keys of the fort to be laid at His Majesty's feet", W. Francklin, *Shah Aulum,* 53.

Particular Sieges. For the period covering the end of Shahjahan's reign and the whole reign of Alamgir, I add a few notes and references in respect of the more notable sieges. I then give an account, in a little more detail, of sieges belonging to the 18th century. In the second half of Alamgir's reign sieges, or at least attacks on forts, were very numerous.

Qandahar. Dara Shukoh had at the siege of Qandahar in 1063 H. (1653) four heavy guns, 30,000 iron shot, great and small, 1500 *mans* (60,000 lbs) of lead, 5000 *mans* (20,000 lbs) of gunpowder, 5000 artillerymen, 10,000 musketeers, 6000 pioneers, sappers and exemen, 500 *pakhalis* (men bringing water in large skins carried on animals), 3000 *ahadis*, 60 war elephants, and a great number of Brinjaris (grain-carriers), Raverty, "Notes", 22. There is a long account of the campaign, id., 23-28.

Bijapur, 1097 H., 1685-86, B.M. 1641, fol. 113a (sixteen entries), id. 138a, Khafi Khan, ii, 322-368, *Maasir-i-Alamgiri*, 275.

Gulkhandah, 1098 H., 1686-87, Abul-Hasan left Haidarabad and took refuge in Gulkhandah in Zul Qadah 1097 H. Possession of Gulkhandah was obtained on the 24th Zul Qadah 1098, *Maasir-i-A.*, 299. The siege lasted eight months and some days, *id.*, 300. Description of the fort, *id.*, 301. See also B.M. 1641, fol. 113a, (forty entries).

Jinji, 1105-9 H., 1693-7 Khafi Kh. ii, 418, *Maasir-i-A.*, 391.

Khelnah, 1113H., 1701-2 Khafi Kh. ii, 499, *Maasir-i-A.*, 445-457.

Kandanah, 1114 H., 1702-3. Khafi Kh. ii, 510, *Maasir-i-A.*, 469.

Wakankhera, 1116 H., 1704-5. Khafi Kh. ii, 527, *Maasir-i-A.*, 490.

Jaitpur. One of the best known sieges of the 18th century was that of Jainpur in Bundelkhand, where Muhammad Khan, Bangash, was invested by the Bundelahs aided by the Mahrattas. This siege is memorable, among other reasons, as the occasion on which the Mahrattas first took a prominent part in imperial politics north of the Narbada. The siege lasted over three months, namely, from the 15th May to the 31st Aug. 1729. Chattarsal, Bundelah, had submitted himself earlier in the year, and Muhammad Khan, quite unsuspicious of danger, was out settling the country at the head of a small force. Suddenly he heard that a large Mahratta army, under Baji Rao and eleven other chiefs, was close at hand. From the 12th March to the 15th May, he maintained himself in his camp, but finally was forced to retreat on Jaitpur. There were no stores of food, and no time to provide any. Soon they were completely surrounded, but the Mahrattas, always poor hands at siege operations, made no impression on the place. They resolved to starve the garrison out. After a month or two there was no longer any grain for food. Recourse was then had to the slaughter of the horses and bullocks. Flour could not be procured even at one hundred rupees the *seer*; the only supplies were those furnished surreptitiously by the Mahrattas outside, and this flour was composed mainly of ground bones. Money was let down by a rope, and the corresponding amount of flour, at the rate of 100 rupees for a *seer*, was attached to the rope and drawn up. Many men died of starvation. But by Baji Rao's orders, any man on giving up his arms was allowed to pass out unmolested. In the end only some thousand or twelve hundred men remained. At last Muhammad Khan was forced to make terms and evacuate the fort (Journal A.S.B. for 1878, p. 300, and *Mirat-i-waridat,* my copy, pp. 25, 26.

Allahabad. This fortress was besieged twice in the 18th century, first in 1131 H. (1719) and again in 1163 H. (1750). On the first occasion the imperial forces were sent to eject the governor, Girdhar Bahadur; on the second, it was attacked by the Pathans of Farrukhabad, when held by the officers of the then governor, Safdar Jang, who was also subahdar of Audh and *wazir* of the empire. The first investment lasted about nine and the second some seven months, but on neither occasion did the besiegers succeed in reducing the fort. In 1131 H. (1719) Girdhar Bahadur yielded on obtaining the government of Audh, and marched out with all the honours of war. In 1163 H. (1750) the Pathans, before they had made the least impression upon the fortress, were recalled hurriedly to defend their homes against a combined attack by Safdar Jang and the Mahrattas.

Bangarh. Almost the last expedition commanded by a Moghul emperor in person involved a siege. Between Abul Mansur Khan, Safdar Jang, governor of Audh, and Ali Muhammad Khan, Rohelah, a man who had recently risen to power in what we now call Rohilkhand, there had long been ill-blood from one cause and another. Now, Amir Khan, Umdat-ul-mulk, a favourite of Muhammad Shah, had been banished from court and sent as governor to Allahabad, the boundary of which runs with Audh. With this noble Safdar Jang struck up an intimacy. After a time, Amir Khan was recalled to Delhi, where he resolved to oust his enemy, the *wazir* Qamr-ud-din Khan. For this purpose he sought the aid of Safdar Jang, and caused the emperor to summon him from his government. Safdar Jang was received with marked favour and appointed *Mir Atash*, or commander of the imperial artillery. Having secured influence at court, he proceeded to use it for the destruction of Ali Muhammad Khan. The latter had, however, a friend in the *wazir*, with whom he had prudently formed a matrimonial connection. Meanwhile Safdar Jang's influence with the emperor was on the increase, and was crowned on the 25th June 1744 by the honour of a visit to his tents from Muhammad Shah in person.

The importance of ejecting Ali Muhammad Khan was so fully impressed on the emperor, that for the first time in his reign he was persuaded to take the field in person. Amir Khan and Safdar Jang worked hard to secure this result, for without the emperor's presence they could effect little or nothing. The *wazir*, Qamr-ud-din Khan, was friendly to Ali Muhammad Khan, Qaim Jang, the nawab of Farrukhabad, was in secret concert and alliance with him, and his army was efficient and well-equipped. On the 24th Muharram, 1158 H. (25th February 1745), making a pretext of a hunting expedition in the Loni preserve, Muhammad Shah crossed the Jamnah, his real purpose being kept secret even from the *wazir*.

Omitting the intervening events, we pass on to the 21st Rabi ii (May 22nd 1745), the day on which the army reached Budaon; and here Muhammad Shah effected a reconciliation between Qaim Jang and Safdar Jang, which was ratified by an exchange of visits. All the same, Safdar Jang continued actively to carry on the campaign. Then, seeing the imperial army so close to him, Ali Muhammad Khan quitted his abode at Anwalah, and took refuge in his stronghold of Bangarh, some *kos* to the south. To this place he was followed by the imperial army. On the one hand, the *wazir* persisted that he could bring in Ali Muhammad Khan; on the other, Safdar Jang urged that if he were given a free hand, he would soon overcome the rebel by force. To strengthen his position, Safdar Jang also sent to Audh for reinforcements. His *bakhshi,* Naval Rae, was ordered to march with this force by way of Shahjahanpur to Bangarh.

Bangarh was now surrounded by the imperialists. Kalyan Singh, rajah of Kumaon, who had recently suffered from an irruption of the Rohelahs, joined the army as an ally. Round the fort was a thick screen of bambus "through which the wind found its way with difficulty". Labourers and axemen were set to work to cut this hedge down, and batteries were erected. But the army and its commanders were only half-hearted in their exertions, many nobles had passed long years at court and had never seen a skirmish or heard the roar of cannon, and others again blamed the *wazir* for bringing them to do a work which he did not care to do himself. The remarks just referred to caused great annoyance to Qamr-ud-din Khan; so much so, that Haiyat-ullah Khan, Hizbar Jang (son of Saif-ud-Daulah Zakariyah Khan, and son-in-law of the *wazir*), begged urgently for leave to advance and end the matter.

In spite of the overwhelming odds, Ali Muhammad Khan held his ground. Khushhal Chand, although an imperial officer, cannot help admiring his courage. He also breaks forth into unstinted praise of the flourishing state of the Rohelah territory, the lands being fully cultivated, the crops good, the peasants well-off. Theft, outrage and highway-robbery were unknown within those boundaries. These results were the fruits of the ruler's strong reason and good understanding :

"The fox carried off the morsel from the wolf,
For the former has great wits, the latter, little".

One day Ali Muhammad Khan came out of the fort, and was attacked by one of Safdar Jang's officers. Safdar Jang mounted and was anxious to make an onset. Muhammad Shah thought this imprudent, when on the one side were the Moghuls (the *wazir's* troops) and on the other the Pathans (Qaim Jang and his men), neither of whom were to be trusted, and might act in collusion with the besieged. Several days elapsed. Then Ali Muhammad Khan fired some balls which fell in the camp of the nobles, some even coming near to the imperial enclosure "to make obeisance". Muhammad Shah sent for the *wazir* and consulted. There was no want of men; one division by itself would have sufficed. Yet nothing was done. Once Muhammad Shah appealed to Rae Hemraj, a Saksena Kayath, a mere clerk in the artillery office; "If I made over this business to you, how long would it take?" The *kayath* replied : "Your Majesty's artillery is so powerful that I could reduce Bangarh to ashes in four *ghari* (about one and a half hours)". But the imperialists continued to discuss helplessly what should be done next. In this interval, Naval Rae arrived with 20,000 horsemen and 40,000 infantry. Safdar Jang went out a *kos* or two to meet him. Naval Rae commenced the siege in earnest, and Ali Muhammad Khan began to think of flight or surrender. He sent an intimation to this effect to this wazir, whose second son, Muin-ud-daulah (commonly called Mir Mannu) was sent to talk the matter over. Having received a promise that his life would be spared, Ali Muhammad Khan came to the Presence on the 3rd Jamadi i, 1158 H. (2nd June 1745), Khushhal Chand, B.M. Or. 1844, fol. 164a—181b.

Agrah. After their defeat by Ahmad Shah, Abdali, in January 1761, the Mahrattas for a time quitted Northern India. Suraj Mall of Bhartpur was then the only powerful ruler left from the gates of Delhi to the banks of the Chambal. The only place of strength remaining to the Moghuls was the fort of Agrah, and in 1763 Suraj Mall determined to acquire it. Since 1754 the commander and troops had received no pay, living on the produce of what they sold from the magazines within the fort. Obviously such people would not be difficult to deal with. Suraj Mall made a pretence of crossing to the north bank of the Jamnah, then turned suddenly and blockaded Agrah. Still, he could never have taken the place, had it been in charge of a good commandant. At this time the command was held by a mere boy, and he was under the thumb of a subordinate, a greedy coward. From this traitor overtures were received, and the fort was given up. The blockade had lasted twenty day, but though the inhabitants of the city suffered from plundering, no damage had been done to the fort. Suraj Mall is supposed to have carried off fifty lakhs of rupees from the town. "When Suraj Mall took Agrah, it had the most numerous and the best artillery in the kingdom, with powder, balls and bullets, and other goods of the Royal Wardrobe, collected during a long course of years. Everything was carried off. The best cannon were removed to Dig and Bhartpur. Two years ago (1765?), Juwahir Singh caused most of the houses to be demolished, imitating what had been done at Allahabad, to allow room for the artillery to play. But the fort guns can do no harm as the bastions are so high. Nay, the *debris* of the houses could be used as ready-made entrenchments and batteries, to secure an approach to the main body of the place. The present commandant and the leaders of the Jats know nothing of war, they are men of low extraction, owing their rise solely to their devotion to young Juwahir Singh", "Orme Collections", p. 4303.

REFERENCES

1. This is not true of Hindustan, outside of Bengal. If "corn" were substituted, the argument would still hold good, and exactitude would not be scarificed.
2. After this date the author also saw Daulatabad, pp. 215-221, and Ahmadnagar, 241, 242.
3. The word actually used is *irtafa,* "height", which evidently means "height" from the floor of the trench to the natural surface of the ground, or to the top of the earth thrown out on each side. In other words, what we call "depth", when speaking of an excavation.
4. See Malleson, "French in India" ([illegible] edition) p. 490.

11

Camps and Camp Equipage

Each soldier seems to have had the shelter of a tent, even if it consisted only of a cotton cloth raised on two sticks. The kinds of tents were numerous, from the *rauti,* a mere low awning, up to the huge imperial tents. The *Ain,* i, 54, names twelve different kinds of tents. I have just spoken of one of these, the *Rauti,* and of another, the *Gulalbar,* not a tent but an enclosure, I shall speak further on. The *sarapardah* No. 11 also is a screen and not a tent. From a perusal of the passage referred to, coupled with plates x and xi, it is fairly easy to understand what each of these tents was like. The *Shamiyanah,* No. 9, is still known and in common use; the name may be from *sham,* evening, that is an awning for use in the evening, or from *shamah* (Steingass, 725), a veil. The *khargah,* No. 8, (Steingass, 456) are spoken of by Bernier, 359, note 4, and 362, where he says they are folding tents with one or two doors, and made in various ways; he calls them "cabinets", and leads us to infer that they were set up inside the large tents. The emperor and the great nobles were provided with tents in duplicate, one set being sent on to the next camping ground while the other set was in use (Bernier, 359). The tents thus sent on were known as the *pesh-khanah* (literally "advance-house").

Camp, description of. The laying out of the emperor's camp, a plan continued to the last, is described in the *Ain,* i, 47, and is shown with more detail in plate iv. In the centre was the imperial enclosure of canvas screens 1530 yards long, and about one fifth of that distance in breadth. It was divided across in its length into four courts. Over the entrance, which faced in the direction of the next march, was the drum-house (*naqar-khanah*), in the second court was the audience tent, in the third a more private hall, and in the fourth the sleeping tents. Behind was a place for Akbar's mother, while outside and still more to the rear were the women's apartments, surrounded on all four sides by guards. Along the outside of the enclosure were ranged on each side the *karkhanahs,* or departments of the household and arsenal, about ten tents on each side. Still further away and towards each corner, the tents of the guards were erected. Outside the gate of the enclosure were the elephants and horses with their establishments on one side; and the records, the carts and litters, the general of artillery, and the hunting leopards on the other. A description of Jahangir's camp will be found in Cambridge, "War", Introd. v, who quotes it from Sir Thomas Roe's journal, the chief impression produced on the ambassador's mind being that of immense size.

A good account of the mode of pitching an imperial camp is to be found in Bernier, 360, 361. First of all the Mir Manzil selected a fit spot for the emperor's tents. This was a square enclosure 300 paces each way. The whole of this was surrounded by screens (*qanat*), seven or eight feet high, secured by cords to pegs and stayed by poles fixed at an angle, one inside and one outside, at every ten paces. The entrance was in the centre of one of the sides. On each side of the gate (Bernier, 363) were two handsome tents, where were kept a number of horses ready saddled and caparisoned.[1] In front of the entrance was a clear space, at the end of which stood the *naqar khanah,* or station for the drums, trumpets and cymbals. Close to it was the *chauki-khanah,* or tent of the officer on guard for the day.

Round the enclosure were the imperial bazars, through which a street led from the gate in the direction of the next day's march, marked out by long poles, which were surmounted by yak tails and placed at 300 paces from each other. The princes and great nobles pitched their camps at various distances, sometimes of several miles, from the emperor's tents. Each was surrounded by the tents of his men and his own bazar, the only order observed being that the chief's tents must face towards the imperial Public Audience-hall (Bernier, 366). Bernier estimates, 367, that where there was ample space for spreading, Alamgir's whole camp would have measured about six miles in circumference. The bazars were marked out (Bernier, 365) by long poles surmounted, as already said, by the tails of the great Tibet cow "which have the appearance of so many periwigs".

The camp is thus described by Catrou, French ed., 4to, p. 128, 12mo, iv, 40, 57, possibly borrowing from Bernier, although he professes to have the Venetian, Manucci, as his authority : "The camp where this numerous army rested was laid out daily in the same manner, so far as the nature of the ground permitted. A great enclosure was roped off of square shape, and this was surrounded by a deep ditch. The heavy artillery was ranged from distance to distance and defended the approaches. The emperor's palace was placed in the centre of the camp. This also was square in shape and the light artillery was disposed all round it. The tents of the generals, of a much less height than those of the emperor, were pitched in the different quarters of the camp. The sutlers and traders of all sorts had streets assigned to them. To sum up it may be said that Aurangzeb dragged in his train a travelling city as large and as peopled as his capital".

Some of the tents were of an enormous size. These was one made by order of Shahjahan which bore the name of *Dil-badil* (Generous Heart). When Bahadur Shah ordered this tent to be erected at Lahor in the year 1711, five hundred tent-pitchers and carpenters were employed for one month in putting it up, and in so doing several persons were killed (*Mirat-ul-Istilah,* 218b). Kamwar Khan, entry of 4th Shaban 1123 H. (16th Sept. 1711), says this tent cost 50,000 rupees. A later writer, *Seir*, i, 25, note 32, says the emperor's camp was about one and a quarter miles in circuit, it contained one hundred and twenty tents, some of them big enough for several hundreds of men, and the largest might admit two thousand or three thousand. All this was surrounded by a *qanat,* or wall of cloth six feet high, outside which is a paling which surrounds the whole : and it is betwixt these two enclosures that live the guards. Further off, there is another paling, and here, too, in the intermediate space reside guards and people attached to the imperial household, such as chairmen, watermen, or taper-bearers. See also Cambridge, "War", Introd. v, for an account of Nasir Jang's camp in 1750, over twenty miles in circumference. There is also a good description of a native camp in Wilks, i, 292, referring to the year 1752, where he tells us of the motley collection of cover, from superb tents down to ragged blankets; tents and animals all intermixed; the only mark of order being the flags set up by each chief, the only regularly laid out lines being those of the traders' booths or shops.

Colour of Tents. The tents of the emperor, his sons, and grandsons were of a red cloth, called *kharwah,* a stout canvas-like cotton cloth, dyed red with the root of the *al* plant. Round the emperor's tents was the enclosure called the *gulalbar.* Some of the great nobles such as the vice-gerent (wakil-i-mutlaq) or the chief minister, (*Jamdat-ul-mulk*) were allowed *patapati* or striped tents, one red stripe and one white stripe alternately. *Pati* is H. For a strip of anything, (*Mirat-ul-Istilah,* fol. 27b and Bernier, 366). The latter writer on p. 362 seems to imply that the imperial tents also were striped outside, but as his phrase is "ornamented with stripes", perhaps the two statements are not absolutely conflicting.

Gulalbar. The name of the screen which Bernier speaks of as being put up round the emperor's tents was the *Gulalbar.* It is mentioned in the *Ain,* i, 45, 54, but a fuller description will not be out of place, since the word frequently appears in histories, and it is well to have a definite idea of what is meant. *Gulal* in Hindi means "red" and *bar,* "anything in the nature of a wall which prevents entrance or passage through it". Thus the whole word is equivalent to "Red Wall". Before Akbar's time the tents of the Gurgani kings were surrounded by a rope called the *tanab-i-quruq* (lit. "the rope of hindrance"). In Akbar's reign the *gulalbar* was devised. It was formed out of bambus coloured red and held together by leather straps like a net-work (*jali*), and so made that it might be extended or gathered up at will. Its height was three *gaz,* or about eight feet, and it had two gateways to the front and one on the side where the harem tents stood. This screen was erected round the imperial tents, which were styled collectively the *Daulat-khanah* (literally, Abode of Prosperity). Outside it a ditch was dug, and red flags, an attribute of sovereignty, were displayed on poles (*Mirat-ul-Istilah,* fol. 203a).

Jali. The word *jali* is similarly met with in reference to the precincts of the emperor's tent. The derivation is from H. *Jal,* a net, and it means lattice, grating, network. From the passage quoted in the last paragraph and another in the same book, we see that this network (*jali*) was the *gulalbar* under another name. But a European observer, who probably had seen an emperor's camp, says the *gulalbar* was the outer paling fifty yards from the *qanats,* or cloth screens seven feet high which enclosed the emperor's tents (*Seir,* i, 159, note 120). For *gulalbar* Khushhal Chand in one place, Berlin Ms. 495, fol. 1010a, uses *salabat-bar* "majestic-enclosure" : and Ashob, fol. 196b, claims it as the invention of Salabat Khan,[2] Mir Atash to Alamgir, *gulal-barah* being nothing more than a popular name Ashob gives a minute description of its construction; this differs in details from that of Anand Ram given above. The tents of princes continued to be protected by the old device of a rope, which still bore the name of *tanab-i-quruq,* or rope of prohibition (*Mirat-ul-I.*)

Rahkalah-bar. This word is literally *rahkalah,* field-piece, plus *bar,* enclosure. It was the park of artillery arranged at the entrance of the imperial quarters, or round them, as a protection against attack. The quarters of the Mir Atash were at the imperial gateway (Danishmand Khan, entry of 4th Zul Hijjah 1119 H., and Bernier, 363).

Harem women with armies (Horn, 57). On all campaigns a harem of women with their attendants seems to have accompanied the emperor and the chief men. On the day of battle these women were put on elephants and carefully guarded by the force forming the rear guard, which was posted at some distance behind the centre, where stood the emperor or other chief commander. Many references might be quoted in illustration of this statement. The habit of being followed by a harem might be justified in cases where the camp was the only home, for perhaps years at a time. But the practice was the same even on short campaigns. For instance, the redoutable Ghazi-ud-din Khan, Imad-ul-mulk, who became wazir at sixteen years of age and had deposed two emperors before he was five and twenty, was born in his maternal grandfather, Qamr-ud-din Khan's camp. This noble, who was Muhammad Shah's wazir, was then on his way to Malwah on an expedition against the Mahrattas. Wilks, ii, 38, writes as if it was a peculiar weakness of the particular noble, that the Nizam of Haidarabad was in 1768 "accompanied in the field by his favourite wives". But in so doing Nizam Ali was only following the usual practice of Moghul commanders.

REFERENCES

1. This is, no doubt, what we read of so often under the name of the *jilau*.
2. According to the *Maasir-ul-umara,* ii, 742, Khwajah Mir, Khwafi, (Salabat Khan) was made Mir Atash in the 23rd year of Alamgir, then removed, but reappointed in the 25th year; he died in 1103 H. (the 36th year). The *Tarikh-i-Muhammadi* says he died in 1104 H. Neither the *Maasir-ul-umara* nor the *Maasir-i-Alamgiri* makes any mention of his having invented the *gulalbar.*

12
Forts and Strongholds

As early as Alexander's time the Indians possessed walled and fortified towns (Mc Crindle, *Invasion of India*, 119). The practice of building such strong places was never abandoned, and by the sixteenth century, when the Moghul rule began, petty forts held by chiefs of Hindu clans or by grantees from Mahomedan sovereigns, were scattered thickly over the country. Speaking of the Mahratta territory at the end of the 18th century, Colonel Blacker, 305, believed that no province of the same extent in India, or perhaps in any part of the world, possessed so many fortresses.

In the plains of the Ganges and Indus, these forts were usually placed on an artificial mound, the earth for which was taken from the foot of the site, thus forming on one or more sides a large pond or marsh, which protected the fort from a sudden attack. As a rule these forts consisted of four high walls, enclosing a rectangular space; they were provided with a bastion or tower at each corner; and had a fortified gate on one side, the entrance lane turning several times at right angles before arriving at the interior of the place. This narrow tortuous entrance lane was generally enfiladed with guns and loop-holed on every side. These gates with their intricate passages are well described by R. Orme ("Mil. Trans." i, 320, Trichinoply), and in the south of India generally by Lake, "Sieges", 56, who considered the gateways the strongest part of the Indian forts. The outer walls were generally of clay and very thick; they were loop-holed for musketry, round earthen-ware pipes being inserted in the walls for this purpose (Fitzclarence, 245, Orme, "Mil. Trans." ii, 203, 255). If the owner were lucky enough to have any wall pieces, they would be mounted on the flat roofs of the houses built against the inside of the wall. These outer walls might be from twenty to thirty feet in height. Such a stronghold was safe against any small force, and with the means then in use, could hardly be reduced except by starvation. At the more important places they added one and sometimes two ditches, together with outworks, so as to render regular approaches necessary (E. Lake, "Sieges", 11). In hilly country and in the Dakhin the fortresses were of much more elaborate construction. Of these I shall speak in a subsequent paragraph.

Bound Hedge. As an additional protection, such places were often surrounded by a thick plantation of thorny trees or an impenetrable screen of bambus. Some of the latter were of great depth and in the operations in Rohilkhand during the suppression of the Mutiny of 1857, our troops came across bambu hedges which a cannon ball was unable to penetrate. This was no new thing. For instance Khushhal Chand, fol. 177a, tells us that when Muhammad Shah came in 1158 H. (1745) to besiege Ali Muhammad Khan, Rohelah, in Bangarh, he found "a great wilderness of bambus round the fort, through which the wind even found its way with difficulty; quick-handed diggers and axemen were collected to cut this down and uproot it". Again, in 1805 we found Rampur in the same province surrounded by a bambu hedge thirty feet thick (Thorn, "War", 435). In the same way, it was in Bundelkhand the usual custom to protect a fort by a wide belt of thorny jungle: and in 1140 H. (1728) Muhammad Khan, Bangash, when reporting to Delhi his campaign there, speaks of these jungles as retarding his operations considerably.

Going to an entirely different part of India, we find that the town adjoining the fortress of Ahmadnagar in the Dakhin had inside a low wall an immense prickly-pear hedge about twenty feet high. No human being could pass it without cutting it down, a work of the utmost difficulty, as it presented on every side the strongest and most pointed thorns imaginable. Being full of sap, fire would not act upon it, and an assailant while employed in clearing it, would be exposed to the enemy's matchlocks from behind it; thus it was stronger than any *abbatis* or other barrier (Fitzclarence 241). We find another good instance of the adoption of these protective belts of jungle in the case of Bobili, 140 miles N.E. of Vizagapatnam, which was attacked by Bussy in 1757: "An area of five hundred yards or more in every direction is preserved clear, of which the circumference joins the high wood, which is kept thick, three or four miles in breadth, around this centre. Few of these forts admit more than one path through the wood... The path admits only three men abreast, winds continually, is everywhere commanded by breast-works in the thicket, and has in its course several redoubts, similar to that at the entrance, and like that flanked by breastworks on each hand" (R. Orme "Mil. Trans.", ii, 256). In early Anglo-Indian writers, for instance Wilks, iii, 217, such plantations are styled a "bound-hedge", of which definitions will be found in the glossaries of Major Dirom's and Lieut. Moor's works. "Bound-hedge" = *quasi* "Boundary hedge"?

Hill Forts. In the parts of India where detached eminences, often of great extent, are found, these were commonly selected for the sites of fortresses. The most celebrated of these in Northern India were the two forts of Ruhtas, one in the Punjab, the other in Babar, Kalinjar in Bundelkhand, Chitor in Mewar. Further south there were Asirgarh in Khandesh, Daulatabad[1] near Aurangabad, and many others equally celebrated. Forts on the tops of hills were extremely numerous in the Dakhin. It that part of the country there was generally a walled town (or *pettah*) at the foot of the hill, and the fort itself was provided with two or more enceintes. In the Dakhin stone walls were common, that material being abundant. Lake, 205, is of opinion that many of these hill forts, if properly defended, were absolutely impregnable, unless by the tedious process of strict blockade. On the contrary, he thought the fortresses in the plains exceedingly weak (id. 208).

Places of Refuge. Most of the petty semi-independent princes were careful to provide themselves with some fort or place of safety, generally situated in a country difficult of access and at some distance from their capital. Here their reserves of treasure and munitions of war were stored and carefully guarded. Ranthambhur used to furnish such a store-house for the rajahs of Jaipur; and as will be recollected, the rajahs of

Banaras provided such places at Latifpur and Bijigarh, in the hills south-east of Mirzapur.

Walled Towns. In the western half of Northern India, walled towns were frequent; all the principal places being provided with a high brick wall. In that part of the country, even the smallest village was capable of some defence, the flat-roofed; clay-built huts being huddled very close together, and the only entry being through a few narrow, tortuous paths between the houses. Some of the largest towns had walls as well as fortresses, as for instance Lahor and Delhi. At these places the fortress was built in one corner of the town, a continuation of the town wall forming its outer side. Such strongholds were palace as well as fortress, and covered a considerable extent of ground. Other towns, such as Agrah and Allahabad, although they possessed first-class fortresses, had no wall round the town itself. In their case, the fortress stood apart from the rest of the town.

Technical words. I insert here such technical terms connected with fortifications as I have come across in my reading. The names for a fort were *hisar* (Steingass 421), *hasin* (id. 422), *qalah, qilah* (id. 984), and H. *garh.* A small fort or redoubt was a *qalahchah* (Steingass, 985) or *garhi.* To be invested was *mahsur* or *mahsun shudan*: to invest was *mahasarah kardan.* The walls were collectively *bnrj o barah,* the former word meaning a bastion, a tower, (Steingass, 170) and the latter, the curtain, the walls, fortifications (id. 142). The Central Asian word for the curtain of a fort was *badan,* see *Mujmil-ut-tarikh* bad *Nadiriyah,* p. 79, line 13. The battlements were *kungur, kungurah,* (St. 1056); the ditch was *khandaq. Fasil* in the dictionary (St. 931) is defined as breastwork inside a fortification, an entrenchment, wall, rampart; but I believe that strictly speaking it meant the platform running round the inside of the wall, on which the guns were mounted, or from which the defenders fired. (J. Shak. 1494). It is apparently what Europeans call the *terre-plein* (Lake, 113, Voyle, 428). *Safil* (Shak. 1292). was a vulgar form of the same word. Ashob, fol. 284a, speaks of the *Chhatah-i-qilah* at Shahjahanabad. I cannot find any meaning for this. Is it only *chhat,* the Hindi for roof?

The word *khakrez* in *Mujmil-ut-tarikh* bad *Nadiriyah,* p. 78, line 12, meaning "foot of the wall", "the glacis", does not seem to have been in use in India.

Goonga. I cannot restore the true form of this word, as I have not found it except in books by Europeans. Can it be intended for *kungur,* battlements? In the "Military Memoir of Col. Skinner", i, 230 we have at the taking of Hansi in Dec. 1801, the passage : "we commenced mining, and advanced to within ten yards of the crown work, called in Hindustani *goongas*". On id., 266, the word is spelt *goonju*; "these brave fellows stood upon the *goonjus* for a full hour, under one of the heaviest fires of musketry and great guns I have seen", (this was at the siege of Aligarh by Lake in 1803).

Kummurgah (Kamrgah). I find this word used for the second line of defence at Asirgarh in the Dakhin (Blacker, "War", 420). This is a metaphorical use of Kamrgah, the place where the belt is placed, the waist (Steingass, 1049). As Lake explains, 156, "it has been aptly styled *kummurgah* (or the belt)."

Raunee, Rainee, Renny. Fitzclarence, 110, saw at Nagpur "a fine piece of masoury" in front of and covering the bottom of the wall "which I suppose to be what is in this country called a *rainee,* similar to a fausse-braye".[2] And again, id. 245 : "though they do not understand the construction or advantages of a glacis, they saw the necessity of covering the foot of the wall from an enemy's fire, and formed a defence, similar to our fausse-braye, which they call *rainee*". Thorn, 400, speaking of Hathras fort (now in the Aligarh district, N.W.P.) says "a *renny* wall, with a deep, dry, broad ditch behind it, surrounds the fort". James Skinner, "Mil. Mem.", i, 172, spells it *rounee,* and Fraser erroneously translates "counterscarp", being as Yule says "nonsense as well as incorrect". Blacker, "War", 299, writes "Sholapur had a fausse-braye of substantial masonry". I suppose this was a *rauni* or *rainee.* Such a wall is shown in his plan and sections of Malligam (Plate 31). This was about twenty feet high, and about fifty feet from the main wall. The word *raunee* is used by him on plate 38 (Asirgarh); and here the secondary wall stood at the foot of a slope, about eighty feet from the main wall. The derivation of the word *rounee* is a puzzle : Yule, 583, says it is the Hindi word *raoni,* but suggests no etymology and admits that it is not in either Shakespear or Wilson. Can it have any connection with a word in J. Shakespear, 1189, *rundhna,* to surround or enclose as with a hedge? Fallon evidently did not know it, and in his "Eng. Hind. Dictionary", 264 renders "fausse-braye by *Dhus, Matti ka pushtah,* equivalents which also show fairly well that he had no clear idea of what a fausse-braye was.

Sang-andaz. Budaoni, ii, 146 uses this word when describing the fort of Surat. This is here evidently "embrasure", and so translated by Lowe, 150. Steingass, 703, has *sangafkan* and *sang-andaz,* a loophole in a fortress. But a passage in the *Maasir-ul-umara,* i, 76, referring to the siege of Dharwar in the Dakhin in Shahjahan's reign, would lead one to infer that *sang-andaz* was a pathway or tunnel, down which stones were literally thrown.

Damaghah. When Sindh was taken by us, we found "Karachi surrounded by a tall wall, tipped with fancy crenelles and perpendicularly striped with what the Persians call *Damag eh,* or nostril holes, down which the besieged could pour hot oil or boiling water" ("Life of Capt. Sir R.F. Burton", i, 126). Possibly the derivation might be from *damaghah* (Steingass, 534), the crest of a falcon or similar bird. We have an instance of the use of boiling oil at Akbar's siege of Asirgarh (Von Noer, French trans., ii, 336, Horn, 128).

Descriptions of small Forts. I find a good description of a petty Rajah's fort in W.H. Russell's "My Diary in India", ii, 318. Although this was written in 1858, it is quite as applicable to an earlier time. "The low bank of earth was the outer parapet of the fort of Amethi (in south-east Audh), with a very deep ditch of irregular profile separating it from the level of the filed. It was some time are we made out the entry. The gateway was approached by a dam across a ditch full of water, which was dominated by a bastion with the embrasures directed upon the dam. A sort of causeway at the other bank led us to, a high gateway in a mud curtain, which was also flanked by a musketry fire and by a few embrasures. The lines of all the works were exceedingly irregular. The gates were of wood, studded and clamped with iron".

Again, this time in Bundelkhand, we get the following description of the ordinary native fort (Fitzclarence, 59) "These forts are in general of mud, but from six to twelve feet at the bottom of the wall are often of masonry. They are surrounded by a deep ditch, and the defences consist of small round-towers connected by curtains. Some of them have two or three lines of these walls and towers within each other. On the glacis are generally large excavations for grain; but this, of course, is only in dry situations. The mud walls receive the shot without being shattered, and they are in consequence very difficult to breach". A similar description applying to the southernmost part of India, is to be found in Wilks, ii, 95.

Blacker, "War", 229, gives a good general description of the small forts in the Dakhin. "Imagine a mound of earth of about one hundred and fifty yards diameter and about sixty or seventy feet high. Then the sides of this are scarped off by labour, and the prominent parts shaped into flanking towers. Let the whole be reveted and surmounted by a parapet, and then only an entrance will be wanted. A gateway pierced in the *revetement* of a reentering angle, something lower than the interior of the fort, will form the inner communication, and on each side will be projected a tower to flank it and to plunge a fire into the next (gateway?). This will be found in a lower wall, the extremities of which will terminate in the *revetement* of the place, inclosing a small space; and it will be likewise flanked by projecting towers, independent of the defences being loop-holed. These works, it is evident, may be frequently repeated; and the form of the traverses as well as the relative position of the gates continually varied; but the general practice avoids placing two successive gates exactly opposite, and the outer aperture is invariably on lower ground than that next within, to favour the ascent. On some occasions so much earth may be scarped off as to form a high glacis, which makes the space left between it and the wall actually a ditch; but in very few cases is a ditch actually excavated round a garhi".

Particular Forts. I have collected from European writers the descriptions of a good many Indian fortresses; and I have no doubt that many more such notices are in existence. I append a list of those I have seen, arranged in alphabetical order with references.

Ahmadnagar. Fitzclarence, 241, a detailed account.

Ajaigarh. Fitzclarence, "Journal", 62; Pogson, "Boondelas", 136, in whose book a plan, a general view of the east face, and of the breach at the N.W. gateway may be seen.

Aligarh. Taken by the English on the 4th Sept., 1803: it was of European design. Thorn, "War", description on p. 102, view on plate 3.

Asirgarh. Blacker, "War", a description on p. 414, two views, one from the north and one from the east, and on Plate 38 plan and sections.

Bhartpur. This town and its fortifications are described in Lord Combermere's "Memoirs". Vol. ii. p. 236.

Chinglapat. Description by John Call, chief Engineer, Madras, in Cambridge, "War", appendix.

Daulatabad. A detailed account in Fitzclarence, 216, and also in Anquetil Duperron, "Zend Avesta", I, ccli. Anquetil visited the place on the 18th April 1758, when it was held by a French officer on behalf of M. Bussy.

Dharwar. A view and description in Moor, "Narrative", 39.

Hathras. Fitzclarence, "Journal", has a plate of it opposite p. 18.

Kalinjar. This place is fully described in Pogson, "Boondelas", 148-157; he tells the story of the siege of 1812 on pp. 139–147.

Nagpur. Described in Fitzclarence, "Journal", 110, Lake, "Sieges", 35.

Trichinopoly. There is a description of this fortress by Col. Stringer Lawrence in R.O. Cambridge, "War", 15.

Imperial Fortresses. In the official manuals we have several lists of these places. The greater number of these forts were in the Dakhin, and in the better days of the Moghul period, the charge of them was committed to imperial officers called *qilahdars*, who were appointed direct from the capital, and were quite independent of the governor of the province. This arrangement was rendered necessary from the importance of these strongholds, both as a means of retaining hold of the country, and owing to their employment as great store-houses and arsenals. Moreover, if left under the control of a governor, he might be tempted to make a try for independence, when the possession of one of these fortresses would contribute largely to his chances of success.

I find from a list referring to the reign of Alamgir (B.M. Or. 1641 fol. 52b), that there were forty-two imperial forts. I cannot read all the names but I have made out the following. 1) Shahjahanabad, 2) Akbarabad, 3) Lahor, 4) Kabul, 5) Kashmir, 6) Atak, 7) Allahabad, 8) Ajmer, 9) Jhansi, 10) Gwaliyar, 11) Kalinjar, 12) Sitapur, 13) Taragarh, 14) Bargarh, 15) Chandu, 16) Ujjain, 17) Raesen, 18) Ranigarh, 19) Dohad, 20) Kakrun, 21) Ranthambhor, 22) Ruhtas Khurd, 23) Surat, 24) Kangrah, 25) Munger, 26) Jodhpur, 27) Mairtah, 28) Sambhar, 29) Ghaznain, 30) Pishawar, 31) Zafarabad, 32) Shergarh, 33) Lankarkot. The identity of Nos. 12, 13, 14, 18, 32, 33, is doubtful; the others are well-enough known places. However, this list, although containing as many as forty-two places, must be looked on as very incomplete. In it are included none of the strongest places in the Dakhin, where to say the least, fortresses were as numerous as in Hindustan.

REFERENCES

1. There is a good view of this fortress as the frontispiece to Fitzclarence's "Journal".
2. Moor, "Narrative", (Glossary, 504) "Fausse-braye, a work between the ditch and curtain: not much adopted by modern engineers". See also E. Lake, "Sieges", 219, and note.

13
Branding and Verification

False musters were an evil from which the Moghul army suffered even in its most palmy days. Nobles would lend each other the men to make up their quota, or needy idlers from the bazaars would be mounted on the first baggage pony that came to hand and counted in with the others as efficient soldiers. Great efforts were made to cope with this evil, and in the earlier times with some success. In the later reigns, notably from the middle of Muhammad Shah's reign (1719–1748), all such precautions fell into abeyance, amid the general confusion and ever-deepening corruption. By 1174 H. (1761) the system had so entirely disappeared from the *sulah* of Ahmadabad, that clerks acquainted with the rules could not be found there (*Mirat-i-Ahmadi*, ii, 118).

Mustapha, the translator of the *Siyar-ul-mutakharin*, gives us an instance of the length to which this cheating was carried (*Seir*, i, 609, note). In Bengal, in the year 1163 H. (1750), when Ali Wirdi Khan, Mahabat Jang, was nazim, an officer receiving pay for 1700 men could not muster more than seventy or eighty. Mustapha, who wrote in 1787–8, adds from his own experience—"Such are, without exception, all the armies and all the troops of India; and were we to rate by this rule those armies of 50,000 and 100,000 that fought or were slaughtered at the decisive battles of Palasi [Plassy] and Baksar [Buxar] (and by some such rule they must be rated), we would have incredible deductions to make. Such a rule, however, would not answer for Mir Qasim's troops (1760–1764), where there was not one single false muster, nor would it answer for Haidar Ali's armies." The admitted difference between recorded and actual numbers in emphazised by Khushhal Chand's expression, Berlin Ms. 495, fol. 1091a, *Munjudi*, nah *kaghazi*, "actually present, not merely on paper", used in reference to the force brought to Delhi by Burhan-ul-mulk at the time of Nadir Shah's invasion.

It was to put down these evil practices that the emperor Akbar revived and enforced more strictly than before a system of descriptive rolls of men and horses, the latter being branded with a hot iron before they were passed for service. This branding, with the consequent periodical musters for the purpose of comparison and verification, formed a separate department under the *Bakhshi* with its own superintendent (*daroghah*), and this was known as the *dagh-o-tashihah,* from *dagh,* a brand, a mark, and *tashihah,* verification. The usual phrase for enlisting was *asp ba dagh rasanidan,* "bringing a horse to be branded." Branding was first introduced by Ala-ud-din Khilji in 712 H. = May, 1312—April, 1313, but on his death it was dropped (*Dastur-ul-Insha,* 233). The emperor Sher Shah, Afghan, started it again in 948 H. = April, 1541—April, 1542. Akbar (*Ain,* i, 233) re-established the practice in the eighteenth year of his reign (about 981 H., 1573–4), and it was continued until the time when the whole system of government finally broke down in the middle of the eighteenth century. At first many difficulties were made (*Dastur-ul-Insha,* 234), and evasions were attempted, but at length the system was made effective. The great nobles, holding the rank of 5000 and upwards, were exempt from the operation of these rules; but when ordered, they were expected to parade their horsemen for inspection (*Dastur-ul-Aml,* B.M., No. 6599, fol. 144b). The technical name for these parades was *mahallah* (Steingass, 1190), a word evidently connected with that used in Akbar's time for branding, *viz. dagh-o-mahalli* (*Ain,* i, 242; *Budnoni,* ii, 190). The germ of the *dagh* system may perhaps be found in the practice in Transoxiana of annually branding the colts. This was done so far back as the twelfth century; see E.G. Browne on the *Chahar Muqalah* of Arudi (composed about 1161 A.D.), Journal R. Asiatic Soc. (1899), pp. 771 and 776.

As said before, the recruit was supposed, at any rate so far as the State was concerned, to furnish his own horse. Orme states the case thus :—"Every man brings his own horse and offers himself to be enlisted. The horse is carefully examined : and according to the size and value of the beast, the master receives his pay. A good horse will bring thirty or forty rupees a month. Sometimes an officer contracts for a whole troop. A horse in Indostan is of four times greater value than in Europe. If the horse is killed the man is ruined, a regulation that makes it the interest of the soldier to fight as little as possible."—"Historical Fragments," 4to edition, 418. Along with his horse the man brought his own arms and armour, the production of certain items of which was obligatory. In actual practice, however, the leaders often provided the recruits with their horses and equipment. When this was the case the leader drew the pay and paid the man whatever he thought fit. Such a man, who rode another's horse, was called a *bargir*(load-taker); while a man riding his own horse was in modern times called a *silahdar* (weapon-holder). The latter word is the origin of the Anglo-Indian phrase of "Sillidar cavalry," applied to men who are paid a lump sum monthly for themselves, horse, uniform, and equipment.

Descriptive Rolls. When an officer entered the service (B.M. No. 6599, fol. 160a) a *Chihrah* or descriptive roll[1] of the new *mansabdar* was first of all drawn up, showing his name, his father's name, his tribe or caste, his place of origin, followed by details of his personal appearance. His complexion might be "wheat-colour" (*gandum-rang*), "milky," *i.e.* white (*shir-fam*), "red" (*surkh-post*), or "auburn" (*maigun-rang*). His forehead was always "open" (*faragh*); his eyebrows either full (*kushadah*) or in whole or in part *moshah* (?); his eyes were sheep-like (*mish*), deer-like (*ahu*), ginger-coloured (*adrak*), or cat's eyes (*gurbah*). His nose might be "prominent" (*buland*) or "flat" (*past*). He might be "beardless" (*amrad*) or "slightly bearded" (*rish o barwat aghaz*); his beard might be "black" (*rish o barwat siyah*), or "slightly red" (*siyah i maigun-numa*), "thin" (*khali*?), "shaven" (*mutarash*), "goat-shaped" (*kosah-i-khurd*), or "twisted up" (*shaqiqah*). So with any moles he might have; the shape of his ears, whether projecting or not, whether the lobes were pierced or not, and whether he was pock-marked or not—all these things were noted. Ashob, *Shahadat*, fol. 84a, tells us that in the imperial service the *chihrahs* were written on red paper sprinkled with gold leaf.

Roll for Troopers. The troopers (*tabinan*) were also described, but not quite so elaborately. A specimen is as follows (B.M. No. 6599, fol. 163a) :

Troopers' Roll (Chihrah-i-tabinan)

Qamr Ali, son of Mir Ali, son of Kabir Ali, wheat complexion, broad forehead, separated eyebrows, sheep's eyes, prominent nose, beard and moustache black, right ear lost from a sword-cut. Total height, about 40 *shanah*.

Horse. Colour *kabud* (iron-grey?). Mark on left of breast. Mark on thigh on mounting side. *Laskar*(?) on thigh on whip side. Brand of four-pointed stamp +

Descriptive Roll of Horses (*Chihrah-i-aspan*)

The next thing done was to make out an elaborate description of the horse or horses (B.M. No. 6599, fol. 106b). There were twenty principal divisions according to colour, and eight of these were again subdivided, so that there were altogether fifty-eight divisions. Then there were fifty-two headings for the marks (*khal-o-khat*) which might occur on the horse's body.

The Imperial Brand

The hot iron was applied on the horse's thigh (*Seir*, i, 481, note 27). The signs used in Akbar's reign are given in the *Ain*, i, 139, 255, 256; but in the end he adopted a system of numerals. In Alamgirs reign and about that time there were twenty different brands (*tamghah*), of which the shapes of fifteen have been preserved and are reproduced below (B.M. No. 6599, fol. 161a). I am not certain of the spelling, and in most instances I am utterly unable to suggest a meaning for the names.

Name	*Form of Brand*
1. *Chahar parha* (four feather?)	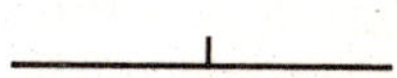
2. *Chahar parha jomar-khaj*	

3. *Chahar parha dur khaj* 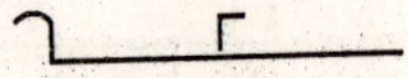

4. *Chahar parha sihsar khaj* 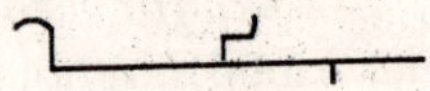

5. *Chakush* 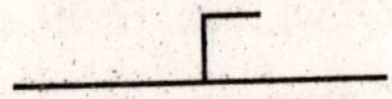

6. *Istad* (upright)

7. *Uftadah* (recumbent) 

8. *Istadah o uftadah* 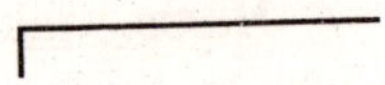

9. *Yak ba do* (one with two) 

10. *Asaran* 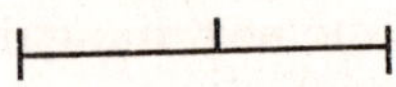

11. *Togh* (horse-tail standard) 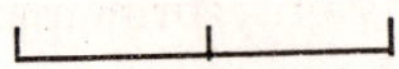

12. *Panjah-i-murgh* (hen's foot) 

13. *Mizan* (balance) 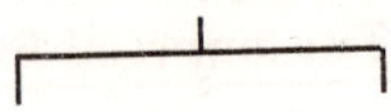

14. *Do darah taur* 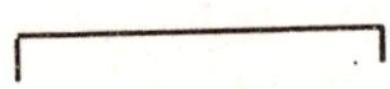

15. *Chahar barah makar khaj* 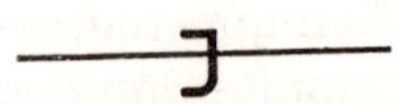

The Noble's Brand

It is obvious that in addition to the imperial brand, a second mark was required by each noble for the recognition of the horses ridden by his own men. Accordingly we find direct evidence of this second marking in Bernier, 216, and again 243, when he speaks of the horses "which bear the omrah's mark on the thigh." Towards the end of the period the great nobles often had the first or last letter of their name as their special brand (*Seir*, i, 481, note 27), as, for instance, the *sin-dagh* of Sadat Ali Khan, nazim of Audh. The brand of Sayyad Abdullah

Khan, was *abd,* according to Khushhal Chand, Berlin Ms. 495, fol. 1020a. Ghulam Ali Khan (B.M., Add. 24,028, fol. 63b) tells us that about 1153 H. (1740 – 41) Muhammad Ishaq Khan used the last letter of his name, a *qaf* , as his brand. The way of selecting the brands is further illustrated by a passage in Kam Raj's *Azam-ul-harb.* When Azam Shah in 1119 H. (1707) was on his march from the Dakhin, some new brands were chosen. "As the brand of the *Wala Shahi* (personal troops) was *Azma,* that of Bedar Bakht, the eldest son, was mankab, and of Wala Jah, the second son, was *khail,* it was thought fit to fix on the word *hashm* (-) as that of Ala Tabar, the youngest son." It is to be inferred from this passage that in each instance the first letter of the word was used.

Classification of Horses

According to the *Ain,* i, 233, there were seven classes of horses founded on their breed—(1) *Arabi,* (2) *Persian,* (3) *Mujannas,* resembling Persian, and mostly Turki or Persian geldings, (4) *Turki,* (5) *Yabu,* (6) *Tazi,* (7) *Janglah.*

In Alamgir's reign we find (B.M. No. 6599, fol. 163a) the following classification (1) *Iraqi,* (2) *Mujannas,* (3) *Turki,* (4) *Yabu,* (5) *Tazi,* (6) *Jangli.* This is practically the same as Akbar's, except that Arab horses are not mentioned. This must be an oversight, since we learn from many passages in the contemporary historians that Arab horses were still in use. The *Tazi* and *Jangli* were Indian horses, what we now call countrybreds, the former being held of superior quality to the latter. The *Yabu* was, I suppose, what we call now the *Kabuli,* stout-built, slow, and of somewhat sluggish temperament. The *Turki* was an animal from Bukhara or the Oxus country; the *Iraqi* came from Mesopotamia.

In Alamgir's reign the proportion in which officers of the different ranks were called on to present horses of these different breeds at the time of branding was as follows :

These figures differ from those in the *Ain,* i, 248 – 9, where the number of horses is given for all *mansabs,* up to the very highest. Some figures are also given in *Mirat-i-Ahmadi,* ii, 118, which agree on the whole with those in the above table.

Rank of of Officer	*Class of Horse*				
	Iraqi	*Mujannas*	*Turki*	*Yabu*	*Total*
400	3	1	1	0	5
300-350	2	1	1	0	4
100-150	0	0	3	0	3
80-90	0	0	2	0	2
50-70	0	0	1	1	2
40	0	0	1	0	1

According as the standard was exceeded or not come up to, the branding officer made an allowance or deduction by a fixed table. This calculation was styled *tafawat-i-aspan* (discrepancy of horses)—B.M. No. 6599, fol. 163a. The extra allowances were as follows :

Horse Required By Regulation	*Horse Produced*	*Additional Allowance*
		Rs.
Turki	*Iraqi*	12
Turki	*Mujannas*	6
Tazi	*Turki*	8
Yabu	*Turki*	9

When an inferior horse was produced the following deduction was made :

Horse Required By Regulation	*Horse Produced*	*Deduction*
		Rs.
Turki	*Jangli*	12
Yabu	*Jangli*	10
Tazi	*Jangli*	8

Subordinate Establishment

An establishment of farriers, blacksmiths' forges, and surgeons had to be maintained by each *mansabdar*, according to the following scale (B.M. no. 1641, fol. 38b) :

The *Mirat-i-Ahmadi*, ii, 118, states that thirty men on foot were required to be entertained for every 1000 of *mansab* rank.

These included water-carriers, farriers, pioneers, matchlockmen and bow-men.

Rank of Officer	Numbers of Establishment: Farriers (Nalband)	Blacksmiths Shops (Ahangar)	Leeches or Surgeons (Jarah)
4000	8	2	2
3500	7	2	2
3000	6	2	2
2500	5	1	0
2000	4	1	2
1500	3	0	1
1000	2	0	1
Or, according to a more recent scale :			
1500-4000	6	3	0

Verification *(Taslahah)*

Something on this subject will be found in the *Ain*, i, 250, where the reference is confined to the *ahadis*; Dr. Horn, so far as he goes into the matter at all, deals with it on p. 49 of his work. In later times, at all events, the rule of mustering and verification seems to have been of almost universal application. For example, in a work called the *Guldastah-i-Bahar*, a collection of letters from Chhabilah Ram, Nagar, compiled in 1139 H. (1726–7), of which I possess a fragment, I find on fol. 18a an instance of the verification rules being enforced against a *mansabdar* in the end of Bahadur Shah's reign (1118–24 H.). Chhabilah Ram, who was then *faujdar* of Karrah Manikpur (subah Allahabad), complains to his patron that the clerks had caused his *jagir*, in parganah Jajmau, bringing in ten lakhs of *dams*, to be taken away from him, because he had not produced vouchers of *dagh-o-tashihah*. He sends the papers by a special messenger, and prays his correspondent, some influential man at Court, to obtain the restoration of the *jagir* in question.

The intervals after which verification was imperative varied according to the nature of the man's pay. If he were paid in *jagir*, he had to muster his men for verification once a year, and, in addition, a period of six months' grace was allowed. If the officer were paid in *naqd* (cash), the time allowed depended upon whether he was—(1) present at Court (*hazir-i-riqab*), or (2) on duty elsewhere (*tainat*). In the first case he had to procure his certificate at six month intervals, or within eight months at the outside. In the second case he was allowed fifteen days after he had reported himself at Court. An *ahadi* seems to have been allowed, in a similar case, no more than seven days. Where an officer drew his pay aprtly in *jagir* (assignment) and partly in *naqd* (cash), if the former made more than half the total pay, the rule for *jagirdars* was followed; if the *jagir* were less than half, the *naqdi* rule was followed (B.M. 1641, fols. 31a, 39b).

When the interval and the period of grace had elapsed, the man was reported for *tawaqquf-i-lashihah* (delay in verification). A *mansabdar* lost the whole of his pay for the period since the last verification; or, if he were important enough to have been presented to the emperor (*ra-shinas,* known by sight), he might succeed in obtaining his personal pay. An *ahadi* lost half his pay, and it was only by an order on a special report that he could be excused the penalty. The proportion of horsemen (*tābinan*) that a *mansabdar* must produce differed when he was at Court and when he was on duty in the provinces. In the first case he was bound to muster one-fourth, and in the second one-third, of his total number or as the case is stated in the *Massir-ul-umara,* ii, 444, "In the reign of Shahjahan it was decided that if an officer held a *jagir* within the *subah* to which he was attached,, he should produce one third of his *tabinan* for Branding. Thus if he were 3000 *zat,* 3000 *suwar,* he would produce 1000 horsemen. If sent to another *subah* of Hindustan, then one forth had to appear. During the campaign in Balkh and Badakhshan, owing to the great distance, one fifth was held to be sufficient." There were three seasons appointed for verification, from the 26th Shawwal to the 15th Zul Qadah (twenty days) the 19th Safar to the 15th Rabi I (twenty-five days), and the 16th Jamadi II to the 15th Rajab (twenty-nine days). (B.M. 1641, fols. 31a, 39b, 58b; B.M. 6599, fol. 148a).

Officials and their duties. At head quarters officers entitled Amin, daroghah, and mushrif were appointed by the emperor to the Verification department, which was under the supervision of the chief bakhshis. The Bakhshis made the appointments for the provinces. In addition to his personal rank (*mansab*), the Amin received a *mansab* of 10 horse while in office (*Mirat-i-Ahmadi*, ii, 118). The duties are thus described by Hidayatullah, Bahari, in his *Hidayat-ul-quwaid*, fol. 13a. The daroghah should compare the marks and points *(khat-o-khat)* of the horses with the descriptive roll (*chihrah*), and inspect the horses to see whether they were fit for the service or not. If fit for branding, he should cause the brand to be imposed, signing the descriptive roll, adding the day, month and year, with the words "Two horses such-and-such branded." If it were a two-horse man, he should certify for two horses and send the original descriptive roll to the office of the Bakhshi, retaining a copy sealed by the Bakhshi among his own records. Two months having passed, he should in the third month inspect and verify according to the copy of the roll, looking to see if the marks correspond. His inspection report was entered on the back of the roll, giving day, month, and year, thus : "So-and-so with his horses and arms was inspected." If it was a one-horse man, the daroghah wrote :

"Man and one horse inspected." If it were a foot match-lock-man or an archer, he wrote on the back of the roll : "Man and arms inspected". For carpet-layers and servants belonging to the court establishment he wrote on the back of the roll. When the paper was full, another sheet was attached. The peshkar (head clerk) of the daroghah drew up according to rule a present state, giving details of those present and absent and the receipts. He then brought it up for orders. The daroghah attached his seal to the report and sent it on to the Bakhshi's office. In accordance therewith an order (*barat*) on the Treasury was prepared for each man. The daroghah ought to see that the horsemen and infantry are present on the march and on guard. He should enjoin on the guard-clerk to make an inspection at midnight of the men posted on guard, and write down the names of those present. According to the *Mirat-i-Ahmadi*, ii, 118, the officials after the mustering and verification made out certificates (*dastak*) bearing the seals of the daroghah, amin, and mushrif, which were delivered to the *mansabdar* concerned.

REFERENCES

1. Literally 'face,' 'countenance.' It must not be confounded with *chirah,* which means (1) a kind of turban, (2) a pay-roll, on which the recipients signed, (3) the pay itself. *Chirah* is used in the second sense in *Alaval-ul-khawaqin,* fol. 230b; and also by Ghulam Hasan, Samin, when telling us of the taunt addressed in 1170 H. (1757) by Ahmad Khan, Bangash, to Najib Khan, Najib-ud-daulah, of having been once a private trooper in Farrukhabad, where his pay-rolls (*charah-hae*) were still in existence.

14
The Evolution of Artillery

1. Organisation and Early Development

The Moghul government was essentially military in nature and every officer of the state held a '*mansab*' or official appointment of rank and profit, which bound him to supply a number of troops for the service of the state. Prior to Babar's invasion, Indian kings had organised their armies into cavalry, infantry and elephants with a few guns as adjunct to the main force. The Moghuls introduced artillery as the third fighting arm of the army along with the cavalry and infantry; they termed this arm the 'lock and key' of the empire.

The Moghul period covers a span of over 300 years (1526-1857) and the artillery arm went through a number of changes in its organization because of political changes, wars and the influence of foreign armies. The stable period and progress lasted till the reign of Aurangzeb; after this, the disintegration of the empire began and no ruler remained in power long enough to think and plan or effect any major change in the pattern of their artillery. Dr. Horn and William Irvine have expressed different views on the progress of the arm. According to the former, artillery had reached the highest point of efficiency under Akbar; Irvine, however, feels that the arm was much more perfect and numerous during Alamgir's time.

Irvine's opinion is probably based on the writing in *Ain-i-Akbari* where the account of the use of cannons is mentioned very briefly, whereas a great deal has been said about matchlocks. The other reason is that during Alamgir's time, the long compaign in the Deccan and the innumerable sieges, some of them of considerable importance, such as those of Bijapore and Jinji, must have brought the use of artillery into much greater importance. And during the 18th century, something was learnt from the example of the French and English armies and from European adventurers who found their way in considerable numbers into the armies of the native powers.

The organisation of the Moghul army as far as cavalry and infantry was concerned was based on the *mansabdari* system, while artillery was kept centrally under the king. A *mansabdar* appointed by the king did not necessarily imply that he held any particular office. Rather, it meant that he was in the employment of the state and was bound, in return, to yield certain services when called for. The object of the system was to settle precedence and gradation of pay. A *mansabdar* was required to provide a fixed number of infantry and cavalry soldiers including horses for the king. In return, the state paid a lump sum yearly to the *mansabdar* for the soldiers and for the upkeep of horses, weapons and equipment. The highest *mansab* during the time of Akbar had a command of 7000 men and the lowest of 20 men. Normally, *mansabdars* who had command of over 500 infantry were also required to have a number of extra horsemen under them and they were styled accordingly, depending upon the number of foot soldiers and horsemen they had. Thus a *mansabdar* could be styled "2500 zat, 1000 sowar". For reasons of simplicity, a *mansabdar* was graded first class, second class or third class depending upon the proportion of horsemen under him in relation to foot soldiers.

Since the artillery arm was directly under the Emperor, on its establishment the men were paid from imperial funds and in this respect were treated differently from cavalry and infantry who were paid by the chief of *mansabdar* under whose banner they had enlisted.

Types of artillery

The artillery arm was termed the *topkhana* and was divided into the following heads :

(a) Manufacture

(b) Artillery in use

(c) Arsenals or magazines

(d) Fortress artillery

Higher Command

Two officers were concerned with the *topkhana* :

(a) The *Khansamah* as the Lord Steward

(b) The *Mir Atash* (the lord of fire) or the "*Daroghah-i-topkhaha*" (Superintendent of the cannon department).

The Lord Steward was in charge of the imperial workshop and concerned with manufacture. It seems likely that during the early period, the Mir *Atash* as *Daroghah-i-topkhana* must have been subordinate to the Lord Steward. But over time, as the artillery branch developed, the office of *Mir Atash* grew in importance until he was equal to or more than equal to his nominal superior, the *Khansamah*. As commander of artillery, he became totally independent and the role of *Khansamah* was confined solely to manufacture.

As the artillery expanded the *Mir Atash* became a most important officer. In 1744, when Safdar Jang was appointed as *Mir Atash*, Khushal Chand wrote that "contrary to former days, the artillery has become the most favoured corps in the army." At times during the reign of Jahandar Shah (1712), we read of two such officers, one as the head of all the artillery and the other in command of the artillery but attached to the person of the emperor. Apart from this case, there is no mention of any emperor who had two officers holding the appointment. The importance of this officer grew, as the *Mir Atash* not only commanded all the imperial artillery but also had direct access to the emperor unlike other *mansabdars* who had to go through the office of *Bakshi-ul-mamalik*, *Mir Bakshi* or one of the other three *bakshis*. Before we go on to look at the role of the *Mir Atash*, we must touch upon the institution of *bakshis* in the Moghul court. *Bakshis* were very senior officers of the court but they were not ministers or *vazirs*. Normally, there were four *bakshis* and the duties assigned to them were different. The seniormost of them, the first *bakshi*, had the title of *Amir-ul-Umara* (noble of nobles). He also held the title of *Bakshi-ul-*

mamalik (*bakshi* of the realms) or Mir *Bakshi* (lord *bakshi*). The other *bakshis* held other department portfolios depending upon the policy of the emperor which varied from time to time. The closest parallel to the current Indian system would be the appointment of a cabinet secretary and other secretaries to the government, the only difference being that *bakshis* took part in campaigns whenever the emperor wished them to.

The prestige of *Mir Atash* was even more enhanced as he not only commanded all the artillery in the field but directly commanded the artillery in the field but directly commanded the artillery which was parked round the fortress, palace or the tents occupied by the emperor, and the appointment carried with it the custody of the person of the emperor, as well as the guarding of the palace gates and walls. Apart from the command function, the *Mir Atash* also functioned as a *bakshi* in relation to all personnel of his department. In administration, he was assisted by a *mushrif* or an executive officer. The *Mir Atash* laid all demands made on his department before the emperor and all orders were passed through him. He checked the pay bills and inspected the diaries of the arsenals before sending them on to the *khansamah*. He saw to the posting of the artillery force and all new appointments and promotions were made at his behest. In the early days, judging from the memoirs of Babar, the *Mir Atash* was supposed to supervise the casting of cannon, but his practice was discontinued later, and the *Mir Atash* confined himself to operational and administrative duties in addition to the security of the emperor. The arsenals, magazines and storehouses of cannon and all other reserve artillery were kept in fortresses such as Agra, Delhi and Lahore under the charge of special commandants called *quiladars* who were officers appointed directly from the court and who were in no way connected with or subordinate to the provincial governor.

In the case of infantry and cavalry a person held a *mansab* when he had as few as 20 men under him, the rank structure of the artillery arm was entirely different from these two arms.

(a) **Hazari/Mink Bashi.** The *hazari* was a *mansabdar* with

1,000 men but in histories, it seems, this term meant an officer of the artillery, equivalent to the rank of captain. A *mansabdar* with 1,000 men would be of an officer of high rank particularly if he had horses as well, while *hazaris* are often referred to in the plural to show that they were numerous. Some writers have used the word *mink bashi* for an artillery officer whereas others have used *hazari*. *Mink bashi* in Turkish means "commander of 1,000" (mink : 1000, bash : head). It is difficult to say how the ranks used in artillery vis-à-vis other arms were equated. But in rank and protocol there is seldom any logic and they often vary according to the views of those in power and the pressure on them by various groups and institutions. Irvine is of the opinion that since the service of Turks from Constantinople, and that of other Europeans, was much prized for artillery, they may have been accorded, at first, the rank of a commander of 1,000 (*mink bashi* or *hazari*) and later, even when Indians themselves became more efficient in the arm, the name stuck. It is also entirely possible that since the *Mir Atash* was closer to the person of the Emperor, he managed to get a higher status for the personnel of artillery. Hazari was also used by the Marathas, but for a *quiladar*.

The other gradation of ranks was :

(a) *Saduwal*: Sadi means a group of 100 and 'wal' is affix for a man, person or possessor.

(b) *Mirdahah* : Mir means lord or master and dahah, a group of 20.

(c) *Sair* : Sair means 'the rest', remainder, the other or in current Indian Army terms "other ranks".

(d) *Golandaz*: This was the formal name of a sepoy in the artillery arm on the same lines as a gunner of the current Indian artillery. It is derived from *'gola'* (ball) and *'andaz'* (to throw).

(e) *Deg andaz*: means a 'pot thrower'. It is not possible to say whether pot throwers were in charge of mortars or they used hand grenades. Irvine feels that possibly it meant the latter as mortars were introduced later in

India by the middle of the eighteenth century and there is a passage in the book by Fitzclarance saying "at times they have recourse to thick earthen-ware pots with fuses and full of powder, the pieces of which wounded dreadfully"

(f) *Ban-andaz/Ban-dar* : These were rocket throwers or rocket holders.

(g) *Firangi* : This is not a rank but refers to Europeans serving in the Moghul army as soldiers. Most of them served in artillery. They were probably mostly native Christians or Portuguese either from Goa or from the colonies of that nation settled in India. Quite a few sailors who were fugitives from ships lying at Surat or Cambay also joined the artillery arm. A number of Frenchmen also served in the artillery. They all lived in a special colony named Firangipurah near Kabul Gate. Some of them were formally designated as nobles and drew their pay accordingly. All the 'firangis' received much higher pay then native soldiers of the Moghul army. Bernier mentions that the garrison of Bakkar in Sind had in 1658 artillery men who were Portuguese, English, French and German. In 1750, the principle artillery officer of Nazir Jang, subedar of the Deccan, was an Irishman. Again in 1774, at the battle of Katrah between the Rohilla chief, Hafiz Rahmat Khan, and Shuja-ud-daulah supported by British, the artillery of the former was commanded by a Spaniard. And as late as 1815, the Nizam had Portuguese artillery men in his service. Lake states, "they had a Portuguese who levelled each gun himself; and appeared to have the direction of the attack. If by chance a shot struck any part of the wall, so as to raise a dust, the air resounded with acclamation in praise of the old Portuguese, who seemed in no small degree flattered thereby."

Foreigners had been welcomed in the armies of Indian rulers since their first advent in the country. Dr. S.N. Sen quoting Cosme da Guarda, tells us that in the seventeenth century every European in India was supposed to be an artillery expert and even an apostate clergyman did not find the least difficulty in securing a lucrative office in the Moghul army without any military training. European artillerymen were of course the most prized. Long before the superiority of the western method of warfare was appreciated, the westerners' efficiency as sailors and artilleymen had been recognised by Indian rulers; even Shivaji had some Portuguese serving under him. In an article written in May 1887, Sir W.W. Hunter gives interesting details of the salaries of native troops in the service of Aurangzeb. These are given below in monthly terms :

(a) Trooper (one horse # *siladar*)	-	£	2	-	20
(b) Four horse *siladar*	-	£	16	-	0
(c) Matchlock man	-	£	2	-	4
(d) Native artillerymen	-	£	3	-	10
(e) European artillerymen	-	£	22	-	0

A *siladar* had to provide his own horse and accoutrements which he let out to troopers called *bagheers.* Taking his investment in horse and equipment into account we can see that an artillerymen was very highly paid in relation to a cavalry or infantry soldier. The extraordinarily high pay given to a European gunner to man the guns and not for manufacture indicates that even during the reign of Aurangzeb the artillery arm perhaps was not so developed as stated by Irvine.

2. Heavy Artillery

It is difficult to establish when the word *top* or tope appeared for the first time in Indian writing but it is probable it came into use first in the Deccan where it was intorduced by officers from Turkey who were employed in the artillery. The word is generally used for large cannon or siege guns but it has been found that later writers used it for all classes of cannon, differentiating the large and the small by calling them *top-i-kalan* and *top-i-khurd* respectively. Babar, however, used the word *zarb-zan* (blow striker) as a general term for *top* without making any distinction.

The Moghul artillery was divided into the following general categories :

*(a)*Heavy artillery

*(b)*Light artillery

(c) Artillery of the stirrup

*(d)*Fortress artillery

The Moghuls were very fond of large guns but such guns were more for show and to impress their enemies rather than for making an impact during battle. They went to extravagant lengths in this. Statistics show clearly that although Europeans may have been the first to invent guns, the Moghuls produced some of the largest and heaviest guns in the world. These made more noise than they did harm and also reduced the mobility of the armies. Their rate of fire was poor. According to Fitzclarance "the oriental idea seems to render this destructive engine from its size more powerful than those of the Western World." All these large guns were given pompous-sounding names and some of them had poetic inscriptions on them apart from other details such as the year of manufacture, the name of the founder and the place. Some of names that appear in various texts are :

(a) Ghazi Khan : (Lord champion); *(b) Sher Dahan* : (Tiger mouth); *(c) Dhumbham* : (The noisy); *(d) Kishwar kusha* : (World opener); *(e) Garch bhanjan* : (Fort demolisher); *(f) Fath-i-lashkar,* (Army conquerer); *(g) Aurangbar.* (Strength of the throne); *(h) Burj shikan* : (Bastion breaker); *(i) Jahan kusha* : (World conquerer); *(j) Alam sitan* : (World capturer).

The size of some of these and other guns can be gauged from historical accounts. The following examples will show to what lengths the Moghuls went to produce large guns :

(a) Malik-i-maidan This has been declared the largest cannon in the world. It was cast at Ahmednagar in 1548 during the reign of Burhan Nizam Shah by the internationally recognised Turkish gun founder Muhammad bin Hassan Roumi. It fell into the hands of Ali Adel Shah of Bijapore in 1562 during retreat of Nizam Shah. It is sometimes also known

as the 'Great Gun of Bijapore'. It was captured by Aurangzeb in 1685 when Bijapore fell. Its particulars were : length 25 feet; weight 40 tons; calibre 28.5 inches; charge 80 pounds of powder; projectile stone 1,000 lb; iron 2,646 lb.

It bears inscriptions in Persian on the upper surface which say :

(i) There is no God but God, and none beside Him.

(ii) Abu I Ghazi Nizam Shah, king; servant of the race of the Apostle and of the House of God, 1548.

(iii) The work of Muhammad bin Hssan Roumi.

(iv) Shah Alamgir (Aurangzeb), the victorious king, defender of the Faith. He who dispensed just judgement, and took dominion of Kings, conquered Bijapore, and for the date of the victory Fortune shewed her face and said, He hath taken possession of the Master of the Field. Executed in the Thirtieth year of the reign of the exalted in dignity, corresponding to the one thousand and ninety-seventh year of Hegira (A.D. 1685).

(b) Jahan kusha (World conquerer) : This weapon was made at Dhakah during the reign of Shahjahan (1637) and was later found in Murshidabad in 1847. It was 17 feet long and had a base diameter of 12 inches and took a charge of 28 *sers* of powder. It had a long poetical inscription on it.

(c) Kishwar kasher (World overcomer): When Dara Shukoh was sent to Qandhar during the reign of Shahjahan, he cast two great guns at Lahore which threw a ball of one man and 5 *sers* (90 lb). Their names were *Kishwar kasher* and *Fateh mubarik* (Blessed Victory).

(d) The great gun of Agra This name was coined by Maj. Thorn. The gun was made of bronze and was taken at the siege of Agra in 1803 by General Lake. Its particulars were :

(i) Calibre	-	22.5 inches
(ii) Length	-	24 feet
(iii) Weight	-	1,469 maunds

(iv) Weight of iron shot - 1,497 lb

(v) Weight of marble shot - 597 lb

(vi) Muzzle - 3 ft., 10.5 inches

(vii) Base ring - 4 ft., 6 inches.

The gun was supposed to contain gold and to have a value of Rs. 1,60,000. General Lake tried to remove it to Calcutta with the idea of taking it to England but despite his best efforts, he could not get a raft made to transport it by river as the raft overturned and the gun sank in the river bed. Twenty years later, it was broken up and sold. It bore the inscription : "In the reign of Akbar Shah, made by Shital Parshad, Weight 1469 maunds". The reference to a Hindu gun founder is interesting, as during the Moghul period all gun founders were Roumies.

(e) Zamzamah (The thunderer) : This famous gun now lies outside the Lahore museum. It was cast by Shah Nazir during the reign of Ahmed Shah Abdali (1747-73). It is made of brass with a length of 14 feet 4.5 inches and a bore diameter of 9.5 inches. It is sometimes called the *Bhangi ki top* as it was removed from the arsenal of Abdali near Lahore by Hari Singh Bhangi, the Sikh leader of the clan. It bears an inscription of 22 lines of which the last two translated mean "After obeisance," he exclaimed, "The dragon-shaped fire-vomiting cannon."

(f) During the reign of Aurangzeb, there were seventy pieces of heavy artillery (mostly of brass) with him in the field. Many of these were so ponderous that twenty yoke of oxen were used to draw them and when the road was rugged or steep, they required the aid of elephants to push the carriage wheels with their heads and trunks. These guns could not move along difficult passes or cross the bridges or boats thrown over rivers. These heavy pieces had often to be left behind because it was impossible to make them keep up with the army. In 1707, when Azam Shah marched from Ahmadnagar to Dholpur, he left all his heavy guns behind at various stages of the march and had none left when he reached the battlefield at Jajan. It is no wonder that history records that "he lost the day as well as his life". Again in 1712, during the contest of thrones between

the sons of Bahadur Shah, three of the largest guns were removed from the fort of Lahore, each being dragged by 250 oxen, aided by five or six elephants and it was ten days before the camp was reached, although it was not more than three or four miles away.

*(g)*During 1715–16, when Rajah Jai Singh was besieging Churaman Jat in his fort of Thun, one of these cannon was sent from Delhi. It was escorted with ceremony and made over to the deputy governor of Agra to be sent to its destination. The shot was one maund in weight. Shien Das further adds that, at the siege of Agra in July/August 1719 several large guns like *Ghazi Khan* and *Sher Dahan* were used which took shot from 60 to 100 pounds. Attached to each gun were upto four elephants and from 600 to 1700 draught oxen. This seems like a very high number but we have another mention on the same lines that Muhammad Shah in 1739, at Karnal had guns requiring 500 to 1,000 bullocks, aided by 5 to 10 elephants.

*(h)*Zufr Bukh (Dispenser of victory) : This gun was cast prior to 1627 and weighed 52 tons and therefore presumably exceeded *Malik-i-Maidan* in size. On its side was inscribed "The work of master Scolatan Muhammad". No further details are available Hogg calculates its calibre to be between 36-40 inches, its length as 16 feet, taking a charge of 350 lb of powder and firing a shot of 2,500 lb.

3. Light artillery

Light artillery has been given different names by various historians. Some of there are :

(a) Topkhanah-i-rezah - Small artillery

(b) Topkhanah-i-jambishi - Moveable artillery

(c) Topkhanah-i-jinsi - Miscellaneous artillery

(d) Topkhanah-i-jilau - Moveable artillery

(e) Topkhanah-i-rikab - Artillery of the stirrup

Artillery of the stirrup. This was a privileged corps. Stirrup (*rikab*) was a figurative expression for the immediate entourage of the emperor. To be at court was to be *hazri-i-*

rikab (present with the stirrup). It was directly under the command of Mir Atash. Bernier has described it thus :

Fifty or sixty small field pieces, all of brass, each piece mounted on a well made and handsomely painted carriage containing two ammunition chests, one behind and one in front and ornamented with a variety of small red streamers. The carriage with the driver was drawn by two fine horses, and attended by a third horse led by an assistant driver as a relay. The light artillery is always intended to be near the king's person, and on that account takes the name of artillery of the stirrup. When he resumes his journey in the morning and is disposed to shoot or hunt in game preserves, the avenues to which are guarded, it moves straight forward and reaches with all possible speed the next place of encampment, where the royal tents and those of the principle omrahs have been pitched since the preceding day. The guns are then ranged in front of the king's quarters and, by way of signal to the army, fire a volley the moment he arrives.

It appears that Sendiah later imitated this practice but called such guns his "orderly artillery".

Types of light guns : For the lighter guns, we come across many names, severel of which are probably different words for the same weapon. These are :

(a) *Jazail/Jazair/Gingall/Janjal.* This was a wall piece or swivel gun. It is difficult to state if this weapon was a large matchlock or artillery weapon. Some of different names which apparently refer to the same type of weapon but spelled, described and pronounced differently are :

(i) Steingass defines *gazail* as a large musket, wall piece, swivel, a rifle used with a prong as rest.

(ii) Shakeshpear says that the *gingall* is either a corruption of *gazail* or from *ganjal* (trouble, difficulty).

(iii) Lake says about *gazail* : "Long matchlocks of various calibres, used as a wall piece by the natives

of India which are commonly fixed like swivels and carry iron balls not exceeding one pound in weight. In the field they are sometimes carried on the backs of camels.

(iv) Grant, speaking of the Chinese 'gingall', says : "This weapon is a species of long heavy duck-gun carrying a ball weighing about two pounds; its range is at least 1,000 yards. It is placed on a tripod, from which tolerable aim can be taken.

(v) Fitzclarance, however says, that a ball of Indian *Jazail* weighed two or more ounces. Williamson says that the ball weighed from one to three ounces and had very substantial barrels, thus was too heavy to used without a rest. Thus is seems that the weapon was a heavier version of a matchlock and not an artillery weapon, although in some cases it carried a round weighing upto one pound or even more. Due to its increased weight it was fired by using a rest or tripod and would have been very effective in defence as it gave greater range, accuracy and had a heavier weight of ball.

(b) *Gajnal/hathnal*: The literal meaning is elephant barrel from 'gaj (elephant)' and 'nal' (tube/gun barrel). They were thus called because they were carried on the backs of elephants. From Jauhar-i-Samsam. It seems that each elephant carried two *gajnal* pieces and two soldiers and suggests that they were fired from the back of the elephant. Irvine however feels that perhaps the gun was placed on an elephant for transport only and dismounted before firing. From the records, it appears that during later times of the Moghul reign, this weapon was not used.

(c) *Shutarnal/Zamburak/Shahin* : This was the same weapon but with different names. An interesting account of the tactical use of camel mounted guns has been given by Sardesai describing the Battle of Panipat :

The Marathas had powerful artillery or more than 200 pieces commanded by Ibraḥim Khan. Abdali, on the other hand, had no heavy guns of the Maratha type; he had, instead an efficient firearm of about two thousand light guns, camel borne swivels which could inflict severe havoc upon the dense mass of the Maratha ranks at short range...

The destruction of the Maratha army was completed by the Afghan squadron of 1500 camel swivels firing from a close range.

(d) *Dhamakah* : The literal Urdu translation of the word is the sound made by a blow or thump or of a heavy body falling on the ground. The word does not appear very often in historical writings. Shakespear defines it as a kind of cannon carried on an elephant. Irvine also feels that it was a kind a light field piece.

(e) *Rahkalah* : This word has been used to describe both a gun carriage and a gun placed on a carriage. Whenever any reference is made to it in the latter form, it obviously refers to a light gun without wheels, which is placed on an apart. The gun must have been of the types placed on elephants or camels described earlier as *hathnal*, *shutarnal* or *zamburak*.

(f) *Arbah*: The interpretation of this word has been discussed earlier. However there is no doubt that whenever *arabah* or *rahkalah* was referred to, it certainly meant a cart, whether a light gun was placed on it or not. We cannot be too critical of this apparent anomaly as certain technical names were used in a very general manner by writers and historians. Evidence shows that light guns without wheels were sometimes transported on small carts or carriages in the same way as they were taken on elephants and camels and at the place of battle, they were either dismounted or sometimes they were fired from the carriage itself. The latter argument can be reinforced by the writings of Lal and Murlidhar.

(g) *Ramjanki/Ramchangi*: A rather unusual word for some sort of a light field piece. There is very little mention of this word in other literature.

(h) *Deg (mortar)* : We have earlier mentioned that *deg andaz* was a pot thrower and that it is not possible to say whether they (*deg andazes*) were in charge of mortars or used a form of pot. Mortars were no doubt used during the later Moghul period. In earlier times however, it meant a fire pot or a hand grenade which the men threw at close quarters or from forts and houses.

(j) *Ban (rockets)* : *Ban* means an arrow in Sanskrit. Although rockets of various types were used by the Moghuls, they did not give them Persian names and continued to refer to rockets as *ban*. They were always part of the equipment of a Moghul army. According to Ashob, the rocket was invented and first used in Dakhin. He speaks of the great number of rockets which fell into Nadir Shah's hands with the rest of Muhammad Shah's artillery in 1739. They were carried on camels, with each carrying ten rockets as well as the rocket man. At times they were also transported on carts, each carrying fifteen rockets along with the attendant. They were used by Dara Shukoh at the battle of Samugarh in 1658.

Wilks says the following :

> The Indian rocket derives its projectile force from the same composition which is used in the rockets of ordinary firework; the cylinder which contains it is of iron; and sometimes gunpowder at its extremity causes it to explode when it has reached its object. A straight sword blade is also not unfrequently affixed to the rocket; and attached bamboo or reed steadies its flight. The rocketmen are all trained to give them an elevation proportioned to the varying dimensions of the cylinder and the distance of the object to be struck; as those projected to any distance describe a parabola of

> considerable height. A single rocket is easily avoidable, but when the flight is numerous, the attempt would be useless and their momentum is always sufficient to destroy a man or a horse.

Moor, quoting Major Dirom, also describes the Moghul rocket :

> It consists of an iron tube of about a foot long and an inch in diameter, fixed to a bamboo rod of ten or twelve feet long. The tube being filled with combustible composition is set fire to, and being directed by the hand, flies like an arrow to the distance of upwards of 1,000 yards. Some of the rockets have a chamber and burst like a shell; others called ground rockets have a serpentine motion and on striking the ground rise again and bound along till their force by spent. They make a great noise and exceedingly annoy the native cavalry in India who move in great bodies; but are easily avoided or seldom take effect against our troops who are formed in lines of great extent and no great depth.

Bans could be dangerous for the handlers. Willamson stresses that they were not very safe engines and apt to turn back on those who use them. He says :

> The contrivance is very simple having a hollow iron cylinder a foot long, two to three inches in diameter, closed at one end with a small apparatus for filling. The cylinder is tied to bamboo or 'lathi ' six to seven feet long. The direction and distance is governed by hand by giving required elevation. When the fuse at the vent is lighted a slight cast of the hand commences the motion. It creates great panic among the enemy's cavalry. The management of the weapon is delicate and unless great precautions are taken, those who discharge them are not safe.

(k) *Field guns :* The Moghul army had a large number of light field guns mounted on wheeled carriages. They were made of iron, bronze and they fired shots varying from one pound upwards. There is no indication of what the demarcation line between light and heavy wheeled artillery was in relation to the weight of shot, the bore of the barrel or the number of animals required to pull the gun.

4. Mobility and Mounting of Guns

Given the large-scale campaigning they undertook, the Moghuls were often on the move. Various scholars have tried to calculate the average movement per day of the Moghul army but have not been able to arrive at any firm figure. Irvine feels that the usual march never exceeded 4.5 *kos* (11.7 miles) per day and was sometimes as little as 1.25 *kos* (3.25 miles). There are of course famous cases of forced marches when this figure was well exceeded, the more well known being that of Akbar whose army covered 600 miles in 11 days. However as the Moghul armies became heavy and cumbersome, the marches became slower and slower.

Order of march. In the order of march, the heavy artillery went first and formed the advance guard. In front of this, thousands of pioneers marched with spades ready to smooth the ground. This was followed by baggage, and the rest of the army with the cavalry leading. The line of march was brought up by the light artillery, each field piece on its carriage drawn by horses.

The most surprising aspect of the march is that is was led by heavy artillery and not by light artillery and cavalry. Now where is it mentioned that the leading heavy artillery had any protection of cavalry or infantry, except at the Battle of Hasanpur in 1719, described later. The only possible reason could be that, of all the elements of the Moghul Court that were on the move, the heavy artillery was the slowest due to its weight and the poor state of the roads en route, and it set the pace for the rest of the main body. We have seen that on quite a few occasions, the heavy artillery was left behind because it could not keep pace with the rest of the army. A modern military analyst will also wonder why the Moghuls put their artillery to lead and that too the heavy artillery drawn by innumerable animals and needing the assistance of elephants to push them over bad roads and gradients, making it extremely vulnerable to attack by cavalry or infantry. We have seen that when Hemu opposed Akbar at panipat in 1556, the former had placed most of his artillery forward, and in the battle the Moghuls (under Ali Quli Khan) captured the whole of Hemu's artillery, leaving the latter under a severe handicap.

Mounting of guns. Weight and size were not the only restricting factors for the mobility of the Moghul army, but the type of mounting also mattered. The gun carriages were of poor quality and technically not very advanced. As late as 1757, when the Battle of Plassey took place, and account of the mounting of the guns of Siraj-ud-daulah is given by Orme :

The cannon were mostly of the largest calibre, 24 and 32 pounders, and these were mounted on the middle of a large stage raised six feet from the ground carrying, besides the cannon, all the ammunition belonging to it, and the gunners themselves who managed the cannon on the stage itself. These machines were drawn by 40 or 50 yokes of white oxen, of the largest size bred in the country of Purnea and behind each cannon walked an elephant trained to assist by shoving with his forehead against the hinder part of the carriage.

Referring to the same battle, Sir Eyre Coote says that the Nawab's cannon were mounted on a bundle of bamboos tied together and each piece was drawn by 20 or 30 pairs of oxen. However, seven years later, after the Battle of Baksar on 23 Oct. 1764, Maj Munro deposed that 133 pieces of different sizes taken from Shuja-ud-daulah were all on carriages and most of them on English carriages. Irvine mentions that in the Dakhin, Blacker found it necessary to employ sixty Carnatic bullocks in yoke to an iron 24 pounder fifty to an iron 18 pounder and forty to an iron 12 pounder.

Other historians of the Moghul period have this to say about guns and carriages :

(a) De la Flott, who was in the south of India from April 1758 to May 1760, declares that Indian cannon when used in fortresses were not mounted on carriages. "They were put on the very embrasures, or supported

by two great movable timbers. The balls are of stone they make many ricochets and then roll a great distance." He also saw at Jinji, a fortress 82 miles from Madras, one of these pieces, twenty feet in length, without any carriage.

(b) In 1746, Clive seems to have fired a big native gun from a mound of earth without having any carriage. Colonel M. Wilks also speaks of an occasion in 1768 when the guns of the Indians were numerous "but unmounted".

Mustapha is much more explicit in his views on the mounting of gun :

> Expressions about a well served artillery are misleading, for it is certain that all their artillery was as cumbersome, ill-mounted and ill-served as was the artillery of Europe three hundred years ago. It is only since the year 1760 that some Indians have put themselves upon the footing of having an artillery mounted and served nearly in the European manner.

An anonymous observer writing in 1768 or 1769 says that Jats took two 24 pounders a mile or two in ten days.

From the slow progress that was made in transporting of heavy guns, we can infer that the carriages on which they were mounted were of a very clumsy and primitive construction. One may speculate that they must have been dragged unmounted along the ground by sheer brute force; otherwise the length of time taken hardly seems credible. It appears that throughout the 18th century, these guns were mounted on low platforms and made to turn on a pivot. Thorn says that such carriages could be termed "country block carriages turning on a large pivot". Fitzclarance adds that the generality of the artillery in the forts was so badly mounted that they would be dismounted at the first discharge.

Since a large number of heavy guns were mounted on block carriages this may explain the delay in the movement of guns, as it would involve the dismantling of barrels from the block, putting these on big wheeled carts, transporting them and then reassembling them at the place of action. In the absence of modern cranes, it must have been quite a feat to assemble the guns considering that some of them weighed as much as 1469 mounds. It is also probable, although no authentic records exist, that for short distances, it would have been easier to move the gun by dragging it along the ground after dismantling it from the block and assembling it at the next place of action, as this would have saved one process *i.e.* loading the gun on carts after dismantling. Alternatively, guns fixed on block carriages could be moved by dragging them without removing the gun.

5. Procurement and Manufacture

The Moghuls not only cast guns themselves but were also keen to procure them from abroad and get the best talent available in India to help in their manufacture. The reigning princes took personal interest in achieving this, as is evident from a *far-man* (directive) issued by Shah Jahan to his Governor of Surat. "You shall endeavour to list ten Christian constables, well versed in their art, into our service; and you shall spare no cost to have some great cannon cast for our use." Again Colonel Hector Munro, the victor of Baksar, speaking of the period 1763-72, held that Indian princes got their artillery from England, Holland and France "there is hardly a ship that comes of India that does not sell them cannon and small arms. Most of the gunpowder they make themselves. They cast shot in abundance, but there is no black prince that casts cannon but the king of Travancore. The cannon and military stores are smuggled into the country." The Moghuls were, however, well versed in the art of manufacture of guns even at the time of Babar. In his memoirs, he describes the founding of a cannon at Agra under the direction of his head of the artillery, Ustad Quli Khan.

> Around the mould they had erected eight furnaces for melting the metal. From the foot of each started a channel which ended in the mould. As soon as I had arrived, the holes to allow the flow of metal were opened. The fused metal rushed into the mould like boiling water. After a time, before the mould was full, the fused metal from the

furnaces began to flow very slowly, either because their size or the amount of material had been wrongly calculated. Ustad Quli Khan, in a state that cannot be described, wished to fling himself into the very midst of the melted copper. I made much of him, ordered him a robe of honour and thus succeeded in calming him. A day or two afterwards, when the mould had cooled down, it was opened. Ustad Quli Khan, overwhelmed with joy, sent me word that the bore of the piece had no fault and that a chamber could easily be made in it. The body of the cannon was then uncovered and a certain number of artificers were set to finish it, while he busied himself with the preparation of the chamber.

Technique of manufacture : Irvine adds that from the records, it seems that this chamber was cast separately and the gun was then tried, and fired a ball for a distance of sixteen hundred paces. On another occasion, a large cannon was fired, the ball went far but the piece burst and eight men were killed. In spite of the evidence in the form of old Moghul guns, foreign writers feel that Indian guns were not cast or founded. De la Flotte, speaking of the 18th century and Dakhin, asserts that Indian cannon were not founded but built up of iron bars bound together and held in place from distance to distance by thick rings of the same metal. Fitzclarance, writing in 1818, says "The artillery in use among the natives is generally an iron cylinder with molten brass cast around it." He again remarks that in their first attempts to make cannon, the Indians employed bars of iron hooped together. In one instance he saw an improvement on this. At Delhi he found a piece made of iron wedges placed as radii, and then hooked together to form the gun.

From all available evidence, it appears that the Moghuls, when they came to India, did not by themselves know much about the manufacture of guns. What they did know was borrowed from the Turks and from Constantinople. In the earlier Moghul period, at any rate, the emperors were dependent for their artillery on the help and instruction of Rumies, that is, Mohamedans from Constantinople or of

Farangis, principally runaway sailors from Surat or Portuguese half castes. Rumi Khan was a well known officer of the first of these classes. It also appears that during the initial period of Moghul rule, they had a considerable number of foreigners employed in their artillery. Bernier has stated that "Formerly, when the Moghuls were little skilled in the management of artillery, the pay of Europeans was more liberal and there are still (1658) some remaining who receive two hundred rupees a month but now the king (Alamgir) admits them with difficulty into the service and limits their pay to thirty-two rupees."

6. Moghul Artillery in Battle

Deployment of arms. For a successful action by the Moghul army open country was one of the first necessities for battle, as without this, their cavalry, which formed the bulk of the army, could not deploy freely. In hills and mountainous terrain, this was a major disadvantage as even the artillery could not be effectively brought into action leaving the fighting to the infantry which, in terms of its training and fighting capability, could not meet the challenge of their foes due to its neglect by the Moghuls.

The order or battle was as fallows :

(a) Skirmishes.

(b) Artillery in a line protected by rocket men and sheltered by a rough field work and guns being chained together.

(c) Advanced guard.

(d) Right and left wing behind the advance guard.

(e) Centre with the emperor/commander on elephant with his protective element of advance guard (*iltmish*) and flank guard (*tarah*).

(f) Rear guard.

The army was made ready for the battle by drawing out the guns in a long line and protecting them by earthworks, the guns being also connected together by chains or hidestraps, to prevent the horsemen of the other side from riding through the line and cutting down the gunners and also to form an obstacle to a cavalry charge. Infantry with matchlocks stood behind the gunners to fire at the charging cavalry and assault by infantry. The practice of chaining guns together started from the days of Babar and continued to the very last as is evident from the following records :

(a) Babar in 1526 chained his guns together by twisted bull hides.

(b) Dara Shukoh used chains at Samugarh in 1658.

(c) In 1748, during the first invasion of Ahmed Shah Abdali, the imperialists joined their cannon together by chains after the fashion of Rum.

(d) Again in 1751, during the third invasion of Ahmed Shah Abdali, the Moghul Governor Muin-ul-mulk resorted to *zanjirah bandi* of guns.

(e) In 1803, the Marathas followed the practice of the Moghuls and chained the guns together at the Battle of Laswari.

A good description of chaining of guns or '*zanjirah band i*, is given by Ashob with reference to Muhammad Shah's camp at Karnal in 1739.

The 'zanjirah bandi' began at the last bastion of the town wall, a narrow path one or two yards wide being left on the bank of the canal for the passage of the guards on their rounds. The swivel guns (rahkalahs) were planted four yards apart with iron chains strongly attached to the wheels of their carriages. Between every two swivel pieces were stationed five men with wall pieces (*jazair*) having breast work thrown up and their pieces ready, side by side, on their tripods.

Role of artillery. A discharge of rockets signalled the start of battle; this was followed by the artillery battle and guns which were deployed all along the line began to bombard the enemy. The guns were all static and because the draught oxen pulling them were slow, it was not possible to move them either during the advance of line or during the withd awal. This was the biggest drawback of the Moghul artillery, as unlike their British counterparts, Indians had never experimented with light galloper guns and horse artillery which were as mobile as cavalry and could be relied upon to provide support to the cavalry and advancing infantry. It is not that the Moghuls did not have guns drawn by horses. The light guns of "Artillery of the Stirrup" were all drawn by horses.

The firing or guns was in fact quite slow as is evident from the following documents :

(a) In Babar's time, the rate of fire was very slow. In his battle near Khanua in 1527, Ustad Quli Khan made very good use of his artillery. The first day he discharged eight projectiles, the second he shot sixteen and continued for three or four days. He used for this the piece called "the cannon of the conquerer".

(b) As late in 1721, the usual rate of fire of the heavy guns was one shot every three hours. He praises Haider Quli Khan's men for the energy with which they cooled their guns, loaded them and fired them at intervals of three quarters of an hour.

(c) During the middle of the 18th century, Orme speaks of their firing once a quarter of an hour.

While the artillery duel went on, the rest of the army was drawn up at some distance behind the guns in the order of battle stated earlier. The role of artillery was to silence the enemy's guns, cause attrition and confusion in their ranks and, if possible, to hit the enemy king or commander riding on the elephant, as due to the nature of composition of the armies with each portion under their own chiefs, the death or disappearance of the chief led to the troops desisting from fighting and taking flight. Once the commander was satisfied that artillery had done their part in action, the infantry and cavalry advanced beyond the line of entrenchment and guns. Due to non-mobility of the guns, the artillery thereafter seldom could take effective part in the battle due to reasons of safety. If the enemy attacked first, because the guns were immobile they had to be left behind or spiked. Blacker says, "In an action, the guns of an Indian army are generally immovable and their cavalry all motion. The object of the batteries is to fire as long as possible previously to being taken, and of the horse to secure their retreat if discomfited, unfettered by any incumbrance."

A perfect artillery battle. Not withstanding the views held by various historians about the immobility of the Moghul artillery and unflattering comments on its tactical handling, an account of the battle fought on 13 November 1720 between Emperor Muhammad Shah and Abdullah Khan, the latter being one of the Sayyad brothers who was conspiring to oust the emperor, will show how the Moghul artillery could be employed to influence the battle, if properly handled. The battle was fought at Hasanpur, 50 miles south of Delhi, and is described in detail by Irvine, who consulted seven histories :

Early in the morning of Wednesday, before the sun rose, Muhammad Shah mounted his elephant and took his place in the centre (the two forces at that time were still apart by six miles and had not been drawn up for battle). Haider Quli Khan, the imperial Mir Atash, was sent on ahead with the strong artillery forces under his command while Khan Dauran and Sabit Khan were ordered to follow and support him with the left wing. When Najm-ud-din Ali Khan at the head of the Sayyad vanguard appeared in the distance from the direction of the river, Mir Atash moved out his heavy cannon into the open, and encountered the advancing enemy with a storm of balls from them and his field pieces. The fire was so continuous and heavy that the artillery of the other side was silenced. After every volley, Haider Quli Khan urged on his men by lavish gifts of gold and silver. As the artillery advanced, the rest of the army followed and occupied the ground. Stimulated by their Commander's liberality, the gunners worked zealously, and a second set of guns were loaded by the time the first were discharged. Khan Dauran's troops moved in support of the imperial artillery. Sanjar Khan and Dost Ali Khan in command of that noble's guns particularly distinguished themselves... During the day, a rocket fell on Sayyad Abdullah Khan's powder magazine exploding it and causing much loss of life. Throughout the day of 13th, the battle was chiefly one of artillery. The Sayyad vanguard commander Najim-ud-din wanted to charge the enemy but was dissuaded by Rajah Mukham Singh, who had deserted from the imperialists. The latter pointed out that to charge down such a powerful artillery as the other side possessed would be to expose themselves to destruction. Their own supply of guns ought, he said, to be entrenched in a good position on the edge of some ravine and there they could await the favour of events. Although Mukham Singh had acquired in the Dakhin the highest reputation as a soldier, his advice was not adopted. The Sayyad's artillery was placed on a high mound, under the shelter of some trees, near a deserted village and it tried to reply to other side's fire to the extent of its ability... In the end, some of Sayyad's field pieces were taken and they were ejected from the sheltered position among the trees. A ball from a swivel gun struck Najim-ud-din on his knee... Abdullah Khan had decided to attack the advanced guard, so as to get near the center where the emperor was located. He tried to approach from his left but found the river an obstacle. He then changed his direction and approached from right. As soon as the movement was spotted, the imperial artillery present with the emperor's division was then despatched to bar the way. The night was a moonlit one and the imperial artillery never ceased its fire. If any man stirred in the Sayyad position or showed himself, a gun was at once pointed in that direction and discharged, and from time to time the guns were dragged forward, the oxen being harnessed to the muzzle instead of, as usual, to the breech end of the gun. Among the guns in use were those named Ghazi Khan and Shah Pasand. These heavy guns were fired oftener than had ever been done before in the recollection of the oldest man. Haider Quli Khan kept up the energy of his men by continual gifts. Abdullah Khan's continued to make off in small parties.

The narrative gives further detail of the battle at which Abdullah Khan was defeated and was handed over on order of the emperor to Mir Atash Haider Quli Khan. This is very significant as it shows how well handled artillery can influence the outcome of the battle and also brings out some remarkable tactical concepts practised by Mir Atash which cannon be faulted, even today, by modern military analysts. Unlike other records of those days which were written in the inflated, rhetorical style of which Persian and Indian writers and so proud, this particular battle narrative can be accepted as accurate and authentic as William Irvine has consulted over seven different authors of that period to describe the battle. Some of the major aspects of the battle are highlighted below :

(a) Mir Atash Ustad Quli Khan not only acted as the head of the artillery and personally stood near the guns to encourage the gun crew but he also acted as commander of part of the force.

(b) Even when the two opposing forces were over six miles apart and still advancing, the Mir Atash went forward with strong artillery force duly escorted by infantry and cavalry to stop the enemy. The artillery arm was being used as a "hitting" arm supported by other two arms.

(c) On seeing the vanguard of the enemy, the Mir Atash deployed his heavy artillery and light field guns and silenced the enemy guns. The heavy guns used by him (*e.g.* Ghazi Khan) were really heavy and it is remarkable indeed that these were brought into action while in sight of the enemy. This is one of the few cases on record where light field guns were also taken ahead as the normal practice in the Moghul order of march was to have heavy guns were immediately deployed ahead under strong protection of the cavalry and infantry and while they took on the enemy, heavy guns were brought into action.

(d) After the initial impact of artillery, the artillery advanced and the rest of the army followed and occupied the ground. This is indeed a remarkable concept and well ahead of thinking even of the British who raised their horse artillery in India in 1797. It is however tragic from the Moghul point of view that such actions and concepts were very rare in the annals of their military history.

(e) The imperial artillery achieved a high and constant rate of fire not only due to the personal encouragement of

their Mir Atash but apparently due to very well practised and disciplined drill by which continuous fire was brought on the enemy.

(f) The Sayyad artillery was ejected from its position by artillery action of the imperial artillery, a perfect example of what in modern warfare is called counter bombardment.

(g) When Abullah Khan tried to get close to the emperor, the imperial artillery present with the emperor was despatched to bar the way: a very flattering compliment can be paid to "artillery of the stirrup" or Topkhanah-i-rikali, the artillery close to the emperor. That such a privileged unit which can "go to seed" due to its proximity to the highest in the land and doing ceremonial functions, can move out for operations and that too a difficult blocking task, speaks well of their training. The credit in this case should surely go to the Mir Atash who also headed this unit in addition to commanding the artillery of the field; Emperor Muhammad Shah at that time being only eighteen (when he was put on the throne in 1719 by Sayyads).

(h) The guns, including heavy guns, were dragged forward as dictated by the situation, and they kept up their fire even at night and were very effective in firing at individuals if they moved in the Sayyad's camp. This speaks highly of the technical expertise accuracy and mobility of the imperial artillery.

15
Rules Connected with Pay and Allowances

In the preceding paragraphs have been shown in general terms the rates of pay for the cavalry, and some of the rules by which pay was governed. When we come to the actual working out in detail of this part of the army administration, our difficulties increase. The official manuals, which are our only guide, are couched in the briefest of language, and naturally presume a knowledge of many things of which we are ignorant. Nor can we be certain whether the rules that they lay down were of general application or were applicable to certain classes of troops only. Thus the data are insufficient for any complete exposition of this part of the general subject. The matters treated of in the next following paragraphs are, moreover, of a somewhat miscellaneous description, and many of them might be better classed under other heads, such as Discipline, Recruiting, and so forth; but as there is not enough-material to yield complete information, I have thought it better to deal with the greater part of them; as the native authors do, in their relation to the calculation of pay.

Rates of Pay. The rates of pay for officers and men of the cavalry, forming numerically far the most important part of the army, have been already stated when dealing with the *mansab* system. The rates for Infantry and Artillery, so far as recorded, will be stated when we come to those branches of the service.

Date from which Pay Drawn. On an officer being first appointed, if by his rank he was exempt from having his horses branded (*dagh*), his pay began from the date of confirmation (*arz-i-mukarrar*). If such branding were necessary, pay began from the date of branding (the day itself being excluded), and as soon as this condition had been complied with, a disbursement was made of one month's pay on account. In the case of promotion, if it were unconditional, the rules were the same as above; if conditional, the pay began from the date of entering on office (*Dastur-ul-Aml,* B.M. 1641. fol. 37a, 58; id. 6599, fol. 146b, *Dastur-ul-Insha,* 233).

Conditional (Mashrul) and Unconditional (Bila-shart) Pay. Rank and pay might be given absolutely, or they might be conditional on the holding of some particular office. The temporary or *mashrut ba Khidmat* rank was given as an addition to the permanent, *bila-shart* rank which a man already occupied. On ceasing to hold the office, such as that of governor (*subahdar*) or military magistrate (*faujdar*), the *mashrut* rank and pay were taken away.

Pay always in Arrears. In later times pay due from the imperial treasure to the *mansabdars,* as well as that due from the *mansabdars* to the private soldiers, was always in arrears. In fact, we should not go far wrong, I think, if we asserted that this was the case in the very best times. The reasons are obvious. More men were entertained than could be easily paid; Indian Mahomedans are very bad financiers; the habit of the East is to stave off payment by any expedient. To owe money to somebody seems in that country the normal condition of mankind. For example, even such a careful manager as Nizam-ul-Mulk, in his alleged testament, dated the 4th Jamadi II, 1161 H. (31st May, 1748), is credited with the boast that he "never withheld pay for *more than three months*" ("Asiatick Miscellany," Calcutta, 1788, vol, iii, 160). Another reason for keeping the men in arrears may have been the feeling that they were thereby prevented from transferring their services to some other chief quite as readily as they might have done if there were nothing owing. Disturbances raised by troops clamouring for their pay were among the unfailing sequels to the disgrace or sudden death of a commander. The instances are too numerous to specify. On this head Haji Mustapha, *Seir,* iii, 35, note 29, says truly enough :—"The troops are wretchedly paid, twenty or thirty months of arrears being no rarity. The ministers, princes, and grandees always keep twice or thrice as many men as they have occasion for, and fancy that by withholding the pay they concern the men in the preservation of their lord's life." We can also quote Lord Clive as to the state of things in the Bengal subah in 1757 ("Minutes of Select Committee of 1772," reprint, 52) – "There were great arrears due to the army by Siraj-ud-Daulah as well as by Mir Jafar, and the sums amounted to three or four millions sterling. It is the custom of the country never to pay the army a fourth part of what they promise them; and it is only in times of distress that the army can get paid at all, and that is the reason why their troops always behave so" (badly)?.

Pay in Naqd and in Jagir. Pay (*tankhwah* : literally, tan 'body,' *khwah* 'need') might be either *Naqd*, that is, given in cash (*naqd*); or Jagir (literally, *ja* 'place,' *gir*, taking, from *giriftan*), that is an assignment (*jagir*) of the land revenue of a certain number of villages (*mauza*) or of a subdivision (*parganah*). A certain number of officers and soldiers, chiefly those of the infantry and artillery, who were, as a rule, on the pay list of the emperor himself, were paid in cash. This seems to have been the case in all reigns up to quite the end. But the favourite mode of payment was by an assignment of the government revenue from land. Such an arrangement seems to have suited both parties. The State was a very centralized organization, fairly strong at the centre, but weak at the extremities. It was glad to be relieved of the duty of collecting and bringing in the revenue from distant places. This task was left to the *jagirdar*, or holder of the *jagir*, and unless such a *mansabdar* were a great noble or high in imperial favour, the assignment was made on the most distant and most imperfectly subdued provinces.[1] On the other hand, a chance of dealing with land and handling the income from it, has had enormous attractions in all parts of the world, and in none more than in India. Nobles and officers by obtaining an assignment of revenue hoped to make certain of some income, instead of depending helplessly for payment on the good pleasure of the Court. Then in negotiating for a *jagir* there were all sorts of possibilities. A judicious bribe might secure to a man a larger *jagir* than was his due; and if he were lucky, he might make it yield more than its nominal return. Many such considerations must have been present to their minds. Whatever be the true reasons, of this there can be no doubt, that the system was highly popular, and that the struggle for *jagirs* was intensely keen. As Abd-ul-Jalil of Bilgram writes to his son : "Service has its foundation on a *jagir*; an employee without a *jagir*, might just as well be out of employ." ("Oriental Miscellany", Calcutta, 1798). A recent French writer, M. Emile Barbe, "Le Nabab Rene Madeo," 117, speaking of a *jagir* given in 1775, says : "Cette apparition des jaguirs dans l' Empire Mogol a son declin est un fait sociologique du plus haut interest." The system of *jagir* grants may be an interesting sociological fact—as to that I have nothing to say for or against; but it was not introduced into the Mogol Empire during its decline. *Jagirs* existed in that empire's most flourishing days having been granted as early as Akbar (Blochmann, *Ain*, i. 261), while under Shahjahan they existed on a most extensive scale.

If the *jagir* were a large one, the officer managed it through his own agents, who exercised on his behalf most of the functions of government. Such *jagirs* were practically outside the control of the local governor of *faujdar*, and formed a sort of *imperium in imperio*. The disastrous effects of the system, in this aspect, need not be further dwelt on here. On the other hand, a small *jagir* was more frequently left by the assignee in the hands of the *faujdar*, through whom the revenue demand was realized. Gradually, as the bonds of authority were relaxed from the centre, the *faujdars* and *subahdars* ignored more and more the claims of these assignees, and finally ceased to remit or make over to them any of the collections.

I append here the first steps of official procedure followed in the grant of a *jagir*. We are to suppose that one Khwajah Rahmatullah has been recalled from duty in some province, and that on appearing at court he has applied for a new *jagir*. Through the *Diwan-i-tan*, a great officer at the head of one of the two revenue departments, a *haqiqat*, or Statement of Facts, was drawn up, in the following form (B.M. No. 6599, fol. 156a to 157b) :—

Statement (*Haqiqat*)

Khwajah Rahmatullah, son of Khwajah Ahmad, a native of Balkh, who was attached to the standards in Province So-and-so, having come to the Presence in pursuance of the exalted orders, and the *jagir* which, up to such-and-such a harvest, was held by him in the said Province, having been granted to So-and-so, in this matter what is the order as to the *tankhwah jagir* of the above-named.

[on the margin] { Presentation (*mulazamat*)
Day so-and-so, month so-and-so

{ Offering (*nazar*).
9 Muhrs (gold coins) and
18 Rupees.

This *haqiqat* was passed on by the *Diwan-i-tan* to the *Diwan-i-ala* (or wazir). The latter placed it before the Emperor. If an order were given for a *jagir* to be granted, the wazir endorsed on the paper, "The pure and noble order issued to grant a *jagir* in *tankhwah* from the commencement of such-and-such a harvest." This paper then became the voucher for the chief clerk to the *Diwan-i-tan*, who wrote out a *siyaha dual*, or Rough Estimate, as follows :

Rough Estimate

Khwajah Rahmatullah, son of Khwajah Ahmad, of Balkh. Whereas he was on duty in Province So-and-so, and according to order has reached the Blessed Stirrup *(i.e.* the Court)—

One thousand, Personal (*zat*)
200 men, Horse (*suwar*)
Pay in dams

	34 lakhs
Personal	Troopers (*tabinan*)
18 lakhs	16 lakhs

= Total, 34 lakhs.

Feed of four-footed animals (*Khurak-i-dawabb*) remitted

Parganah So-and-so, situated in Province So-and-so, 20 lakhs of Dams.	Parganah So-and-so, situated in Province So-and-so, 14 lakhs of Dams.

It will be seen, on referring to a previous page, that as the man was 1000 *zat*, but had only 200 *suwar* rank, he was third class *Hazari.* By the table this gives him 18 lakhs, and then 200 horsemen at 8000 dams each comes to 16 lakhs, making the 34 lakhs which are sanctioned in the above.

The *daul*, or estimate, was made over to the diary-writer (*waqiah navis*), who, after he had entered it in the *waqiah* (diary), prepared an extract called a memorandum (*yad-dasht*) for submission to the office of the confirmation of orders (*arz-i-mukarrar*, lit. second petition). The *yad-dasht* repeated the facts much in the same form as the *haqiqat* and the daul. On it the wazir wrote : "Let this be compared with the diary (*waqiah*) and then sent on to the confirmation office (*arz-i-mukarrar*)." On the margin the diary-writer (*waqiah navis*) then reported : "This *yad-dasht* accords with the waqiah." Next the superintendent (*daroghah*) of the confirmation office wrote : "On such-and-such a date of such-and-such a month of such-and-such a year this reached the confirmation office. The order given was—'Approved." We need not follow here the further fate of the order after it left the Court and reached the governor of the province referred to.

Loans, Advances, and Gifts. The technical name for a loan or advance of pay was *musaadat* (Steingass, 1225, A, helping, favour, assistance, aid), and the conditions as to interest and repayment are given in Book ii, *Ain* 15, of the *Ain-i-Akbari* (Blochmaan, i, 265). Historians frequently mention the advance of money under this name. In later times, especially from the reign of Muhammad Shah, no commander ever took the field without the grant of the most liberal cash advances to meet his expenses. Possibly these were never repaid, or were from the first intended as free gifts. When we meet with the phrase *tankhwah-i-inam*, I presume that there can be no doubt of the payment being a gift. Here the word *tankhwah* seems to denote the order or cheque on the treasury, and the word *inam* (gift, present), differentiates it from other *tankhwah*, which were in the nature of payments to be repeated periodically. The recovery of loans and advances came under a head in the accounts called *mutalibah* (Steingass, 1259, asking, claim, due). Another term of somewhat similar import, *baz-yaft* (Steingass, 146, the resumption of anything, deduction, stoppage), seems to have been confined to the recovery of items put under objection in the revenue accounts by the *mustaufis*, or auditors. At one time the recovery of an advance was made from a man's pay in four instalments; but towards the end of Alamgir's reign, it was taken in eight instalments (B.M. No. 1641, fol. 58b).

Deductions. Of these I have found the following : *kasur-i-do-dami* (fraction of the two dams), *kharch-i-sikkah* (expenses of minting), *ayyam-i-hilali* (days of the moon's rise), *hissah-i-ijnas* (share in kind), *khurak-i-dawabb* (feed of four-footed animals).

Kasur-i-do dami. *Kasur* is, literally, fractions, deficiencies, faults. This item was a discount of five per cent., that is, of two dams in every forty, and therefore styled "do-dami" (B.M. 1641, fol. 37a). The origin of this is to be found possibly in Akbar's five per cent. Deductions from the Ahadi troopers on account of horses and other expenses (*Ain*, i, 250, line 14). The rate of deduction is differently stated in fol. 58b, B.M. 1641, as four dams in the 100, if the officer drew seven or eight months pay, and two dams in the 100, if he drew less than that number of months.

Khurch-i-sikkah was also deducted: in Alamgir's reign the rates were Rs. 1. 12a 0p. per cent. On Shahjahan's coinage, and Rs. 1 8a 0p. per cent. On the coin of the reigning emperor. Under the rules then in force, the Shahjahani coins, not being those of the reigning emperor, were uncurrent, and therefore subject to a discount. Why a deduction was made on the coins of the reigning emperor, is harder to explain. It was not till Farrukhsiyar's reign, I believe, that the coinage was called in annually, from which time only coins of the current year were accepted, even by the government itself, at full face value.

Ayyam-i-hilan. This was a deduction of one day's pay in every month except Ramazan. *Mansabdars, Ahadis,* and *barqandaz* (matchlockmen) were all subject to it. But, towards the end of 'Alamgir's reign, it was remitted until the Narbada, was crossed, that is, I presume, so long as a man served in the Dakhin (B.M. 1641, fol. 55b, 62b). The reason for making this deduction is difficult to fathom; and about the name itself there is some doubt. In the first of the two entries just quoted, I read the word as *talafi* (Steingass, 321, obtaining, making amends, compensation, reparation); but this variant, instead of throwing light on the subject, leaves it as obscure as before.

Hissah-i-ijnas. *Jins* (goods) is used in opposition to *naqd* (cash), and this item (*hissah* = share, *ijnas* = goods) seems to mean the part of a man's pay delivered to him in kind. Apparently this item did not apply to the cavalry. In the case of the matchlock men, artillerymen, and artificers, the deduction was 1/24 if the man were mounted, and 1/12 if he were not. This represented the value of the rations supplied to him. There is another entry of *rasad-i-jins* (supplies of food?), the exact nature of which I cannot determine (B.M. 1641, fol. 62b).

Khurak-i-dawabb. This is, literally, *khurak,* feed, *dawabb,* four-footed animals. It was a deduction from a *mansabdar's* pay on account of a certain number of horses and elephants belonging to the emperor, with whose maintenance such officer was saddled. The germ of this exaction can, I think, be found in Akbar's system of making over elephants to the charge of grandees (*Ain.* i. 126). "He (Akbar) therefore put several *halkahs* (groups of baggage elephants) in charge of every grandee, and required them to look after them." Akbar would seem to have paid the expenses; but in process of time, we can suppose, the charge was transferred to the officer's shoulders entirely, and in the end he had to submit to the deduction without even the use of the animals being given to him. At any rate, the burden became a subject of great complaint. This is shown by a passage in Khafi Khan. ii, 602.

"In the reign of Alamgir the *mansabdars* for a long period were reduced to wanting their evening meal, owing to the lowness of the assignments (*paebaqi*) granted by the emperor. His stinginess reminds one of the proverb 'one pomegranate for a hundred sick men,' *yak anar, sau bimar*. After many efforts and exertions, some small assignment (*jagir*) on the land revenue would be obtained. The lands were probably uncultivated, and the total income of the *jagir* might not amount to a half or even a third of the money required for the expenses of the animals. If these were realized from the officer, whence could come the money to preserve his children and family from death by starvation? In spite of this, the Akhtah Begi (Master of the Horse) and other accursed clerks caused the cost of feeding the emperor's animals to be imposed on the *mansabdars*, and, imprisoning their agents at court, used force and oppression of all kinds to obtain the money.

"When the agents (*wakils*) complained of this oppression to the emperor, the head of the elephant stables and the Akhtah Begi so impressed matters on the emperor's mind, that the complaints were not listened to, and all the men were reduced to such an extremity by this oppression, that the agents resigned their agency. In Bahadur Shah's reign, the *Khan-i-Khanan* decided that when the *mansabdars* received a *jagir* for their support, the number of *dams* required for the cost of feeding cattle should be deducted first from the total estimated income, and the balance should be assigned as the income. In this way, the obligation for meeting the cost of feeding the animals was entirely received from the heads of the *mansabdars* and their agents. Indeed, to speak the truth, it was an order to absolve them from the cost of the cattle provender." Dowson (Elliot, vii, 408) could make nothing of this passage.

In the case of officers below a certain rank, the deduction of *khurak-i-dawabb* was not make. The rule says that where the pay (*tankkwah*) did not come up to 15 lakhs of *dams*, the deduction was not made; but apparently no lower rank than that of 400 *zat*, 200 *suwar*, was liable. This rank would by the tables draw a pay of 20 lakhs of *dams*. As to the rate of deduction, the records are so obscure that I am unable to come to any conclusions. Sometimes we are told that the calculation was made at so many *dams* on each 100,000 *dams* of pay; at others, that for each 100,000 *dams* one riding and five baggage elephants were charged for. A distinction in rates was made between Mahomedans and Hindus, the former paying more; also between officers holding *jagirs* in Hindustan and those holding them in the Dakhin and Ahmadabad, the former paying slightly less than the latter.

Fines. We come now to the subject of fines, which were of various sorts, such as *tafawat-i-asp* (deficiency in horses), *tafawat-i-silah* (deficiency in equipment), *tafawat-i-tabinan* (deficiency in troopers), also called, it would seem, *kami-i-baradari, tawaqquf o adam-i-tashihah* (non-verification), saqali (casualties), *bartarafi* (rejections).

Tafawat-i-asp. This is literally "difference of horses," and refers to a classification of horses by their breed and size, which will be referred to more fully under the head of Branding and Verification. In each rank or *mansab* a certain number of each class of horse had-to be maintained, and if at Verification it was found that this regulation had not been complied with, the result was a fine. In the section on Branding I give the rates so far as recorded.

Tafawat-i-silah. This "difference in armour" was a fine for not producing at inspection arms and armour according to the required scale. The amount of fine and so forth I have stated further on under the head of Equipment.

Tafáwat-i-tabinan (difference of followers) or *kami-i-baradari* (deficiency in relations) was a fine imposed on an officer for non-production of the number of men stipulated for by the *suwar* rank. The following rates are stated in B.M. 1641, fol. 37a, and I presume that the deductions apply to *mansabdars* as well as to *Ahadis*, and that they were made from the monthly pay for each man deficient, although the entry is so brief as to remain very obscure :

In another passage, fol. 41, the same authority explains the matter thus. In the twenty-first year of Alamgir, a report on this subject having been made, the emperor allowed a term of four turns of guard (*chauki*) for a *mansabdar* to produce men of his own class or family (*baradari*), and for this period pay for the men was passed as if they had been present. But subsequently, on the first Rabi of the twenty-third year, the delay was extended to two months, and for the time during which such men were not actually present, pay at half-rates was sanctioned.

	Number of Months for Which Pay was Drawn				
	Four Months	Five Months	Six Months	Seven Months	Eight Months
Amount of fine in Rupees.	R. A. P. 2 8 0	R. A. P. 3 0 0	R. A. P. 4 0 0	R. A. P. 7 0 0	R. A. P. 8 0 0

Ahsham. In the case of the *Ahsham*, or troops belonging to the infantry and artillery, we have a little more definite information under this head (B.M. 1641, fol. 64a). Officers of this calls fell into three subdivisions, *hazari* (of a thousand), *sadiwal* (hundred-man), and *mirdahah* (lord of ten). The first class was always mounted (*suwar*) and the second sometimes; these mounted officers might be two-horse (*duaspah*) or only one-horse *yakaspah*) men. Working on these distinctions, we get the following scheme of pay. *Dulaspah Suwar*: Where, inclusive of the officer's own retainers (*khasah*), there were one hundred men present per 100 of rank, pay was drawn at *duaspah* rates. But if the number were under fifty per 100 of rank, pay was passed to the *hazari* as if he were a mounted *sadiwal*; subject to restoration to *duaspah* pay when his muster again conformed to the standard. *Yakaspah* : If, including *khasah* men, there were fifty men present per 100 of rank, full pay was given; if only thirty-one or under, then the *hazari* was paid as a *sadiwal piyadah* (unmounted), and certain other deductions were made. *Piyadah* (unmounted officer). If a *sadiwal* produced under thirty-one men out of his hundred, he received nothing but his rations. When the numbers rose above thirty, he was paid as a *mirdahah* till his full quota was mustered. In the case of a *mirdahah*, the production of two men entitled him to his pay. If one man only was paraded for inspection, a deduction from the pay was made, varying, on conditions which I have not mastered, from one to three annas per man.

Tawaqquf-i-tashihah (Delay in Verification). The rules for Branding and Verification will be found further on. If the periods fixed were allowed to elapse without the verification having been made, a man was reported for delay; and then a *mansabdar* was cut the whole, and an *ahadi* the half, of his pay (B.M. 1641, fol. 58b).

***Saqati* and *Bartarafi*.** The first word is from *saqat shudan* 'to die' (applied to animals, Steingass, 687), and may be translated casualties. The other word means setting aside or rejecting, in other words to cast a horse as unfit. We find the groundwork of the *saqati* system in the *Ain-i-Akbari*. Blochmann, -i, 250. In later times there were the following rules for regulating pay in such cases. First it was seen whether the man was *duaspah* (paid for two horses) or *yakaspah* (paid for one horse). In the first case, (1) if one horse died (*saqat shavvad*) or was cast (*bar taraf shud*), the man was paid at the *yakaspah* rate; (2) if both horses died or were turned out, the man obtained his personal pay for one month, and if after one month he had still no horse, his personal pay was also stopped. In the second case, that of a *yakaspah*, if there were no horse personal pay was disbursed for one month; but after one month nothing was given (B.M. 1641), fol. 41a).

If an *ahadi's* horse died while he was at headquarters, the clerk of the casualties, after having inspected the hide, wrote out his certificate (*saqat-namah*), and pay was disbursed according to it. If the man were on detached duty when his horse died, the brand (*dagh*), and the tail were sent in to headquarters (B.M. 1641, fol. 29b).

***Other incidents of military service considered as affecting pay*.** Among these may be mentioned : (1) *Ghair-haziri* (absence without leave); (2) *Bimari* (illness); (3) *Rukhsat* (leave and furlough); (4) *Farari* (desertion); (5) *Bartarafi* discharge or resignation); (6) Pension; (7) *Fauti* (death).

(1) *Ghair-haziri*. If a man were absent from three consecutive turns of guard (*chauki*), his pay was cut; but if he did not attend the fourth time, the penalty was dismissal, and all pay due was confiscated. Absence from night guard or at

roll-call (*jaizah*) involved the loss of a day's pay. If absent at the time of the emperor's public or private audience, or on a day of festival (id), half a day's pay was taken (B.M. 1641, fol. 39a, 62b).

(2) *Bimari.* Absence on the ground of illness was over looked for three turns of guard (*chauki*), but after that period all pay was stopped, and a medical certificate *(bimari-namah*) from a physician was demanded (B.M. 1641, fol. 39a, 58a). The rule is somewhat differently stated in B.M. 6599, fol. 163b.

(3) *Rukhsat.* Men who went on leave for their own business received no pay while doing no duty (B.M. 1641, fol. 41b). In another place in the same work, fol. 64b, we find a different statement. We are there told that for one month a man received half-pay; if he overstayed his leave it was reduced to one-fifth or one-tenth; and after three months' absence he was classed as an absconder. Leave on account of family rejoicings or mournings was allowed for one turn of duty; if the man were absent longer his pay was cut (B.M. 1641, fol. 39a). Again, on fol. 57b, a rule is stated of which I am not bale to understand the bearing. It seems to be that not more than two months of arrears were to be paid to a man who took leave; but whether that means the arrears due to him when he left, or the pay accruing during his absence, I cannot say.

(4) *Farari.* If, among the *Ahsham*, an absconder who had been some time in the service, left after drawing his pay in full, the amount was shown on the margin (*hasho*) of the pay-bill (*qabz*) as recoverable, and one month's pay was realized from the man's surety. If a recruit absconded after drawing money on account, the whole advance was recovered, but a present of one month's pay was allowed. If a matchlockman deserted the service of one leader to enter that of another, he was cut half a month's pay (*nim-mahah*). But, if it were found that the *mirdahah* or *sadiwal*, to whom he had gone, had induced him to desert, such officer had to pay the fine himself (B.M. 1641, fol. 64b). Pay of absconders was reckoned up to the date of the last verification, and three month's time was allowed (*idem*, fol. 57b). By the last phrase I understand that they were allowed

that time to reappear, if they chose. If they were again entertained, their rations only were passed, that is, I presume for the interval of absence (*idem*, fol. 64a).

(5) *Bartarafi*. If the discharged *mansabdar* produced a clear verification roll, he received half of the pay of his *zat* rank, and the full pay of his horsemen (*tabinan*). Matchlockmen received their pay in full up to the date of discharge (B.M. 1641, fols. 57b, 62a).

(6) *Pension*. So far as I have ascertained, there was no pension list, under that express name. No retiring allowances could be claimed as of right. When a man retired from active service, we hear sometimes of his being granted a daily or yearly allowance. Such was the case, for instance, when Nizam-ul-Mulk in Bahadur Saha's reign threw up the whole of his offices and titles, and retired into private life. But the ordinary method of providing for an old servant was to leave him till his death in undisturbed possession of his rank and jagir.

(7) *Fauti*. It seems that in the case of deaths a different rule prevailed, according to whether the death was a natural one or the man lost his life on active service. In the one case half-pay and in the other full-pay was disbursed to the heirs on the production of a certificate of heirship (*waris-namah*) attested by the *qazi*.

16
Ahsham

The *Ahsham* is the heading under which the later native writers place all connected with the army, who were neither *mansabdars, tabinan,* nor *ahadis.* I retain the heading, with one change only; I place the artillery by themselves, as of sufficient importance for separate treatment.

In the *Ain,* i, 251-254, there is a chapter headed *Piyadagan* which corresponds generally to the *Ahsham* of the later books. Under the same head as Akbar's 12,000 matchlockmen, who are the only men in the group at all entitled to be reckoned as soldiers, come the doorkeepers, the palace guards, the letter carriers and spies, the swordsmen, wrestlers, slaves, litter-bearers, carpenters, water-carriers and so forth. In the *Ain,* i, 254, there is a class of troops called *Dakhili* (extra, additional) which seems no longer to have existed in 'Alamgir's reign, at least the name has dropped out of the official manuals.

The vague word *Ahsham* is defined in the dictionary as servants, domestics, followers, attendants, retainers, a kind of militia or armed police. In the official manuals *(Dastur-ul'-Aml)* it comprehends the infantry, the *personnel* of the artillery, the artificers, and the attendants on the court. The incident of service which was common to all these men, and caused their inclusion under one head, was the fact that they were all borne direct on the imperial books, and received their pay from the imperial treasury, without the intervention of a *mansabdar.* This fact also accounts for Abul Fazl's apparently anomalous classification of the artillery as part of the Household in Book i of the *Ain,* instead of with the rest of the army in Book, ii, *Ain* 1 to 10. I have also found *Ahsham* used with three more restricted meanings : (1) The light artillery which attended the emperor's person wherever he went were called the *Ahsham*

This artillery is described by Bernier, who calls it "artillery of the stirrup" *(i.e.* rikab); (2) the word *Ahsham* is used constantly in the 18th century for the gunners of the garrison artillery; and (3) we find *Ahsham* used as a general term for petty zamindars serving in any campaign, and the half-armed militia or levies which they brought in their train. Khafi Khan, names the *daroghah-i-ahsham* separately, between the *mir atash* and the *daroghah-i-top-khanah-i-jinsi,* which would make the *Ahsham* something distinct from both the artillery generally and the light artillery.

Infantry. This arm of the service held a very inferior position and was of little or no consideration. Writing about 1760, and referring more particularly to the south, De la Flotte, 258, says that the less numerous body gave way at the first meeting, especially infantry before cavalry; "nay, seldom would 50,000 infantry stand before 20,000 cavalry". Another observer, Orme, "says the infantry consisted in a multitude of people assembled together without regard to rank or file: some with swords and targets, who could never stand the shock of a body of horse; some bearing matchlocks, which in the best of order can produce but a very uncertain fire : some armed with lances, too long or too weak to be of any service, even if ranged with the utmost regularity of discipline. Little reliance was placed on them. To keep night watches and to plunder defenceless people was their greatest service, except their being a perquisite to their commanders, who received a fixed sum for every man, and hired every man at a different and less price. In short, the infantry were more a rabble of half-armed men than anything else, being cheifly levies brought into the field by petty zamindars, or men belonging to the jungle tribes. Any Mahomedan or Rajput, who respected himself, managed somehow or other to provide himself with a mount and obtained enrolment as a cavalry soldier, who was in popular estimation a gentleman. The high figures for Infantry in each district and province, shown in volume ii of the *Ain-i-Akbari,* can only be accepted under considerable reservation. These numbers can only represent the men called on to render strictly local duty, and they must have consisted almost entirely of villagers armed with long pikes, or swords and shields, perhaps even with only an iron-bound bambu staff *(lathi).*

Bernier tells us, that the foot soldiers received the smallest pay : "and to be sure, the musketeers cut a sorry figure at the best of times, which may be said to be when squatting on the ground and resting their muskets on a kind of wooden fork which hangs to them. Even then they are terribly afraid of burning their eyes or their long heards, and above all least some *jinn,* or evil spirit, should cause the bursting of their musket. Some have twenty rupees a month some fifteen, some ten". And again, "I have said that the infantry was inconsiderable. I do not think that in the army immediately about the king the infantry can exceed 15,000, including musketeers, foot-artillery, and generally every person connected with that artillery. From this an estimate may be formed of the number of infantry in the provinces. I cannot account for the prodigiuos amount of infantry with which some people swell the armies of the Great Mogol, otherwise than by supposing that with the fighting men they confound servants, sutlers, tradesmen, and all those individuals belonging to bazars or markets, who accompany the troops. Including these followers, I can well conceive that the army immediately about the king's person, particularly when it is known that he intends to absent himself some time from his capital, may amount to two or even three hundred thousand infantry. This will not be an extravagant computation, if we bear in mind the immense quantity of tents, kitchens, baggage, furniture, and even women, usually attendant on the army"

Nagas. These bodies of so-called Hindu devotees were common in the armies of the 18th century, and I believe that to this day the Rajah of Jaipur entertains a large number of them. There was a corps of them in the Audh service from about 1752 to the end of the century. The last leader of these was Rajah Himmat Bahadur, whose name appears so frequently in our own early connection with Bundelkhand. With this exception the Mahomedans do not seem to have retained any of these *fakirs* in their employ. Anquetil Duperron "Zend Avesta", describes a body of these armed vagabonds, numbering some 3000 men, that he met in 1757 on their way to Jagannath. The three leaders marched first, a long pike in one hand and a buckler in the other. The main body was armed with swords, bows and matchlocks. Haji Mustapha, during his adventurous attempt in 1758 to reach Masulipatam via Western Bengal and Pachet, came across five thousand of these devotees on their way to the Ganges at Sagar; "they are all of them tall, stout, well-limbed min, in general stark naked, but very well armed" A description of corps of these Nagas commanded by a disciple (*chela*) of Himmat Bahadur, and then in the employ of Daulat Rao, Sendhiah, says the "Gossyes" *i.e.* Gusains or Nagas, "have always been considered good troops"

'Alighol. In the later years we find a class of troops known as *'Alighol,* who would seem to have been the equivalent of the *ghazis,* as we now style them, so frequently heard of on our Afghan frontier. Fraser defines them as "a sort of chosen light infantry of the Rohilla Patans : sometimes the term appears to be applied to other troops supposed to be used generally for desperate service". Tone, makes out the *'Alighol* to be one of the divisions of the Nezib *(Najib).*

Silah-posh. In 1799 the Jaipur Rajah had a body-guard of sixteen hundred men, armed with matchlocks and sabres, who were called the *silahposh,* no doubt from their being clad in armour.

Najib. The word means literally "noble", and Blacker, tells us they were irregular infantry, who disdained uniform and carrying a musket, their arms being a matchlock, or blunderbuss, and a sword. They disdained to stand sentry or do any fatiguing duty, considering it their only business to fight and to protect the person of their prince. Tone, says that long practice had enabled them to load with sufficient readiness, while their matchlock carried farther and infinitely truer than the firelock of those days. The Najibs was also excellent swordsmen.

With regard to the Najibs in the Nawab of Oudh's service

in 1780, Captain Thomas Williamson, tells us that they were clothed in blue vests and drawers, furnishing their own arms and ammunition (matchlock, sword, shield, bow and arrows). Their discipline was very contemptible; they answered very well for garrison duty, but could not stand the charge of cavalry, having no bayonets, while their arms were totally unfit for prompt execution. As for the Nawab's troops organized in imitation of the E. I. Company's battalions, they were, even on actual service, nothing but "food for powder". Such as had bayonets had no locks; those that had hammers to their locks, had no cock, or at any rate the flints were wanting. Such ammunition and cartridges as there were had, through damp and time, become so incorporated with the wooden pouch-blocks, that when touched the tops came off, leaving the powder and ball a fixture. A battalion of Najibs could with ease cut to atoms half a dozen of those mock regiments.

Pathabaz. The author of the *Husain Shahi* mentions, that in 1760-1 Sendhiah had several thousand *Pathahbaz*, "a word which in the idiom of the Dakhin is applied to courageous men and expert swordsmen". They received their name, no doubt, from their weapon, the *patta* or straight rapier.

Dhalait. This Hindi word meaning literally "shield bearer", I have met with in three writers. Ashob applies it to one of the three foot soldiers who followed Sad-ud-din Khan, the Mir Atash, when forced in 1738, much against his will, to accompany Nadir Shah's general of artillery into the streets of Delhi, to put the inhabitants to the sword. This *Dhalait* was sent as a messenger to carry a note to the Wazir, Qamr-ud-din Khan. The word is also found in *Tarikh-i-Alamgir*, referring to the year (1756-7); and in the *Tahmas-namah* of Miskin.

Amazons. At the end of the 18th century the Nizam at Haidarabad had two battalions of female sepoys, of one thousand each, which mounted guard in the interior of the palace, and accompanied the ladies of his family whenever they moved. They were with the Nizam during the war against the Maharattas in, 1795, and at the battle of Kurdlah did not behave worse than the rest of his army. They were dressed as our sepoys used to be, and performed the French drill with tolerable precision. The corps was called the *Zafar-pallan* or victorious battalion, and the women *gardani,* a corruption of the word "guard". The pay was five rupees a month. This Nizam seems to have had a penchant for female warriors. Moor, tells us of an Italian lady, a dancer, who so entranced him, that he conferred on her a title and placed a battalion under her command. She now learnt the manual exercise and evidently took her military position. Soon afterwards a foreign male dancer arrived, and the lady was directed to appear in a *pas de deux.* Full of her new dignity, she objected; and as the Nizam insisted, she resigned her command and retired to Poona.

Sihbandi. This was the name for the armed men entertained by local officers when engaged in collecting the land revenue. Colonel Sir R.C. Temple in an article on the Andaman Sibandi Corps, suggests that this word found its way into Anglo-Indian use from Madras, and that originally it was unknown in Northern India. This opinion seems untenable. The word is also used for local levies by Danishmand Khan, *Bahadur Shah-namah.* Or we may go still farther back, to the year (1526), when we find it applied by Babar to the Indian levies of Ibrahim Lodi.

Barqandaz. This name (literally *barq,* lightening, *andaz,* thrower), which came to be the commonest name of a foot soldier using a musket, appears rarely, if at all, in earlier writings, unless as a mere metaphor. An early use of it as a name for a matchlock man is found in *Ahwal-i-khawadqin.*

Matchlockmen, Rates of pay. The following table shows the rates of pay for the various classes of the matchlockmen; it may be presumed, perhaps, that the mounted men were in the position of officers, or were perhaps what we should call mounted infantry. First we have the pay of the regular matchlockmen *(Banduqchi-i-jangi* or *Tufang-chi)* who were either Baksariyahs or Bundelahs. Of these some drew rates of pay specially fixed, and entered in the official diary at the time when they were entertained (*hukmi*). The usual rates, which every one else got, were as follows :

Class	*Rank*	*Qadimi (Old)*	*Jadidi (New)*	
Suwar, (mounted).	*Hazari Duaspah* (two horsed).	Rs. 45, 40, 32	Rs. 40, 35	
	Id. *Yakaspah* (one horsed).	Rs. 22, 20, 17½	Rs. 20, 17½	
Piyadah, (foot).	*Sadi-wal.*	Rs. 9	Rs. 8	Cash Rs. 6, and conditional *Jagir,* 8 annas.
	Mirdahah.	Rs. 8	Rs. 7	
	Sair (the rest).	Rs. 6, 5½, 5	Rs. 6½	

Akbar's rates for these men, *Ain*, i, 116, work out as follows:

Class	*1st Grade*	*2nd Grade*	*3rd Grade*	*4th Grade*	*5th Grade*
Mirdahahs	Rs. 7½	Rs. 7	Rs. 6½	Rs. 6½	
	1st 2nd 3rd	1st 2nd 3rd	1st 2nd 3rd	1st 2nd 3rd	1st 2nd 3rd
Others Rs.	6 1/4 6 5 3/5	5½ 5 1/4 5	4 3/5 4½ 4 1/4	4 3 1/4 3 1/2	3 1/4 3 2 1/4

The later rates for the *Mirdahahs* would thus appear to have been a little higher than those first fixed; those for the common soldiers, on the whole, much higher.

There are some words which occur in the above which call for some explanation :

Baksariyah is a curious word, and suggests to us at its origin the town of Baksar on the Ganges in the Bhojpur country. The region is one which still supplies from its Rajput and Bhuinhar clans the stalwart clubmen of the zamindars in Bengal proper, the door-keepers of private houses in Calcutta, and many of the finest sepoys in our Hindustani regiments. Bhojpur shared with Audh the supply of men to our native army in Bengal from its earliest to its latest days, that is, from the middle of the 18th to the middle of the 19th century. That these men crowded to our standards, as soon as the Company began to raise an army, was due, no doubt, to their having already been accustomed, for generations, to serve as matchlockmen and gunners in the army of our predecessors, the Moghuls. When in 1756 Calcutta was threatened by Siraj-ud-Daulah and preparations for defence were made, we find that "the number of Buxeries" (*i.e.* Baksariyahs), "or Indian matchlockmen, was therefore augmented to 1500". (Orme, Mil. Trans., ii, 59). See also the Glossary prefixed to an Address to the Proprietors of East India Stock (J. Z. Holwell's *India Tracts,* 3^d^ ed. 1774),— "*Bucksérrias*—foot soldiers whose common arms are sword and target only".

The connection between the Baksariyahs of the army and the town of Baksar in Bahar was evidently a matter of common belief and acceptance. In the *Chahar Gulshan* of Rae Chatarman (my copy, fol. 127b), written in 1178 H. (1759), in the itinerary from Rae Bareli to Patnah, when the author comes to Baksar, he adds "original home-country of the Baksariyahs" (*asl watn-i-Baksariyah-ha*). It is strange that they should have been known by the name of the town rather than by that of the subdivision of the country, that is, parganah Bhojpur, sirkar Ruhtas, Subah Bahar (*Ain,* ii, 157). We call the nowadays Bhojpuris and not Baksariyah. In the historians belonging to the 18th century, I find that the men of the garrison artillery are usually designated Baksariyah.

Bandelahs. Bundelahs are, of course, the Rajput clan whose home is in the country south of the Jamnah and east of the Betwah river (J. Rennell, "Memoir of a Map...", p. 234, but for the northern limit read *Jamnah* instead of *Ganges*). Their appearance in this list shows that originally they were held to be an inferior class of troops, and employed principally as matchlockmen. They were always renowned, howerver, for their bravery. In the end, through the rise of the Orchhah rajah, the head of their clan, and that of the so-called Dhangya State, formed by Champat Rae and extended by his more famous son, Chattarsal, their position was much enhanced, and during the 18th century they played an extremely prominent part, fighting first on the side of the Moghuls and subsequently against them.

Arabs. In later times, in the Dakhin at any rate, the best infantry were held to be the Arabs, who received higher pay than others. They received Rs. 12 a mouth, while the lowest pay was only Rs. 5 a mouth. The Arabs were in general fully to be depended on, but particularly so in the defence of walls (Blacker, "War", 21).

Other classes under this general head of *Ahsham* were Bhilah, Mewati, Karnataki, Mughal (B.M,. 1641, fol. 59b, 60a). For a mention of Bhilah and Karnataki in 1133 H. (1721), see Khushhal Chand, Berlin Ms. 495, fol. 1013b.

The *golandaz* (*golah*, ball, *andaz*, thrower) or artilleryman, the *Degandaz* (*deg*, pot, *andaz*, thrower) and the *Bandar* (*ban*, rocket, *dar*, holder) are included in this section, but I have classed them under the head of Artillery. In one battle, that against Abdullah Khan, Khushhal Chand, Berlin Ms. 495, fol. 1013b, speaks of certain men immediately around the emperor's elephant as *qurqchis*, there being two kinds, those in yellow and those in red. The word, an unusual one in Indian works, is defined by Steingass as "a gamekeeper, a sentinel over the women's apartments".

Bhilah. These were men of the wild tribe whose home is in the rugged country between Ajmer and Gujarat. They are described by an 18th century writer, (Anand Ram, Mukhlis, *Mirat-ul-Istilah*, fol. 184b) as being in their own country nothing but highway robbers and skilful hunters, wearing clothes mostly of leaves. Their principal weapon, which no doubt they brought with them when in the emperor's service, was the long bow of bambu called *kamanth*, which has been already described (p. 95).

Mewati. These men are further designated *Tir-andaz* (archers, lit. "arrow throwers"). Mewat is the hilly country south and west of the Jamnah, between Agrah and Delhi (J. Rennell, "Memoir, cxx). It derives its name from the tribe inhabiting it, the Meos. In the *Ayn*, i, 252, the men from Mewat are called Mewrahs, and they are described as post-runners and spies. Neither the name nor these duties seem to have belonged to the Mewatis in the 18th century; though *mewrah* had survived as a name for a post-runner of any kind. From Mewat, the name of the country, comes the word Mewati, an inhabitant of Mewat. They are now Mahomedans and were famed, until our time, for their turbulence. Their depredations made the imperial highway from Agrah to Delhi, via Mathura, at all times unsafe; and it was necessary to travel in large parties, or to hire armed men, who were probably themselves Mewatis, on the principle of setting a thief to catch a thief. A good description of the state of things about 1710 will be seen in Yar Muhammad's *Dastur-ul-Insha,* p. 130, 131. The E. I. Company's envoy, Mr. John Surman, who travelled this way to Court in June 1715, mentions in his diary that at Agrah they were forced to hire an armed guard for their protection (Orme Collections, p. 1694, under date of June 8th).

Karnataki. These must have been men from the south of India, the word Karnatak by the Moghul usage applying to the whole of peninsular India south of the Tungah-bhadra, except Adoni (J. Rennell, "Memoir" (Peninsula), 20). I suppose these men in the Moghul army were of the same class as those who formed our first sepoy battalions in the south of India. In Northern India, which they reached in 1757 as part of Clive's force sent for the relief of Calcutta, they were known as Talingahs, that is, men of the Talagu country; and *Talingah* is still the common village word in Hindustan for a sepoy in one of our regiments. De la Flotte, 258, who served in South India from 1758 to 1760, says the infantry (no doubt the same men as these Karnatakis) carried on their heads a bundle of rice and their cooking utensils, their women carrying the husband's sword and other arms. Those were a very long and heavy matchlock called *kaitoke* (*ante,* p. 107). The whole family followed.

Kala Piyadah. Kamwar Khan (Ms. of the Royal Asiatic Society, Morley's Catalogue No. 97) when speaking of the army led against Nizam-ul-Mulk by Mubariz Khan, *subahdar* of Haidarabad, says there were in it 30,000 matchlockmen of the Dakhin known as *Kala piyadah,* (lit. "black foot-soldiers"). These if not identical with, must have been very similar to the Karnataki.

Rawat. This is a name which in Northern India indicates generally any respectable Hindu landholder who is not of very high caste. Mahomedan writers not infrequently apply it to the general body of Mahrattah soldiery, most of whom were of the *kumbi* caste, for which such an epithet would be appropriate. It is applied in this sense by the author of the *Husain-shahi* to 12,000 men, who served in Sendhiah (Scindiah) Patel's army during the campaign ending in the battle of Panipat (1760-1761).

Bargi. Another general name used by some writers, when speaking of the Mahrattah soldiery, is *Bargi.* See *Maasirul-umard,* iii, 740, line 17, and J. Shakespear "Dict." 319; its use is also referred to in Grant Duff, 37. I do not know the etymology of this word.

Mughal. As to these men I can suggest no reason for their appearance in this list of men serving in the infantry, but it is curious to find that there were any Mughals, who would deign to serve in this inferior branch of the service.

Farangi. These must have been Europeans serving in the capacity of common soldiers. They were probably for the most part native Christians, or so-called Portuguese, either from Goa, or from the colonies of that nation settled about the mouth of the Ganges and Brahmputra. There may have been among them some fugitive sailors from ships lying at Surat or Cambay. More usually, however, such men entered the artillery. Ashob, fol. 266a, informs us that in 1739 there were still Franks in the Mughal service. They were all Frenchmen, either attached to the artillery or practising as surgeons, bone-setters (*shikastah-band*), or physicians. The chief of them, Farangi Khan and Farashish Khan, were accounted nobles and drew nobles' pay. These Europeans lived in a special quarter called Farangipurah just outside the Kabul gate, close under the hill Kali Pahar. They killed some of Nadir Shah's provosts (*nasaqchi*) and in retaliation the colony was wiped out.

Pay. They pay of the classes above enumerated is given as follows (B.M. 1641, fol. 59b, 60a). The word *sair,* which I would render "Private soldier", will be found used in that sense in the Institutes of Taimur, Davy and White, 232, "common soldiers".

Name	Mounted (Suwar)		Foot (Piyadah			Remarks
	Hazari Duaspah	Sadiwal Yakaspah	Sadiwal	Mirdahah	Sair	
	Rs.	Rs.	Rs.	R. a. p.	R. a. p.	
Bhilah	52	26	10	8 12 0	6 4 0	Formerly they received rations, but no pay in cash. Receiving rations. Without rations.
Mewati	50	25	—	4 8 0	4 0 0	
"	—	—	8	6 0 0	5 0 0	
Karnataki	50	25	8	7 0 0	5 0 0	
				6 0 0	4 8 0	
Mughul	—	—	—	8 0 0	7 0 0	
					6 8 0	
Farangi	—	According to order	8	6 4 0	6 0 0	
					5 12 0	
					5 8 0	
					5 4 0	

Name		Class		Remarks
Persian	*English*	*Suwar Yakaspah*	*Piyadah*	
Kahardah Turani	—	Rs. 40	Rs. 14, 11, 7	
" Hindustani	—	(as ordered)	Rs. 8, 7, 6, 5½	
	—	(as ordered)	Rs. 15	
Najjar	Carpenters	(as ordered)	Rs. 8, 7, 5	
Basali	—	—	Rs. 10	An armourer? Steing. 187, Basal, aniron helmet. *Musufi* (double?) Rs. 9½
Ahangar	Blacksmiths	—	Rs. 6½, 6 1/4, 6	
Dhunch	Cotton-carders	—	Rs. 6	
Badaha	—	—	Rs. 6, 5	
Sahalki	—	—	Rs. 8, 7	
Khor bakliyah	—	—	Qadim, Rs. 9 Usual, Rs. 8, 7	*Baheliyah*, a bird snarer?
Sang-tarash	Stone masons	—	Rs. 8, 7, 6	
Mochi	Leather workers	—	Rs. 8	
Atashbaz	Firework makers	—	Rs. 7, 6, 5	
Kharati	Turners	—	Rs. 7	
Arah-kash	Sawyers	—	Rs. 6	
Beldar	Diggers	—	(blank)	
Naqb-kun	Miners	Rs. 20, 17	Rs. 4 3/4, 4½, 4	
Tabrdar	Axemen	—	Mirdahah, Rs. 5½ Private, Rs. 4 1/4	
Salotri	Farriers	Rs. 15	—	

Bernier, 217, gives the pay of foot soldiers at Rs. 20, 15, and 10 a month, and the pay of Farangis as Rs. 22 a month. Rations, when issued to the above men, were as follows : Flour (*arad*), 1.1/4 sir, Split peas (*dal*) 3/4 sir, Salt (*namak*) 3/4 of *dam*, ghi (*roghani-i-zard*), 2 *dams*.

Artificers, or other men classed under Infantry. Of these there were a number, artisans and labourers, who can scarcely be designated soldiers at all; they were really camp-followers, though they may possibly have carried some sort of weapons for their own protection, just as we furnish litter-bearers with swords when on active service. The *Beldars* were used to make difficult roads passable (Horn, 24, "*Alamgir-namah,* 653); they also threw up the fieldworks usually made to protect the guns. One duty of the carpenters and axemen was to cut a road through the thorny jungle with which most petty strongholds were surrounded. The use of some of the others, as bearing on the service of the army, are obvious enough; others, less so. Dr. Horn, 24, seems to translate *beldar* by "beiltrager", a word meaning, I believe, an axeman. But *bel* is a spade, hoe, or mattock, and a *beldar* is a digger up of earth, an excavator, not an axeman.

The following table gives the names and pay of some of these artificers (B.M., 1641, fol. 60b). Many of the words I am unable to make out.

17
The Different Branches of the Service

Although in writing this essay I think it better to retain the divisions of the original authorities, who distribute the army into *mansabdars* (with their *tabinan*), *ahadis,* and *ahsham*' it is quite true that, as Dr. Horn says, p. 11, the Moghul army consisted of cavalry, infantry, and artillery. But the second and third branches held a very subordinate position towards the first. The army was essentially an army of horsemen. The Moghuls from beyond the Oxus were accustomed to fight on horseback only; the foot-soldier they despised; and in artillery they never became very proficient. Until the middle of the eighteenth century, when the French and English had demonstrated the vast superiority of disciplined infantry, the Indian foot-soldier was little more than a night-watchman, and guardian over baggage, either in camp or on the line of march. Under the Moghuls, as Orme justly says "Hist. Frag.," 4to, p. 418, the strain of all war rested upon the numbers and goodness of the horse which were found in an army. Their preference for hand to hand fighting and cavalry charges in well illustrated by the remarks attributed to Prince Azam Shah in 1707 by Bhim Sen, *Nuskhah-i-dilkusha,* fol. 162a, that "to fight with artillery was a stripling's pastime, the only true weapon was the sword."

There was no division into regiments. Single troopers, as we have already said, enlisted under the banner of some man a little richer or better known than themselves. These inferior leaders again joined greater commanders, and thus, by successive aggregations of groups, a great noble's division was gathered together. But from the highest to the lowest rank, the officer or soldier looked first to his immediate leader and followed his fortunes, studying his interests rather than those of the army as a whole.[1] It was not till quite the end of the period that, under the influence of European example, and also partly in imitation of the Persian invaders, it became usual for the great nobles to raise and equip at their own expense whole regiments without the intervention of petty chiefs. In Audh, Safdar Jang and Shuja-ud-Daulah had such regiments, as, for instance, the *Qizzilbash,* the *Sher-bachah,* and others, which were all clad alike, and apparently were mounted and equipped by the Nawab himself.

When Akbar first introduced the *mansab* system, which ranked his officers according to the number of men supposed to be under the command of each, these figures had possibly some connection with the number of men present under those officers' orders, and actually serving in the army (Horn, 39). But it is tolerably certain that this connection between the two things did not endure very long : it was, I should say, quite at an end by the reign of Shahjahan (1627-58). Indeed, if the totals of all the personal (*zat*) *mansabs* in existence at one time were added together, we should arrive at so huge an army that it would have been impossible for the country, however heavily taxed, to meet such an expense. If paid in cash, the army would have absorbed all the revenue; if paid by assignments, all the land revenue would have gone direct into the hands of the soldiery, leaving next to nothing to maintain the Court or meet the expenses of the other branches of the government. The inference I wish to draw is, that from the grant of rank it does not follow that the soldiers implied by such rank were really added to the army. The system required that a man's rank should be stated in terms of so many soldiers; but there is abundant testimony in the later historians that *mansab* and the number of men in the ranks of the army had ceased to have any close correspondence.

Thus it seems to me a hopeless task to attempt, as Dr. Horn does, p. 36, following Blockhmann (*Ain,* i, 244-7), to build up the total strength of the army from the figures giving the personal (*zat*) rank of the officers (*mansabdars*). The difficulty would still exist, even if we had sufficiently reliable accounts of the number of such officers on the list at any one time. For we must remember that the number of men kept up by any officer was incessantly varying. On a compaign, or on active employment in one of the provinces, either as its governor or in a subordinate position, an officer kept up a large force, generally as many as, if not more than, he could find pay for. On the other hand, while attached to the Court at Delhi, his chief or only duty might be to attend the emperor's public audience twice a day (a duty which was very sharply enforced), and take his turn in mounting guard at the palace. For duties of this sort a much smaller number of men would suffice. If we reckoned the number of men in the *suwar* rank, for whom allowances at so much per man were given by the State to the *mansabdar,* we might obtain a safer estimate of the probable strength of the army. But for this also materials fail, and in spite of musterings and brandings, we may safely assume that very few *mansabdars* kept up at full strength even the quota of horseman (*tabinan*) for which they received separate pay. In these matters the difference between one noble and another was very great. While one man maintained his troops at their full number, all efficiently mounted and equipped, another would evade the duty altogether. As, for instance, one write, Khushhal Chand, in his *Nadir-uz-zamani* (B. M. Or. 1844, fol. 140a) says : Lutfullah Khan Sadiq, although he held the rank of 7,000, "never entertained even seven asses, much less horses or riders on horses." In Muhammad Shah's reign he lived quietly at home at Panipat, 30 or 40 miles from Delhi, his attention engrossed by his efforts to get hold of all the land for many miles round that town, and passing his days, in spite of his great nominal rank, like a mere villager.

It seems to me equally hopeless to attempt a reconstruction of the force actually present at any particular battle by adding together the numerical rank held by the commanders who were at that battle. This Dr. Horn has tried to do on p. 67, without feeling satisfied with the results. But, as far as I can see, there was little, if any, connection between the two matters. The truth is that, like all things in Oriental countries, there existed no rules which were not broken in practice. A man of high rank would, no doubt, be selected for the command of a division. But it was quite an accident whether that division had more or fewer men in it than the number in his nominal rank. The strength of division depended upon the total number of men available, and the extent of the contingents brought into the field by such subordinate leaders as might be put under the orders of its commander. It was altogether a matter of accident whether the number of men present corresponded or not to the rank of the commanders.

Bernier, 43, has an excellent remark on the vague way that numbers were dealt with by historians : "Camp-followers and bazar-dealers...I suspect, are often included in the number of combatants." Again, on p. 380, he seems to come to the conclusion that it would be a fair estimate to take the fighting men at about one-third of the total numbers in a Moghul camp. I have seen somewhere (I have lost the reference, but I think it was in Khafi Khan) an admission that the gross number of a so-called "fauj" (army) was always reckoned as including no more than one-third or one-fourth that number of fighting men. I give below, for what it is worth, a tabular summary of Dr. Horn's figures (pp. 39-45).

ESTIMATED NUMBERS OF MOGHUL ARMY

Period	*Cavalry*	*Matchlockmen and Infantry*	*Artillery-men*	*Authority*
Akbar	12,000	12,000	1000	Blochmann, i, 246.
Do.	384,758	3,877,557	-	*Ain-i-Akbari.**
Shahjahan	200,000	40,000	-	*Badshahmamah*, ii, 715; *Ain*, I, 244.
Aurangzeb	240,000	15,000	-	Bernier.
Do.	300,000	600,000	-	Catrou.
Mhd. Shah	200,000	800,000		*Tarikh-i-Hindi* of Rustam Ali'.

*These include all the milita levies and zamindar's retainers throughout the provinces, besides the army proper.

NUMBERS PRESENT ON PARTICULAR OCCASIONS

Name of Battle or Commander	Number of Imperialists				Number of Enemy				Authority
	Cavalry	Infantry	Artillery	Elephants	Cavalry	Infantry	Artillery	Elephants	
Sarkhej...	10,000	—	—	100	40,000	100,000	—	—	*Akbarnamah*, iii, 424
Under Khan Azim...	10,000	—	—	—	30,000	—	—	—	*Id.* iii, 593.
Under Khan Khanan	1200	—	—	—	5000	—	—	—	*Id.* iii, 603.
Sadiq Khan...	3000	—		—	8000	—	—	80	*Id.* iii, 714.
Qandahar (1061 H)....	50,000	10,000	—	10	—	—	—	—	Elliot, vii, 99.
Jahangir (1016 H)...	12,500	2000	—	60	—	—	—	—	*Id.* vi, 318.
Ahmad Abdali (1174 H.)...	60,000	20,000	—	—	—	—	—	—	—

18
Mughal Naval Organisation

Babar and Humayun used boats in their wars against the Afghans in the Eastern provinces, although none of them could develop a naval organisation or a naval force as such. Of course it is to be admitted that none of them felt the necessity of building up a naval fleet as a special branch of armament. It was due to strategic necessity that Babar impressed into his service a large number of boats which constituted a fitting reply to the numerous war-boats of the Afghan rebels of the Eastern provinces.

Balban and Firuz Tughluq did the same thing while marching upon the Eastern provinces. But while Balban and Firuz Tughluq utilised the fleet as an auxiliary to the land army, Babar carried his entire army in his boats. Again there is no mention of fire-arms carried by the fleet of Balban and Firuz-Tughluq. But the fleet of Babar and Humayun was furnished with guns along with other war instruments. Babar and Humayun, however, laid the foundation of the Mughal navy which took a definite shape in the time of Akbar.

Akbar's conquest of Gujarat in 1573 A.D. pushed his western frontier to the sea and brought him into contact with the Portuguese. Gujarat at that time was a rich emporium of commerce between India, Turkey, Syria, Persia and the countries of Europe and therefore very wealthy.

Moreover, Gujarat lay on the way to Mecca and Akbar therefore was anxious to bring it under his control. It was at Gujarat that the emperor saw the strength of the Portuguese naval squadron. Like Gujarat, other ports on the western coast like Cambay, Surat and Sarnal were noted for trade and commerce. The conquest of Gujarat opened the emperor's eyes to the vast prospect of revenue from trade and commerce. Moreover, he was interested in providing a safe conduct for the Mecca pilgrims.

But Akbar was quite aware of the fact that shipping on the western coast was dependent on the goodwill of the Portuguese.[1] Although the emperor courted friendship with the Portugese who were afraid of the irresistible landforce of the emperor. He made serious efforts in building a naval force on the western coast.

With the extension of the Mughal frontiers to the Eastern provinces by the second half of the 16th century and the consequent hostilities with the local rulers who were strong in naval power, it became incumbent upon the Mughal Government to create a powerful fleet and organise a naval force. Moreover, a naval establishment on a permanent basis in that region was necessitated, from the side of the Mughals, by the depredations of the Magh and Feringhi sea-rovers as well as of the Ahoms who used to come often by the numerous water-routes and hence constituted a serious menace to Mughal rule in the Eastern provinces and particularly in Bengal. Like the Sultans of Bengal in the preceding epoch, the Mughals also experienced great difficulty in extending their imperial sway over the whole of Bengal due to physical factors.

"The cavalry, hitherto the mainstay of the Mughal army, proved practically useless in traversing the numerous rivers and streams of South-eastern Bengal...Above all, the Mughals (in their initial stage of conquest in Bengal) were weak in war-boats, the only effective instrument of war in Bengal and weaker still in trained soldiers and they had to depend on the war-boats of their allies and vassal zamindars."[2] Moreover, prolonged rains and floods in the rivers made it absolutely impossible for any military campaign without a strong fleet.

A department of admiralty was considered very useful by Akbar for the benefit of the country in general as it furnished means of obtaining things of value, provided for agriculture and the emperor's household. Hence the Mughal Government under Akbar gave a great impetus of Indian shipping and as a matter of fact an imperial naval establishment was founded. The department came to be known as 'Nawara'. Akbar looked upon "promoting the efficiency of this department as an act of divine worship."[3]

For the first time, Akbar framed a set of elaborate regulations for the organisation of the department of Admiralty or the office of the 'Meer Bahar' ('Amir-ul-Bahar') as it came to be called.

Akbar's admiralty had, broadly speaking, four functions to perform.[4]

The first duty was to fit out strong boats for the purpose of navigation, transportation of elephants and conveyance of merchandise. Some boats were to be built in such a manner as to be of use in sieges and for the conquest of strong forts. The officers were to "look upon the ships as if they were houses and dromedaries and use them as excellent means of conquest."[5]

The second duty of the admiralty was "to appoint experienced seamen acquainted with the tides, the depths of the ocean, the time when the several winds blow and their advantages and disadvantages. They must be familiar with shallows and banks. Besides, a seaman must be hale and strong, a good swimmer, kind hearted, hard-working, capable of bearing fatigue, patient; in fact, he must possess all good qualities."[6] Men of such character could only be found after much trouble. The seamen for the Mughal navy came from Malabar and Bengal.

The third duty was to appoint experienced, impressive and fearless men with loud voices to look after the rivers, to settle the ferries and to provide the travellers with boats. Abul Fazl writes, "As he possesses experience, he settles every difficulty which arises regarding foods, and takes care that such places are not overcrowded, or too narrow or very un-even or full of mud. He regulates the number of passengers which a ferry may carry; he must not allow travellers to be delayed and sees that poor people are passed over gratis. He ought not to allow people to swim across or wares to be deposited anywhere else but at fording places. He should also prevent people from crossing at night unless in cases of necessity."[7]

The fourth duty was in regard to the imposition, realisation and remission of custom duties. "He (Emperor) wished that boatmen should get their wages."

The vessels were built of various sizes and the number of sailors in a vessel varied according to the size. In large ships there were officers and men of the following titles and description.

(1) The 'Nakhuda' or the captain of the vessel, Abul Fazl calls him the owner of the vessel. He directed the course of the ship.

(2) The 'Muallim' or the mate. Abul Fazl calls him the captain. He must be acquainted with the depths and shallow places of the ocean and must know astronomy. It was he who guided the ship to its destination and prevented her falling into danger.

(3) The 'Tandil' or the chief of the 'Khalasis' or Sailors. Possibly his duty was to recruit Khalasis and to look after their discipline and well-being.

(4) The 'Nakhuda-Khashab' whose duty it was to supply the passengers with fire-wood and straw and to assist in loading and un-loading the cargo.

(5) The 'Sarhang' whose duty was to supervise the docking and landing of the ship and he often acted for the 'Muallim'.

(6) The 'Bhandari' was in charge of stores.

(7) The 'Keranee' or the ship's clerk who kept the accounts of the ship and served out water to the passengers.

(8) The 'Sukhangeer' or helmsman. He steered the ship according to the orders of the 'Muallim'. Some ships carried several helmsmen but never more than twenty.

(9) The 'Panjaree' whose duty it was to look out from the top of the mast and to give notice when he saw land or a ship or a coming storm. In the English navy during

the days of Elizabeth we find the same thing. A barrel was fixed at the mast-head of a man-of-war as a shelter for the lookout-man. It was called 'crow's nest'. Little boys with sharp eyes were put on the mast-head to give warning when they happened to come across any ship, land or storm.

(10) The 'Gumtee'. He belonged to the class of Khalasis. He threw out the water which had leaked through the ship.

(11) The 'Top-andaz' or gunners were required in naval fights and their number depended on the size of the ship.

(12) The 'Karwa' or common sailors. Their duty was to set and furl and sails. Some of them also performed the duty of divers and stopped leaks or set free the anchor when it sticked fast.

In their earnestness to have a strong fleet, the Central Government took all possible care to keep the harbours in excellent condition, to appoint hard-warking and experienced seamen and to look after their well-being. Emperor Akbar set down the rules regulating the wages of the seamen which of course varied from region to region depended on the course of the voyage or 'Kush' as the seamen called it. For instance, in the harbour of Satgaon (Hughli) a 'Nakhuda' used to get rupees four hundred per month as his salary; besides he was allowed four 'malikhs' or cabins which he filled with merchandise for his own profit. The Muallim used to draw rupees two hundred and two 'malikhs'; the Tandil rupees one hundred and twenty; the Keranee rupees fifty and one 'malikh'; the Nakhuda Khashab rupees thirty; the Sarhand rupees twentyfive; the Sukhangeer, the Panjari and Bhandari, each rupees fifteen; each Kharwa or common sailor rupees forty and his daily food in addition; the Top-andaz or gunner rupees twelve.[8]

In Cambay, a Nakhuda used to get rupees eight hundred and the other men in the same proportion. In Lahari, a Nakhuda used to get rupees three hundred and the rest in proportion. The boatmen on rivers got wages varying from rupees one hundred to five-hundred per month.[9]

The Mughal Government had to incur heavy expenses for building vessels and maintaining the naval establishment. The Mughal flotilla at the time it was established by Akbar, consisted of 3000 vessels of various sizes. Besides a large number of boats were furnished by the vassal allies and landlords. The flotilla was principally stationed at Gujarat and Surat on the western coast and at Dacca in the east as their headquarters. Under the jurisdiction of the admiralty of Dacca was placed the whole coast from Mundelghat, near the confluence of the Damodor and the Rupnarayan rivers to the coast of Balasore to the west and the whole of the Brahmaputra and the Meghna coasts to the east.

Understandably, the naval defensive measures involved a huge expense. "In fact", writes Grant, "the ordinary established rental of the whole country was then almost absorbed actually or fraudulently in jagirs in protecting the sea coasts from the ravages of the Arakanese aided by the Portuguese".[10] The flotilla was maintained not only for defence but also for the purpose of offence. A large number of boats had to be built, a huge number of personnel to be impressed into service and naturally huge expenses had to be incurred.

Raja Man Singh as Mughal governor of Bengal, considerably increased the revenue of Bengal by conquering the maritime region of Bhati (Lower Bengal) near the mouth of the Ganges and by levying a tribute from Raja Lakshminarayan of Kuch Behar. This did not, however, augment the public income as the gains achieved were absorbed in maintaining a huge flotilla. It was during Man Singh's viceroyalty that we find a remarkable ourburst of naval activity in eastern Bengal in which the Mughals and the local independent landlords played an equal part.

Regarding the details relating to the financial aspect of the naval establishment, we have to refer to the abstract of the 'Ausil Toomar Jumma' (original-established revenue) of Bengal as settled about the year 1582 by Raja Todar Mal. The whole expenses of maintaining the 768 armed cruisers and other boats of the imperial 'nawara' stationed at Dacca including the wages of 923 Portuguese sailors "was estimated monthly at Rs. 29,282 which with constructing new vessels and repairing the old amounted annually to Rs. 8,43,452 levied altogether from 112 entire or broken parganahs chiefly in the 'chakla' of Jahangirnagar (Dacca) and composed a great part of the richest and most productive lands of the great province...".[11] On this account, a large amount was also raised from Sylhet. The jagirs that were assigned in the Dacca district for the support of the imperial flotilla were computed to comprise 1/8th of its whole extent.

Besides the vessels built and maintained by the Mughals in Bengal, the landlords of the province also supplied their boats to the imperial 'nawar' whenever called upon to do so and in return they were assigned lands under the head, 'Omleh Nawara'.

For the support of the 'nawara', another source of revenue was derived from a tax called 'Meer Baree' levied on the building of boats varying from eight annas to one rupee and four annas according to the size of the vessels. This tax was realised from all boats arriving at or leaving the naval headquarters "whose crews were not residents of the district".[12] It is to be noted that the tax 'Meer-Baree' thus collected was entirely spent on the naval establishment. As regards the river-tolls, Abul Fazl writes, "for every boat, 1 R. per kos at the rate of 1000 'mans', provided the boat and the men belong to one and the same owner. But if the boat belong to another man and everything in the boat to the man who has hired it, the tax is 1 R. for every 2 1/3 kos. At ferry places, an elephant has to pay 10d. for crossing; a laden cart 4d; do empty 2d; a laden camel 1d; empty camels, horses, cattle with their thing ½ d; do empty ¼d. Other beasts of burden pay 1/10d. which includes the toll due by the river...The rule is that one-half or one-third of the tolls thus collected go to the state (the other half goes to the boatmen)".[13] Throughout the reign of Akbar, the 'nawara-jagirs' and river-tolls (Meer-Baree) constituted the principal sources of income for maintaining the naval establishment. During the reign of the succeeding emperors, other sources like customs collected from the Europeans were also utilised for the same purpose.

Although boats and ships were collected from many places, it was nowhere other than in Bengal, Kashmir, Massulipatam and Sind that sea-going war-vessels of superior quality were built. After the conquest of Gujarat, Akbar appointed one Mir-Saman to supervise the construction of boats of various sizes. Mir Saman was entrusted with the task of recruiting expert shipwrights. Along the coast of the ocean, in the West, South and East, large ships were built suitable for long voyages. Each of them carried some times 1,700 men on board. These ships sailed for purpose of trade and pilgrimage to Mecca and Jeddah in the month of January returning in September or October. Also long voyages were made to Arakan, Pegu and Tenasarim. But possibly voyages to Mecca for pilgrimage were forbidden by Akbar's famous decree of 1579.

From countries abroad, Akbar imported many carpenters and artificers and got constructed war-vessels and pleasure-boats at Lahore and Allahabad.[14] But these boats seldom came to Bengal. When Akbar came to Bihar to suppress Daud Karrani in 1574, he brought along with him numerous boats built at Lahore and Allahabad. Mostly the boats that were built in Bengal were used in Bengal. A large variety of vessels were built and stationed at Dacca. The Emperor "had the sterns of the boats made in shapes of wonderful animals and thus combined terror with amusement." Like his father, Akbar had a special fancy for floating markets and floating gardens. During his voyage of Bengal (1574) two large vessels were appropriated for the residence of the Emperor himself and they were followed by a great fleet carrying the high officials with necessary equipments and baggage of every kind. Even "gardens such as clever craftsmen could not make on land" were built on some of the boats.[15] Kasim Khan was the Emperor's chief craftsman,[16] skilled in constructing bridges of boats for the passage of the imperial army. Besides the vessels of the Mughal 'nawara' and the Emperor's personal boats, two state-barges for the use of the subahdars were always stationed at Dacca. The subahdars or viceroys were under obligation, as Akbar had imposed, to send two magnificent vessels annually to the Emperor at Agra.

The Emperor's personal boat bore a special dignity and respect and it was commanded that the provincial governors should show a befitting respect and perform an obeisance to it whenever they happened to meet it. For instance, Murshid-Kuli Khan's (of Bengal) sense of respect for the Emperor's barge was so deep that "he would not sit down in a royal boat and when in the rainy season, the Emperor's boat came from Jahangirnagar for an exhibition, he went out (from Murshidabad) to meet it and turning his face towards the seat the Emperor used to occupy, made his obeisance, presented his 'nazars' and kissed the deck of the state-boat".[17]

Did Akbar employ European sailors in his navy? We have reason to believe that he did. Europeans had earned the reputation of being good gunners and expert sailors since the days of Vasco da Gama and Indian merchants were very eager to employ European mariners in their sea-going vessels. It was at Gujarat that Akbar came into contact with the Portuguese and he was impressed by their superior seamanship. "There must have been Eupropeans serving in the capacity of common soldiers...and some fugitive sailors from ships lying at Surat or Cambay..."[18] The Emperor impressed the Portuguese "either from Goa or from the Colonies of that nation settled about the mouth of the Ganges and Brahmaputra"[19], in the naval department as craftsmen and artillerymen and thus set the precedent of appointing Europeans which was followed by his successors. The sailors were recruited from the seafaring tribes.

Akbar's Government took some steps for regulating the entry of ships into ports after the Portuguese on the western coast had tried to plunder the port of Thatta (Sind). The Tarikh-i-Tahiri records the port-regulation thus, "whenever a ship enters the creek it intimates its approach by firing a gun which is responded to by the guard-house (chowkie) by that signal, to inform the people at the port of the arrival of a strange vessel. These again instantly send word of its arrival to the merchants of Thatta and then embarking on boats repair to the place where the guard is posted. Ere they reach it, those on the look-out have already enquired into the nature of the ship. Every vessel and trader must undergo this question. All concerned in the business, now go in their boats (ghrabs) to the mouth of the creek (communicating with the port). Between the ocean and the port, there is one inhabited spot called Sui Miani. Here a guard belonging to the Mir Bandar or port-master, with a loaded piece of ordnance is always stationed. If the ship (incoming) belongs to the port it is allowed to move up and anchor under Lahori Bandar; if it belongs to some other port, it can go no further; its cargo is transpired into boats and forwarded to the city."[20]

It should be noted that the rules and regulations as framed by Akbar's Government were not rigid. The working of the Mughal naval department as well as the rules relating to the officers and sailors engaged in the 'nawara' and their wages underwent alterations during the reigns of the succeeding Emperors.

Mughal Navy After Akbar

Of the Emperors following Akbar, Aurangzeb took a keen interest in maintaining and strengthening the imperial 'nawara' both in western and eastern India. Jahangir and Shah Jahan do not appear to have taken such active interest in developing the naval department as was expected of them in the face of growing naval strength of the European maritime nations in Indian waters.

Again of the imperial viceroy posted at the imperial provinces, only Islam Khan, Mir Jumla and Shaista Khan as viceroys in Bengal, are found to have been alive to the necessity of organising and strengthening the naval force in Bengal and it is under them that the Mughal 'nawara' is seen at its best.

The maintenance of the flotilla was the work more of the provincial governors than the Emperors, because ultimately they were charged with the responsibility of preserving peace and security in the provinces, fighting out the enemies and extending the imperial frontiers. So far as the Mughal navy in eastern and western waters is concerned, neither Jahangir nor

Shah Jahan exerted themselves in making it a real fighting force and protecting the coasts.

On the contrary, the naval organisation, particularly in Bengal, showed signs of declining to a considerable extent after Islam Shah's viceroyalty (1608-13) till Aurangzeb and his capable viceroy did their best to revive it and made it fit both for defensive and offensive purposes.

Like his father, and great grand-father, Emperor Jahangir had a special fancy for pleasure trips in boats, although we are not told whether like his great grand-father, he used to take along with him any drinking party. "Everyday, I sat in a boat", Jahangir writes, "and went to hunt waterfowl and wander over the river." With a view to gaining the Emperor's favour, some Europeans 'ghrabs' (ghurabs) well decorated, were showed to him but "it does not seem likely", observes Roger "that Jahangir interested himself in foreign ships."

In the time of Emperor Shah Jahan, there was no navy worth the name. Manrique attributes the want of an efficient navy to the timidity of the Mughals.[21] However, in Shah Jahan's time, the flotilla of boats for transport purposes called 'nawara' was there and this 'nawara' was used as a fighting arm, once against the Portuguese of Hugli and again against the Ahoms in Assam.

Emperor Aurangzeb was a man of different calibre whose over-powering ambition "would not allow any earthly power to defy the Emperor's authority." Hence he took a keen interest in developing and strengthening the naval force. Certain incidents drew his attention to the problem of protecting the sea coasts both in western and eastern India.

While in Kashmir, Aurangzeb received a report that one of the imperial ships that was carrying pilgrims to Mecca had been captured by a European pirate. And unfortunately some of the pilgrims were ladies belonging to the imperial 'harem' who had been manhandled by their European captors. In the east, the Arakan flotilla had attacked the Mughal flotilla in the waters of Dacca, destroying 160 of the boats and this happened just after the Mughal disaster in Assam followed by the return and death of Mir Jumla.[22] Aurangzeb was much exasperated at these unhappy incidents and hence resolved to re-build the flotilla for the purpose of suppressing piracy in Indian waters and hence asked his Bengal viceroy to take "fitting steps in this regard." Besides, Aurangzeb was much interested in augmenting his revenue derived from customs. The sea-ports yielded him a large revenue. Among them were those of Sind, Broach, Surat, Cambay and Hughli. Surat alone brought him in about thirty lakhs of rupees annually. Also he earned huge customs from the whole coast of Coromandal, from Masulipatam and from the coast of Orissa.[23] Hence the Emperor was anxious to build up a sufficient naval strength to protect his coastal trade and commerce.

The Department at Work

Emperor Akbar laid the foundation of the Mughal naval department, as we have already seen. Further developments were made in the organisation although the details are lacking. However, the Mughal naval organisation, as we find in Eastern India, was developed considerably.

Like other departments of the Mughal government, the Naval department was placed in charge of high ranking imperial officer of integrity and having knowledge of naval warfare, called Mir Bahar. Along with Islam Khan and Mutaqid Khan, appointed viceroy and 'diwan' of Bengal respectively, Ihtimam Khan was appointed Mir Bahar of the imperial 'nawara' by Emperor Jahangir.[24] All the personal boats of the Mughal officers in Bengal were under overall control of the Mir Bahar. The personal boats of the officers furnished with cannon bore special marks for their use in times of war. Although the Mir Bahar was the chief officer of the 'nawara', he was subject to the command of the viceroy and as a matter of fact, no naval warfare could be undertaken without the latter's permission. Sometimes the land army was placed at the command of the Mir Bahar.[25] The latter was to recruit boatmen and crew and provide other equipments necessary for naval campaigns. A large number of menials were always kept in service on a permanent basis. The persons employed in the navy were paid by the chief admiral for which the latter was assigned jagirs in several parganas. The chief admiral was to supply money and other provisions to the land-troopers when demanded by the general of the army. During the Assam campaign in 1663, we find the Mir Bahar Ibn Husain despatching "six boats, two laden with gold and four with silver" to Mir Jumla, the supreme commander of the Mughal army.[26] The post of the Mir Bahar, carried high respect. When Ihtimam Khan, the Mir Bahar of the Mughal 'nawara' arrived at Akbar-nagar from Delhi, the Bengal viceroy Islam Khan and the diwan Mutaqud Khan came to the bank of the Ganges to welcome the Mir Bahar in a befitting manner.[27] The Mir Bahar used to receive a robe of honour, a sword, a special gun with the rank of 1000 'zat' (personal) and kettle-drums.[28]

It was the duty of the 'diwan' to settle the wages of the boatmen, sailors and other personnel employed in the department. Sometimes he was to accompany the troops and supply ration to the workmen engaged temporarily in the construction of bridges, mud-forts and barricades. Accountants were appointed to look into the financial matter of the naval department and to keep the accounts properly as it was subject to audit. The exact number of the accountants is not known. Along with these officers are mentioned captains, stewards (Mir Samana), 'sardars' and 'darogahs'. A group of boats was put in charge of a captain; the steward had the responsibility of inspecting the boats and keeping them in good order. The 'sardars' were to recruit sailors and other labourers in the times of campaigns. In the Baharistan we find the 'sardars' sometimes in charge of posts. Those in charge of posts were appointed on a permanent basis, while some of them were employed temporarily to assist the 'nawara' in the war-fronts. The 'darogahs' were superintendents of the boats. Their duty was never fixed.[29]

Besides the imperial fleet in charge of the chief admiral, the viceroy, other imperial officers and the vassal zamindars had their personal boats to be used in times of naval war. Although the personnel of these boats were the personal employees of the officers and zamindars concerned, in times of naval engagements, they were subject to the control of the Mir Bahar of the imperial 'nawara' and normally the viceroy was not expected to engage them without Mir Bahar's approval, but exceptions were always there. The boats were arranged into groups, each placed in charge of superintendents or captains and Mir Samana under the direct control of the chief admiral. The boats of the Zamindars' fleet were likewise grouped according to their respective strength and placed in charge of the imperial superintendents. The latter were probably deputed to prevent the desertion of the zamindars' boats. The desertion of the zamindars' boats in times of naval engagements was a normal phenomenon. Besides the superintendents, commanders were also appointed over the zamindars' boats. Of course, in most cases, they were appointed from amongst the zamindars themselves who and none else had control over their sailors and crews.[30]

For supplying provisions to the naval troopers and others engaged in war, the boats of the 'beparis' (traders) full of ration always accompanied the fleet. These boats followed the fleet but they were always kept at a safe distance from the actual war-field as they were the objects of the enemy to be plundered.[31]

The imperial flotilla was often inspected and reviewed by the Emperors and the viceroys. For instance, on the eve of departing for Bengal, on 4th July 1607 the newly appointed Mir Bahar Ihtimam Khan arranged the fleet under his command for a review by the Emperor. The Mir Bahar held a grand review of his 295 war-boats of which seventy were designed for carrying loads, properly equipped with heavy cannon and other necessary requisites. It is reported by Mirza Nathan that the artillerymen from the fleet had produced such a sound and the numerous 'mountain like boats' had created such a horror that "the crocodiles of the river (Jamuna) fled from the banks and shallows and ran to deep waters."[32] During the progress of the imperial flotilla towards the Bhati (lower Bengal), the viceroy Islam Khan often inspected and reviewed it, rewarding the naval officers for their excellent jobs and reprimanding others for negligence.

While the imperial army under the viceroy Islam Khan and the imperial fleet under Ihtimam Khan had been proceeding towards Dacca against Musa Khan (1610 A.D.), Ihtimam Khan was ordered to hold a review of the fleet on the river Ichhamati. Referring to this review, Mirza Nathan writes that as ordered by his father Ihtimam Khan, he arranged the review of the fleet in the following way, "He (Mirza Nathan) beautifully arranged the 'Katari', 'maniki' and 'bathila' boats by putting big cannon on them and made such a floating bridge as has never been done by any leader during any time. Behind it, he placed the 'kusas' of war and other boats of this type for review. After preparing the floating bridge, the big boats which contained large cannon and 'zabarzangs' (field pieces) were arrayed like battlements. On the gangway of each of these boats, he arrayed (a line of) wagons called 'thatari' and on them he arrayed a series of towers and on each of these towers a red flag was hoisted...Every boat was covered with a gold embroidered canopy. It was arranged in such a way that if it was desired to discharge the artillery, these wagons which stood like the wall of a fort on the boats extending from one side of the river of the other, could all at once be made to lie flat on the boats and when the dreadful cannon were discharged by the time their smoke disappeared, these wagons could be raised to their former position. A large number of soldiers dressed in steel uniform was posted on the aforesaid boats. Six fully equipped war-kusas were placed in front of the above mentioned (floating) bridge as 'qarawal' (vanguard). Tying those 'kusas' with the bridge by means of strong ropes, six expert men were made to board the stern of these 'kusas' with the instruction that when it was necessary to keep the bridge in straight order, they would row each of the six 'kusas' in a straight line so that the bridge might proceed in that direction. When it was necessary to turn it from the right to the left, they should stop rowing the three on the right and ply very swiftly the other three on the left so that it might turn to the right and they would row all the six equally. When it was necessary to turn the bridge from the left to the right, they should similarly stop rowing the 'kusas' of the left and put all their strength on the 'kusas' of the right. When the firing of the cannon would begin, they should take the three 'kusas' on the left to the left bank of the river and the other three to the right; and at the end of the firing, all these six must be employed in carrying the bridge. In the rear he (Mirza Nathan) arrayed all the small and large boats of the fleet...At the time of the arrival of the imperial officers (to attend at the review) Mirza Nathan ordered the ropes of the wagons to be pulled so as to make them fall flat on the gangway of the boats and he fired the cannon all at once with a wick of a lamp. The dreadful sound of the artillery resounded from land and water...No sooner did the smoke of the artillery clear up than the wagons were pulled up and were made to stand again like the wall of a fort...when the bridge (floating) approached the boat of Islam Khan...Mirza Nathan disjoined the connecting links of the bridge and placed each one of these boats of the bridge separately before Islam Khan and the imperial officers."[33] The dexterity of Mirza Nathan in building a floating bridge and his placement of the fleet in a battle array, the excellent equipment of the boats and the skill displayed in handling them excited the admiration of the viceroy and other imperial officers. Normally the viceroy, who was also the chief commander of the imperial army, used to send 'couriers' to the admirals beforehand asking them to keep the flotilla in a battle array for his inspection and he used to come on the spot on horse. After reviewing the arrangement from the bank, sometimes he used to inspect the number of sailors and crew as well as the war equipments for his personal satisfaction.

It was the duty of the admirals of the fleet, whether imperial, officers' or zamindars' to collect carpenters, blacksmiths and other menials for the repair of the boats in case of damage. Sufficient quantity of gun-powder, bundles of straw, bamboo-pikes, pieces of stones and other materials were always kept ready in the boats for the purpose of constructing bridges, mud-forts and barricades.[34]

Elephants were used in fighting. Elephants were carried on boats and for this purpose two or more boats were tied together with a platform over them which was called 'mands'.

To carry them 'biras' or a kind of raft made of wood and plaintain trees tied together called 'bir' were also used. Then there are references to 'gondolas' to carry men and horses.[35] Mirza Nathan says that in the time of the Assam campaign (during Qasim Khan's viceroyalty 1614-17) several 'gondolas' were procured from the fishermen to carry the general and others.[36] The elephants were covered with iron-jackets to protect them from the fire of the enemy. A huge number of blacksmiths were always kept employed at Dacca to make the iron-jackets for the elephants and it was the duty of the chief admiral to inspect the 'karkhanas' from time to time.

Kettle-drums, big and small were always taken in times of naval expeditions and were used in times of marching as well as in rallying the fugitives hiding in the forests and jungles adjoining the battle-field. Unlike the Portuguese sea-rovers who threw wounded or half-dead soldiers into the water, the Mughals took proper care of them. They were supplied with cooked-food, raw corn, 'bhang' and clothes. "Whoever", writes Mirza Nathan, "was addicted to intoxicating drugs was given intoxicants." Opium mixed with soup was poured down the throats of the wounded soldiers and sailors alike. "First give us some intoxicants so that we may take something" was the common reply of them when asked if they would take any food.[37]

In the time of naval war, temporary bridges were often constructed for transporting infantry serving as an auxiliary to the naval army as well as cavalry, elephants and other heavy loads. Any river, if unfordable, was crossed by a temporary bridge of boats such as are still to be found in the present days. The Mir Bahar himself was to supervise the construction work and to supply flat-bottomed boats for the purpose.[38] It seems that purely native system of making a bridge of boats suffered from one glaring defect. The native made no use of grapnels. Instead of these, they followed the tedius mode of driving stakes into the riverbed. The result was that the bridge became less secure and what might have been ready in one day took 8 or 10 days to complete.[39]

It is interesting to know how this huge Mughal naval establishment in Bengal was financed. Akbar's government worked out some procedures in this regard in a general way. So far as the imperial 'nawara' in Bengal is concerned, we find two modes of paying the persons employed in the naval department *viz.* assignments of lands and cash payments. The naval officers like the officers of the land-army were granted 'jagirs'. Here a distinction was made between the officers' personal jagir and those assigned for the maintenance of their soldiers or for such specific purposes as the up-keep of the flotilla. Mirza Nathan says, "Islam, Khan (the viceroy) was assigned as much of the territories of Ramchandra (Raja of Bakla) to him as was necessary for the maintenance of his fleet, the rest was given to the 'kroris' and jagirdar." It should be noted that the chief admiral, being in charge of the imperial navy was assigned land. Besides, as he was to maintain his personal boats to be pressed into the imperial service, further assignments were made. For instance, Ihtimam Khan, the Mir Bahar, received 22 'mahals' in Bhati and Ghoraghat as his personal jagir and several parganas of Jahanabad, Tamluk and other places in Orissa, Burdwan and Midnapur "in lieu of the salaries of his men."[40] Mirza Nathan, as an officer having his personal boats at his disposal, likewise received grants of land in several parganas. Mirza Nathan gives an interesting account about the rates of boats that the officers used to receive. Ihtimam Khan, the Mir Bahar was entitled to draw Rs. 1,200 for the each boat at his disposal. But later Islam Khan, the viceroy, reduced the rate to Rs. 400 for each boat.[41]

As a result, Ihtimam Khan had to suffer a great loss. He required one hundred and twenty thousand rupees for his three hundred boats but he was given only eighty thousand rupees. However in order to meet the remaining forty thousand rupees, he obtained the assignment of ten 'mahals' or parganas.[42]

As regards the vassal zamindars like the Raja of Chandradwipa and the Thakurtas of Banaripara who helped the Mughals in conquest and pacification, were assigned two kinds of rent free lands called 'nawara' and 'hissajat'. The 'nawara' lands were granted in order to enable the zamindars to contribute boats and sailors during the campaigns against the Maghs and the Feringhis. The 'hissajat' lands were assigned to them as reward for their personal participation in those campaigns. Dr. Wise has referred to three sanads relating to 'nawara' lands.[43] He writes "The Jangalbari family (of Isa Khan of Sonargaon) have only preserved three sanads of any importance. The one is dated 1059 A.H. (1649) and is sent by Shah Shuja (Governor of Bengal) to the mansabdars and other officials and directs them to leave the land owned by Masum and to give over to him the 'Nawara Karkhana' or dockyards which had previously been worked by the government. The other (Sanad) bears the name of Shahzadah Muhammad Azim (Governor of Bengal), better known as Azimusshan dated 44th Julus of Alamgir (1700). In it Haibat Muhammad, son of Hayat Muhammad, is ordered to have in readiness 37 'Kosa' boats with 32 boatmen in each; to pay rupees 10,261-7, the revenue of pargana Buldakhal etc. and to remit the rental of the 'paibaqi' or reserved lands, then held by Luthfullah, and Inayatullah." It is clear therefore, that the vassal zamindars were assigned nawara-lands to maintain a fixed number of boats and sailors to be pressed into imperial service when called for. Dr. Wise has also referred to some nawara-lands in some districts. He writes "The modern tradition in Tippera is that the old name of the district was Jahaznagar or the 'city of ships'. This is evidently founded on the circumstance that at a much later period, the revenue for the support of the Nawara or imperial fleet was derived from lands in the district."[44] Dr. Wise writes further that the Haibatnagar family still possess a sanad issued by Shah Shuja in 1649 and another by Shaista Khan in 1667. Both were addressed to Masum Khan "but they contain nothing excepting order about war-boats."[45]

But all the zamindars were not assigned 'nawara'-lands and they had to supply boats and sailors to the imperial flotilla when occasion arose and the expenses had to be borne by themselves. For instance, Musa Khan, 'when defeated by the Mughals (1611), was left but little of his territories, the greater portion being absorbed by the victors, although often he had to contribute quite a good number of boats to the imperial flotilla for which he received neither 'nawara' lands nor cash payments. Raja Satrajit of Bhusna, a vassal of the Mughals, similarly had to supply boats and naval armaments at his own cost, of course, according to the terms of his vassalage.

So far as the boatmen, crew and other menials are concerned we come across some arrangements for their payments. Here again, a distinction was made between those employed on a permanent basis directly under the Mir Bahar and those recruited on temporary basis according to necessity. Sometimes lands under the head 'nawara jagir' were assigned to them for their maintenance. Generally a plot of land was divided into 'taluks' and each such division was assigned to each boatman. As Taylor writes, "The following were the principal assignments (in the district of Dacca) (1) 'Omleh Nawara' for the support of the armed vessels to guard the coast against the incursions of the Maghs...(besides the imperial fleet as established by Akbar) a number of boats and men were furnished by the zamindars in return for the lands...(2) The 'Nawara jagir' was the principal assignment in the district and included the best lands of the Nizamat and was subdivided into a number of 'taluks' which were granted to the boatment and artificers of the fleet instead of wages.[46] In the Ain-i-Akbari, the rates of wages in cash of the workers employed are given, which of course, were not strictly followed.[47] The rates varied from region to region. Generally, the diwan was to settle the wages of the sailors, crew and artificers of the fleet. As we have already noted, in times of war 'sardars' were appointed to recruit the menials for the fleet. For their wages the Mughal government entered into contracts with the 'sardars' acting as agents who were paid in lump-sum to be distributed amongst the workers and in certain cases these poor people were defrauded by these agents. As a result the sailors and other menials often deserted the fleet. Referring to such incidents, Mirza Nathan writes "All the sailors of the fleet fled away on account of their distressed condition, because neither the Diwan Mutaqid Khan had settled their dues, nor had Islam Khan made him to do so. In the morning at the time of march, it was found that in the whole fleet of three hundred war and cargo boats, there were only seven hundred men."[48]

Contributions of Mir Jumla and Shaista Khan to Mughal Navy

The Mughal navy is seen at its best during the reign of Emperor Aurangzeb both on the eastern and western coasts. The imperial viceroys in Bengal, Mir Jumla and Shaista Khan introduced certain new elements in the naval organisation to make it a 'real force' in the eastern waters and as a matter of fact, the Mughal navy came to acquire such a standard of strength and efficiency that it caused nervousness even among the Europeans, as the Madras Council might write to the Court of Directors at London thus "Your (company's) warships must consider that these people (Mughals) are grown more powerful than formerly and will not be so subject to us as they have been...They accounted us formerly very powerful there (in Bengal), but they (the Mughals) look not upon us now-a-days after that rate and begin to slight our passes."[49] So long the Europeans with their superior naval power used to defy Mughal authority in Indian waters. But during Aurangzeb's reign the Mughal navy grew to be a serious challenge to the European maritime nations. What Mir Jumla and Shaista Khan did in Bengal, the Sidis of Janjira as Mughal admirals did the same in the western waters. The Mughal navy under the Sidis threw a great challenge to the European navies.

The Mughal naval strength showed signs of declining since the closing years of Jahangir's reign till Aurangzeb came to the throne when attempts were made afresh by his viceroys Mir Jumla and Shaista Khan to revive it. During the reign of Emperor Shah Jahan the established rental of Bengal was almost entirely absorbed in jagirs assigned to protect the coasts from the depredations of the Arakanese and the Feringhi pirates. Matter instead of improving grew worse and worse due to the gradual dilapidaton of the Mughal flotilla on the one hand and the growing power of the Magh and Feringhi fleets on the other. When Prince Shuja was appointed viceroy of Bengal in 1639, great confusion was caused by his negligence and the extortion and violence of the nawara mutasaddis (clerks) ruined the 'nawara' parganas assigned for maintaining the 'nawara'. Many naval officers and sailors holding nawara jagirs and stipends were overpowered by poverty and starvation.[50] "The navy (nawara) so necessary for the defence of the Bengal delta at last fell into decay and despair through official parsimony or peculation".[51] The parganas assigned for the maintenance of the 'nawara' and yielding 14 lakhs of rupees annually had become desolate on account of the extortion and violence of the rent collectors. Moreover 'scorched-earth' policy of Shuja while fighting with the imperialists left only a few and rotten boats in Bengal constituting the 'nawara'.[52] The loss of the revenue from the nawara-parganas made it impossible to maintain a large number of boats. The most pressing problem before Mir Jumla was to protect the coastal regions from the ravages of the Maghs (Arakanese) and Feringhi sea-rovers. To fight them without a strong fleet was well-nigh impossible. Hence Mir Jumla and Shaista Khan had to undertake the task of defending the coastal regions, building up new war-boats, financing their maintenance and extending the Mughal frontiers to the north-east and south-east.

Mir Jumla "an expert, clever and hardworking officer" was sent to Bengal (1660-63) with definite instructions from Aurangzeb to regulate, supervise and 'bring to order' the Mughal nawara. Mir Jumla's first concern was to build new vessels and repair the old ones. And to do this he engaged a number of European shipwrights and European captains. Of course, the employment of Europeans in the Mughal navy was not a new thing. Akbar had given the start long before. Due to their superior skill as carpenters, gunners and fighters, Mir Jumla took them into imperial service on a grand scale. Glanius, a Dutch sailor says "..we went on board one of the vessels belonging to the Nawab (Mir Jumla) where we found four Englishmen, few Portuguese and two men of our company.[53] The viceroy was always on the look-out for European sailors and carpenters. For instance, upon the arrival of Glanius and his party, the viceroy at once sent for him, offered him three hundred rupees as wages and assigned him a number of 'ghurabs', one of which carried 14 guns and 60 men. Each 'ghurab' was attended by 4 'Kosas'. A good many of the officers were Portuguese and "the General (Mir Jumla)," writes Glanius, "had so good an opinion of the Christians that if a Moor could speak but a little of that language, he commonly preferred him to some considerable office."[54]

Mir Jumla required two of the Dutch carpenters' assistance to build for him a stately vessel from a model he showed them. These carpenters were in the company of Glanius whom he promised their liberty if they could furnish him with the required vessel. They accepted the offer, came to Dacca and finished their undertaking within the stipulated time.[55] Mir Jumla utilised the services of the European shipwrights for his boats and paid them handsomely. But in certain cases we find him employing them forcibly without paying their wages. He pressed the Dutch, Portuguese and English to lend him vessels to reconquer Hijli. He also put pressure on the Dutch to despatch a vessel to Arakan in pursuit of the fugitive Mughal Prince Shah Shuja. It is admitted by the English factors that the Dutch assistance made the enterprise a grand success and Hijli was reconquered. Moreover a 'gallivat' which the Dutch had built at Hughli and manned by 6 or 7 English runaways under the command of Captain John Durson was sent to Dacca for the use of the Mughal viceroy towards the end of May 1661. But Mir Jumla had little gratitude for the services rendered by the Dutch.

It will not be true to suppose that Mir Jumla employed Englishmen indiscriminately in the 'nawara' department. For instance, at Dacca there was residing a certain William Pitt with five English sailors. He quartered himself at the ship's timber 'wharf' superintending the building of a 'gallivat' though he was not entertained by the viceroy for this purpose. William Pitt had no admittance to the viceroy nor he had any influence of any sort.[56] According to the English factors at Dacca, William Pitt demanded exhorbitant wages for constructing a single vessel. On the other hand, Thomas Pratt, another Englishman "high in favour with Mir Jumla" was employed by the viceroy in building boats and making ammunition for river-fighting.[57]

In an undated letter but probably of October or November, 1663, Pratt is found demanding 180 rupees for his salary and servants' wages and apparently it was agreed upon to pay him that amount."[58] But Manucci writes that Pratt demanded 500 rupees and he was offered that sum. He was master of the riverside and employed in building boats and making ammunition for river fighting.[59] After the death of Mir Jumla, Thomas Pratt had certain difficulties in realising his wages from the Mughal government. So he left Dacca with four Englishmen and reached Rajmahal in a sloop furnished with four guns, "his object being to offer to the new Nawab (Shaista Khan) his services in building ships and making cannon."[60] A Madras letter of 12th January 1665 mentions that William Blake, the Bengal factor, "is forced to continue Mr. Pratt at Dacca at a great charge."

Besides improving the quality of the war-boats with the assistance of the Europeans and making them thereby more efficient for naval wars, Mir Jumla took an equal interest in protecting the sea-coasts by raising a number of naval forts about the confluence of the Lakhiya and the Ichhamati rivers and constructing several good military roads and bridges in and around Dacca. The Khizrpur fort bears the name of Mir Jumla. From Khizrpur towards the West can be traced an old road with several ruined bridges on the banks of the Buriganga.[61]

Mir Jumla made a new financial arrangement for defraying the cost of maintaining the flotilla which amounted to 14 lakhs of rupees annually. For defraying partly the costs of maintaining the flotilla, customs were realised more vigorously from the Europeans. Sometimes anchorage charges were levied on the Europeans ships and on this issue a dispute arose with the English upon their refusal to pay Rs. 3,000 as the anchorage charges in addition to annual customs. The exasperated English agent at Hughli seized a country vessel belonging to Mir Jumla at Balasore. Mir Jumla, thereupon, ordered the faujdar at Balasore to levy a duty of 40% on all English exports besides anchorage duties on their ships. However the dispute was brought to a settlement. The grant under the head "Omleh Ahshan' was appropriated for maintenance of the naval troops and artillery to defend the forts on the coasts.[62] The Jahanshahi pargana in Mymensingh district supplied 20 'Kosa' boats to the imperial 'nawara' and "the two shares into which it is now divided and which paid for the equipment of 10 1/3 and 9 1/3 Kosas respectively are still known as the 'daghkosa' and 'nankosa' zamindars."[63]

A large area in Jessore was distributed among the 'Kaibartas' who were expert sailors, for their employment in the imperial fleet. These people manned Raja Pratapaditya's navy but were reduced to great straits after the fall of the Raja. Mir Jumla made fresh grants to these people and thus got a great supply of them as sailors. Mir Jumla also revived Pratapaditya's dockyard called 'Jahajghata' for rebuilding the imperial 'nawara'.

Doubtless, the 'nawara' under Mir Jumla was in a progressive state and as many as 323 war-boats he employed in his Assam campaign (1662-63). Besides, several other boats laden with provisions and war-ammunition were always kept ready at the headquarters to be engaged in times of emergency.[64] Glanius says that "Mir Jumla had 500 (boats) for his share".[65]

In spite of his best endeavours, Mir Jumla could not bring any lasting improvement in the naval organisation. With a view to reorganising the nawara, he abolished the old system but before he could start a new one and make it permanent, he had to set out on his fateful Assam campaign.

The disastrous Assam campaign of Mir Jumla affected the Mughal nawara very adversely. Many expert naval officers and crew perished in the course of the campaign and the flotilla utterly ruined. On the resignation of its admiral Ibn Husain, Mahamad Beg was appointed its superintendent and he was asked by Aurangzeb to send a report after ascertaining the quality, the number and the true state of the Bengal nawara. The destruction of the Mughal navy endangered the security of the Subah and aggravated the menace of the Magh and

Feringhi pirates. Early in 1664 the Arakan fleet appeared before Dacca, made an attack upon the Mughal flotilla in the Dacca river and destroyed 160 of the Mughal war-boats.[66] The cruising Mughal admiral (sardar-i-sairab) Munawar Khan who was stationed there with the relies of the 'nawara' took to flight in confusion and the few boats that still belonged to the nawara were thus lost and its name alone remained in Bengal.[67]

Hence upon his arrival in Bengal as the next viceroy, Shaista Khan had to face an unhappy situation. But he was equal to the occasion and employed his whole time and energy to revive the imperial nawara, and to his credit, it should be admitted that his energy and perseverance overcame every obstacle.

Shaista Khan's first concern was to have a suitable shipyard for constructing new boats and repairing the old ones. Dacca served the purpose, and accordingly it was turned into a great and busy shipyard. In the great dockyards that lined the channel passing through the city of Dacca in the quarter known as Tanti Bazar, began busy activities for building boats on a large scale.[68] As timber and shipwrights were required for repairing and fitting out the ships, bailiffs were sent with parwanas to fetch timber and carpenters from every 'mauza' of the province and to bring them to Dacca.'[69] The viceroy ordered as many boats as possible to be built at the ports of Hughli, Balasore, Murang, Chilmary, Jessore and Karibari and desired them, when finished, to be sent to Dacca. From his vigorous exertions and busy activities, it seems that he put the entire province on war-footing and it must be admitted that he left no stone unturned to make the flotilla a real force to fight the enemies, particularly the Maghs and the Feringhis whose "war-vessel were more numerous than the waves of the sea." Talish writes "Not for a moment did he (Shaista Khan) forget to mature plans for assembling the crew, providing their rations and needments and collecting the materials for ship-building and shipwrights" and in a short time about 300 war vessels were built ready in wartrim and employed against the Feringhi pirates of Chittagong.[70] At Lalbagh, Shaista Khan built a large red-brick fort to command over the river which once washed its south face.[71]

Expert officers were chosen for the fleet. Hakím Muhammad Husain, a mansabdar, "an old, able, learned, trustworthy and virtuous servant of the Nawab" was appointed head of the ship-building department. Qazi Samu was made superintendent of the dockyard. Kishore Das, "an imperial officer and a well-informed and experienced clerk" was entrusted with the duty of supervising the 'nawara' parganas and the stipend of the jagirs assigned to the naval officers and others. The viceroy was careful enough to appoint only expert officers having had previous experiences. Balchand was made the superintendent of the customs at Hughli with Parameswar Das as his assistant. Ibn Husain, who resigned from the admiralty after Mir Jumla's Assam expedition, was again appointed chief admiral.

Like Mir Jumla, Shaista Khan also engaged the English, Dutch and Portuguese in the Mughal navy and we find him often demanding of them their vessels. "You make vast amounts every year", Shaista Khan told the Dutch Captain, "by your trade in the imperial dominions for which you have to pay no duty or tithe. For this reason, the path of the profit of Muslim and Hindu 'beparis', and merchants in the imperial dominions especially in Bengal, has been closed. In gratitude for such favour and bounty, you should call for your ships from your country and co-operate with the imperial forces in the expedition against Arakan for extirpating the Maghs which I have in view"...[72] The Dutch Captain asked his permission to write to their Governor-General (of the Dutch Indies) as it was a "serious proposal". Although Shaista Khan appreciated the Captain's suggestion, he instead of depending on the assurance of the Captain, despatched an envoy to Batavia with suitable presents, soliciting the Dutch Governor-General's favour in this regard.[73] Talish says that their help was at last found unnecessary.

Shaista Khan put forth the same demand to the English. A letter from Madras to Hughli dated 8th October 1664 contains the following passage upon the subject. The letter runs, "you say, there is an absolute necessity to furnish the Nawab with a 'sloope' and men and it will be a great furtherance to our masters' business...You must endeavour to get men and a 'sloope' to assist him (the viceroy) ... but he must allow the charges of the sloope and men".[74] By threats and allurement, the viceroy also succeeded in effecting a desertion of a large number of Portuguese sailors and soldiers from the side of the Arakan king. Lands were assigned for their settlement near Dacca and two thousand rupees were distributed amongst them from the viceroy's private purse. Also a monthly stipend of Rs. 500 was settled on the Portuguese captain from the imperial treasury.[75]

According to Bowrey, Shaista Khan imposed a sort of 'shipmoney' on the merchants to build up the naval power of the Subah both for defensive and offensive purposes. A boat proceeding to Murshidabad was charged at the rate of 8 annas per oar; to Calcutta 10 annas; and to Burdwan one rupee and eight annas; while boats coming from these places were taxed at the rate of 1, 2, and 4 rupees per boat respectively. These rates were likewise exacted by the 'zamindars from every boat that passed their territories.'[76]

Bowray writes futher that the viceroy sent his 'paiks' to the merchants at Hughli, Jessore, Pipli and Balasore for a ship or two in each respective place of 400, 500 or 600 tons to be sent to Dacca and also 10, 20 or 30 'jalia' boats to attend them, and "the Moor's governor having strict order to see them finished with all speed and gunned and well manned and sent up the Ganges as high as Dacca."[77]

Of Shaista Khan's marine, Bowrey says that it consisted of about "twenty sail of ships of considerable burden that annually trade to sea from Dacca, Balasore and Pipli, some to Ceylon, some to Tenassarim".

To the credit of Shaista Khan, it should be admitted that he not only revived the imperial flotilla and built it afresh but also inspired the demoralised Bengali sailors and mariners into a fighting mood and at last succeeded in crushing the naval power of the Maghs and Feringhi's in the year 1666 A.D.

REFERENCES

1. V. A. Smith, *Akbar the Great Mogul,* p. 81.
2. *History of Bengal* (Dacca University), Vol. II, pp. 245-46.
3. Blochmann, *Ain-i-Akbari,* p. 289.
4. Blochmann, *Ain-i-Akbari,* pp. 289-92
5. *Ibid.*
6. *Ibid.*
7. *Ibid.*
8. *Ibid.*
9. *Ibid.*
10. Grant, *Analysis etc.,* p. 131.
11. *Ibid.,* p. 203.
12. R. K. Mukherjee, *Indian Shipping,* p. 211.
13. Blochmann, *Ain-i-Akbari,* p. 292.
14. *Ibid.,* p. 279.
15. *Akbarname,* Vol. III, p. 120.
16. *Mirat-i-Ahmadi,* trans. by Lokhandwala, p. 99.
17. Gladwin, *Narrative of transactions etc.,* p. 113.
18. Irvine, *The army of the Indian Moghuls,* p. 172.
19. *Ibid.*
20. *Tarikhi-i-Tahiri,* Vide, Elliot and Dawson, Vol. I, p. 277.
21. Manrique in Bengal, Vide *Bengal – Past & Present,* Vol. XII, p. 218.
22. Foster, *English Factories in India,* 1661-64, p. 397.
23. Manucci, *Storia do Mogor,* Vol. II, tr. Irvine, p. 417.
24. Tuzuk, p. 144; *Baharistan,* Vol. I, p. 4.
25. *Baharistan,* Vol. I, p. 6.
26. Glanius's Accounts, Vide *Bengal—Past & Present,* Vol. XXIX, p. 20.
27. *Baharistan,* Vol. I, p. 11.
28. *Ibid.,* p. 5.

29. *Baharistan,* Vol. I, pp. 29, 34, 35.
30. *Ibid.,* pp. 21, 29.
31. *Ibid.,* p. 48.
32. *Ibid.,* p. 6.
33. *Ibid.,* pp. 48-51.
34. *Ibid.,* p. 32.
35. *Ibid.,* p. 422.
36. *Ibid.,* pp. 358, 362.
37. *Ibid.,* pp. 400-401.
38. Vide, Elliot & Dowson, Vol. VI, p. 363.
39. R. E. Roberts, *Asiatic Miscell,* Vol. I, p. 419
40. *Baharistan,* Vol. I, pp.12-13
41. *Ibid.,* p. 34.
42. *Ibid.,* p. 35.
43. Vide *J.A.S.B.,* 1874, Part I, p. 214.
44. *Ibid.,* F. N. p. 83.
45. *Ibid.,* 1872, Part I, p. 57; 1874, Part I, p. 210.
46. Taylor, *Topography of Dacca,* pp. 193-94
47. Irvine, *The Army of the Indian Moghuls,* p. 174.
48. *Baharistan,* Vol. I, pp. 29-30.
49. Foster, *English Factories in India,* 1661-64,p. 401.
50. J.A.S.B., Vol. III, 1907, p. 405.
51. *Proceedings of Indian History Congress,* Vol. XI, pp. 296-97.
52. J. N. Sarkar, *Life of Mir Jumla,* p. 160.
53. Glanius, Vide, *Bengal–Past & Present,* 1925, Vol. XXIX, p. 13.
54. *Ibid.,* p. 15.
55. Foster, *English Factories in India,* 1661-64, p. 70.
56. *Ibid.,* p. 71.
57. *Ibid.,* p. 294.
58. Ibid., *Manucci,* Vol. II, p. 87.
59. *Manucci,* Vol. II, p. 102.
60. Foster, *English Factories in India,* 1661-64, p. 393.

61. *J.A.S.B.,* 1874, Part I, p. 211.
62. Taylor, *op. cit.,* p. 194.
63. Glanius, vide, *op. cit., p.* 13.
64. *Ibid.*
65. *Ibid.*
66. Foster,—*English Factories in India,* 1661-64, p. 397.
67. *J.A.S.B.,* 1907, pp. 205-6.
68. *History of Bengal (*Dacca Univ.), Vol. II, p. 397.
69. *J.A.S.B.,* Vol. III, 1907, p. 406.
70. Vide Sarkar, *Studies in Mughal India,* p. 134.
71. Wilson, *Early Annals,* Vol. I, p. 81.
72. *J.A.S.B.,* Vol. III, 1907, p. 406.
73. Foster, *English Factories in India,* 1661-64, p. 403.
74. *Ibid.,* p. 399.
75. Sarkar, *Studies etc.,* p. 130.
76. Bowrey, *Countries Round Bay of Bengal.*
77. *Ibid.*

19

Rewards and Distinctions

The promise of honorary distinctions has been in all ages and in all countries one of the most potent agencies employed to incite men to exertion. We have our medals, crosses, orders, and peerages. The Moghul sovereigns were even more ingenious in converting things mostly worthless in themselves into objects to be ardently striven for and dearly prized. Among these were : (1) Titles; (2) Robes of Honour; (3) Gifts of Money and other articles; (4) Kettle-drums; (5) Standards and Ensigns.

1. ***Titles.*** The system of entitlature was most elaborate and based on strict rule. This subject belongs, however, to the general scheme of government, and need not be set forth at length here. Suffice it to say, that a man would begin by becoming a *Khan* or Lord (added to his own name). After that, he might receive some name supposed to be appropriate to his qualities, coupled with the word *Khan,* such as Ikhlas Khan, Lord Sincerity; an artillery officer might be dubbed Ra'd-andaz Khan, Lord Thunder-thrower, or a skilful horseman, Yakah-Taz Khan, Lord Single Combat, and so on. Round such a title as a nucleus, accreted all the remaining titles with which a man might from time to time be invested. As the empire declined in strength, so did the titles increase in pomposity, and long before the end of the dynasty the discrepancy between a man's real qualities and his titles was so great as often to be ridiculous. Still, these titles were never given quite at random, nor were they self-adopted. Yet I read quite recently in a history of India, by a well-known and esteemed author, that one governor of Bengal was "a Brahman convert *calling himself* Murshid Kuli Khan." Now Murshid Quli Khan no more called *himself* by that name than has Earl Roberts of Candahar called himself by the title he bears. Both titles were derived from the accepted

fountain of honour, the sovereigns of the states which those bearing them respectively served.

2. ***Robes of Honour.*** The *khilat* was not peculiar to the military department. These robes of honour were given to everyone presented at court. Distinction was, however, made according to the position of the receiver. There were five degrees of *khilat,* those of three, five, six or seven pieces; or they might as a special mark of favour consist of clothes that the emperor had actually worn (*malbus-i-khas*). A three-piece *khilat,* given from the general wardrobe (*khilat-khanah*), consisted of a turban (*dastar*), a long coat with very full skirts (*jamah*), and a scarf for the waist (*kamrband*). A five-piece robe came from the *toshah-khanah* (storehouse for presents), the extra pieces being a turban ornament called a *sarpech* and a band for tying across the turban (*balaband*). For the next grade a tight-fitting jacket with short sleeves, called a Half-sleeve (*nimah-aslin*), was added. A European writer, Tavernier (Ball, i, 163), thus details the seven-piece *khilat*: (1) a cap, (2) a long gown (*kabah*), (3) a close-fitting coat (*arkalon*), which I take to be *alkhaliq,* a tight coat, (4) two pairs of trousers, (5) two shirts, (6) two girdles, (7) a scarf for the head or neck.

3. ***Gifts, other than Money.*** These were naturally of considerable variety. I have drawn up the following list from Danishmand Khan's history of the first two years of Bahadur Shah's reign (1708-1710): Jewelled ornaments, weapons, principally swords and daggers with jewelled hilts, palkis with fringes of gold lace and pearls, horses with gold-mounted and jewelled trappings, and elephants. The order in which the above are given indicates roughly both the frequency with which these presents were granted and the relative value set upon them, beginning with those most frequently given and the least esteemed.

4. ***Kettledrums.*** As one of the attributes of sovereignty, kettledrums were beaten at the head of the army when the emperor was on the march; and in quarters they were beaten every three hours at the gate of his camp. The instruments in use, in addition to the drums, will be found in the *Ain-i-Akbari*

(Blochmann, i, 51). As a mark of favour, kettledrums (*naqqarah*)[1] and the right to play them (*naubat*) might be granted to a subject. But he must be a man of the rank of 2000 *suwar* or upwards. As an invariable condition, moreover, it was stipulated that they should never be used where the emperor was present, nor within a certain distance from his residence. Marching through the middle of Delhi with drums beating was one of the signs by which Sayyad Husain 'Ali Khan, Amir-ul-Umara, notified defiance of constituted authority, when he returned from the Dakhin in 1719, preparatory to dethroning the Emperor Farrukhsiyar. The drums when granted were placed on the recipient's back, and, thus accoutred, he did homage for them in the public audience hall. In Lord Lake's case the investment was thus carried out : "Two small drums of silver, each about the size of a thirty-two pound shot, the apertures covered with parchments, are hung round the neck of the person on whom the honour is conferred, then struck a few times, after which drums of the proper size are made." – Thorn, "War," 356. There is on record another instance of miniature drums being used in this way, as a symbol. When conferring on him the right to the *naubat*, Ahmad Shah (1748-1754) gave such drums to Daim Khan, a favorite *chela* of Ahmad Khan, Bangash, of Farrukhabad. ("Bangash Nawabs," Journal A.S.B., 1879, p. 161.)

5. ***Flags and Ensigns.*** The flags and ensigns displayed, along with a supply of spare weapons, at the door of the audience hall and at the entrance to the emperor's encampment, or carried before him on elephants, were called collectively the *Qur* (Pavet de Courteille, "Dict.," 425, ceinture, arme, garde), and their charge was committed to a responsible officer called the *Qur-begi.* An alternative general name sometimes employed was *mahi-o-maratib* (Fish and Dignities), or more rarely, the *panjah* (literally, Open Hand). It is, no doubt, the *Qur* which Gemelli Careri describes thus (French ed. iii, 182) : "Outside the audience tent I saw nine men in red velvet coats embroidered with gold, with wide sleeves and pointed collars hanging down behind, who carried the imperial ensigns displayed at the end of pikes. The man in the middle carried a

sun, the two on each side of him had each a gilt hand, the next two carried horse-tails dyed red. The remaining four, having covers on their pikes, it could not be seen what it was they held."

In the *Ain*, i, 50, we are told of eight ensigns of reyalty, of which the first four were reserved exclusively for the sovereign. The use of the others might, we must assume, be granted to subject. The eight ensigns are—(1) *Aurang*, the throne; (2) *Chatr*, the State umbrella; (3) *Saiban* or *Aftabgir*, a sunshade; (4) *Kaukabah* (plate ix, No. 2); (5) "*Alam*, or flag; (6) *Chatr-tok*, or yak-tails; (7) *Tuman-tok*, another shape of yak-tails; (8) *Jhanda*, or Indian flag. To these we must add (9) *Mahi-o-maratib*, or the fish and dignities.

The origin and meaning of the different ensigns displayed by the Moghul Emperors in India have been thus described, *Mirat-ul-Istilah*, fol. 5 :

(1) *Panjah*, an open hand, is said to mean the hand of 'Ali. Taimur ordered it to be carried before him for a charm and as a sacred relic. It was said that he captured it when he overcame the Siyahposh tribe. In 1753 Gentil saw four different "pondjehs" (*i.e. panjahs*) carried on horseback in Salabat Jang's cavalcade; they were copper hands fixed on the end of a staff ("Memoires," 61).

(2) *'Alam*, a flag or standard—This was supposed to be the flag of Husain, and obtained by Taimur at Karbalah. To it he attributed his victory over Bayazid, the Kaisar of Rum.

(3) *Mizan*, a balance, was a reference to the equal scales of Justice, and was adopted as having been the emblem of Nushirwan the Just. There is a figure on a plate in Gentil's "Memoires," which is probably the *Mizan*.

(4) *Aftab*, or Sun, was obtained from the fire-worshippers when they were conquered; it was an article used in their worship.

(5) *Azhdaha-paikar*, Dragon-face—From the time of Sikandar of the Two Horns, the rajahs of Hind had worshipped this emblem in their temples, and when Taimur made his

irruption into India it was presented to him as an offering. It consisted of two pieces, one carried in front and the other behind the emperor.

(6) *Mahi,* or Fish, was said to have been an offering from the islands of the ocean, where it was worshipped.

(7) *Qumqumah* (Steingass, 989, a bowl, a jug, a round shade, a lantern). This also was obtained from the Indian rajahs. The *Ain-i-Akbari,* I, 50, has *kaukabah* for apparently the same thing (see figure No. 2 on plate ix). There is also what looks like the *kaukabah* in a plate in Gentil's "Memoires." The definition of *kaukabah* in Steingass, 1063, corresponds with the figure in the *Ain, viz.* "a polished steel ball suspended from a long pole and carried as an ensign before the king." Careri, iii, 182, tells us that he saw a golden ball hanging by a chain between two gilt hands, and adds that "it was a royal ensign carried on an elephant when the army was on the march."

All these emblems, we are told, were carried before the emperor as a sign of conquest over the Seven Climes, or, in other words, over the whole world.

Mahi-o-maratib. Some words must be added with special reference to this dignity, which was borne on elephants or camels in a man's retinue. It was one of the very highest honours, as it was not granted to nobles below the rank of 6000 *zat,* 6000 *suwar* (*Mirat-ul-Islilah,* fol. 3). *Mahi* (literally, a fish), was made in the figure of a fish, four feet in length, of copper gilt, and it was placed horizontally on the point of a spear (*Seir,* I, 218, note 150, and 743, note 51). Steingass, 1,147, defines *mahi-maratib* as "certain honours denoted by the figure of a fish with other insignia (two balls)." But in careful writers I have always found it as *mahi-o-maratib,* "fish and dignities," and, as I take it, the first word refers to the fish emblem and the second to the balls or other adjuncts which went with it. The *maratib* Thorn, "War," 356, describes as a ball of copper gilt encircled by a *jhalar* or fringe about two feet in length, placed on a long pole, and, like the *mahi,* carried on an elephant. Can this be Gemelli Careri's "golden ball"? Perhaps it was identical with the *qumqumah* or *kaukabah* already described above. The translator of the *Seir-Mutaq-herin,* i, 218, note 150, tells us that the fish was always accompanied by the figure of a man's head in copper gilt. This must have been in addition to the gilt balls. The *mahi,* as conferred on Lord Lake on the 14th August, 1804 (Thorn, "War," 356), is described as "representing a fish with a head of gilt copper and the body and tail formed of silk, fixed to a long staff and carried on an elephant." James Skinner, who recovered Mahadaji-Sendhia's *mahi-o-maratib* in a fight with the Rajputs, speaks of it as "a brass fish with two chourees (horse-hair tails) hanging to it like moustachios" (Fraser, "Memoir," i, 152), Gentil, "Memoires," 62, calls the *mahi* simply "the head of a fish on the end of a pole." As a sign of the rarity of this dignity, he adds that while in the Dakhin (1752-1761) he only saw four of them.

Sher-maratib, or lion dignity. This is a name only found, so far as I know, in Gentil, "Memoires," 62; and he only saw it displayed by Salabat Jang, nazim of the Dakhin. At the head of the dedication of the above work to the memory of Shuja-ud-Daulah, are the figures of two elephants; one of which bears a standard that is most likely identical with this *Sher-maratib.* The flag bears a lion embroidered on it, and the head of the staff is adorned with the figure of a lion.

Alam. The flags seem to have been triangular in shape, either scarlet or green in colour, having a figure embroidered in gold, and a gold fringe. The staff was surmounted by a figure corresponding to the one embroidered on the flag. A plate in Gentil's "Memoires" shows four of these embroidered emblems—1st, a *panjah*, or open hand; 2nd, a man's face with rays; 3rd, a lion (*sher*); and 4th, a fish. A flag, or *alam*, could be granted to no man under the rank of 1000 *suwar.*

Aftabgiri. This sun screen (*aftab,* sun; *gir,* root of *giriftan,* to take), shaped like an open palm-leaf fan, was also called *Suraj-mukhi* (Hindi, literally, sun-face). By the Moghul rules it could only be granted to royal princes (*Mirat-ul-Istilah,* fol. 3). In the eighteenth century, however, the Mahrattas adopted it as one of their commonest ensigns, and even the smallest group of their cavalry was in the habit of carrying one.

Tuman-togh. This is one of the two *togh* mentioned in Akbar's list, *Ain* i, 50, and figured on plate ix of that volume. Pavet de Courteille, "Dit.," 236, has *togh*, "etendard se composant d'une queue de *qatas* ou boeuf de montagne (*i.e.* yak) fixce a une hampe, au dessus d'un pavillon triangulaire." This yak's-tail standard was not unfrequently granted to officers of rank, by whom it was esteemed a high honour. The *togh* consisted generally of three tails attached to a cross-bar, which was fixed at the end of a long pole or staff.

Summary. Thus, apart from titles or money rewards, or ordinary gifts, a man might be awarded any of the following honorary distinctions, of a more permanent character – (1) the right to carry a flag or simple standard, (2) the right to display a yak-tail standard, (3) the right to use kettle-drums and beat the *naubat,* (4) the right to display the fish and its accompanying emblems, (5) the right to use a litter adorned with gold fringes and strings of pearls. Of course, all these things wee dependent on the caprice of the monarch; for in the Moghul, like in all Oriental states—*Ba yak nuktah mahram mujrim shavvad:* By one spot " confidant" becomes "criminal."

Glossary

Aftabgir (*or Aftabgiri, Aftagir*)—'This sun screen (*aftab*, sun; *gir*, root of *giriftan*, to take), shaped like an open palm-leaf fan, was also called *suraj-mukhi* (Hindi, literally, sun-face). By the Moghul rules it could only be granted to royal princes (*Mirat-ul-Istilah*, fol. 3). In the eighteenth century, however, the Maharattas adopted it as one of their commonest ensigns, and even the smallest group of their cavalry was in the habit of carrying one.' Irvine, *The Army of the Indian Moghuls*, p. 34.

Alvara—Charter or prince's letters-patent. Lacerda, *A New Dictionary of the Portuguese and English Languages*, p. 65.

Amin—'The word is Arabic *Amin*, meaning a "trustworthy person"; and then an inspector, intendant, *Hobson Jobson*, p. 17.

Arrack—'This word is the Arabic *arak* properly "perspiration", and then first the exudation or sap drawn from the date palm (*arak al-tamar*); secondly, any strong drink, "distilled spirit", "essence"; etc. In India it is applied to a variety of common spirits; in S. India to those distilled from the fermented sap of sundry palms; in E. and N. India to the spirit distilled from cane-molasses, and also to that from rice.' Crooke, *Hobson Jobson*, p. 36.

Balparveshi—(A compound of *bal*, child, and *parwardan*, to rear or foster.) 'A pension or maintenance granted by a Government to the family of a soldier or servant who died in its service,' Molesworth, *A Dictionary—Marathi and English*, p. 579.

Bania—Merchant, a man of the trading caste.

Bazar—Market.

Beldar Lugare—Beldar, a wandering caste of quarrymen. 'They are strong and dark and the men wear the moustache and top-knot. They speak Marathi. They are stone-cutters and bricklayers, digging wells, blasting rocks, and breaking stones. Their houses are like those of cultivating Marathas. The men wear the loin cloth, waist cloth, and short tight trousers or *cholnas*, the jacket, and the Maratha turban; and the women dress in the ordinary Maratha robe and bodice and do not tuck the end of the robe back between the feet. They eat fish and flesh and drink liquor. They are hard working, orderly, and hospitable but fond of drink. They have caste councils, do not send their boys to school, and are a steady people earning enough to maintain themselves.' *Gazetteer of the Bombay Presidency,* Vol. XX, pp. 91-92. *Lugadu* means a robber or plunderer. *Beldar Lugare,* therefore, stands for a plunderer of the Beldar caste.

Bildar—The same as Beldar, but when used in relation to the army the word means a digger or pioneer. See *Hobson Jobson,* p. 94; Irvine, *The Army of the Indian Moghuls,* pp. 173-74.

Bhaldar—Mace-bearer. 'An attendant on great men who waits with wand in his hand—an usher. Molesworth, *A Dictionary—Marathi and English,* p. 611.

Bunga—Baggage of an army. See p. 149; also *Molesworth, A Dictionary—Marathi and English,* p. 572.

Cafilla—'Arabic *Kafila*; a body or convoy of travellers. Also used for a sea convoy.' *Hobson Jobson,* p. 142; Dalgado, *Glossario Duso-Asiatico,* Vol. I, pp. 169-70.

Cartaz—Permit or passport.

Charrua—Ship of burden, merchant ship, store ship.

Chitnis—(From *Chithi,* letter, and *navishtan,* to write). Correspondence clerk or secretary.

Cozzy—Arabic *Kadi,* a judge.

Daftardar—'An ancient public officer. His duty was to collect and frame in order the accounts of the waste-book as prepared by the Fadnis, and to transmit monthly abstract accounts to the Huzur.' Molesworth, *A Dictionary—Marathi and English,* p. 402.

Dakshini—Southerner, a man hailing from the Deccan.

Darakhdar—'A holder of a hereditary public office especially Diwan, Mazumdar, Fadnis, Sabnis, Karkhannis, Chitnis, Jamdar and potnis.' Sen, *Administrative System of the Marathas,* p. 665.

Desy—More correctly Desai. 'An hereditary Officer, the head of a Pergunnah. He is the same as the Deshmukh.' Molesworth, *A Dictionary—Marathi and English,* p. 426. 'In W. and S India a native official in charge of a district, often held hereditarily, a petty chief.' *Hobson Jobson,* p. 306.

Dhal—Shield. A shield was made of either steel or hide. Brahmans often used a shield made of forty or fifty folds of silk. Irvine, *The Army of the Indian Moghuls,* pp. 77-78; Egerton of Tatton, *Indian and Oriental Armour,* p. 111-18, 134, 139.

Duan—More correctly, Diwan or Dewan. 'A prime minister.' Molesworth, *A Dictionary—Marathi and English,* p. 413. 'The head financial minister, whether of the state or a province. . . .charged, in the latter, with the collection of the revenue, the remittance of it to the imperial treasury, and invested with extensive judicial powers in all civil and financial causes'. Wilson quoted in *Hobson Jobson,* p. 309.

Durbar—More correctly, Darbar. Court or levee.

Fadnis—'A public officer—the keeper of the registers, etc. By him were issued al grants, commissions, and orders; and to him were rendered all accounts from the other departments.'—Molesworth, *A Dictionary—Marathi and English,* pp. 547.

Farman—Royal mandate, grant or patent.

Faujdari—The *Faujdar* was a military governor of a small

district; *Faujdari* was an *abwab* or *abwabs* exacted by the *Faujdar.*

Gariwan—Carter.

Ghat—Mountain pass, landing-place.

Golandaz—(From *gola,* a ball, and *andakhtan,* to throw) Gunner.

Gumashta—Agent or factor.

Hon—Gold coin (from Canarese *honnu,* gold). Wilson quoted in *Hobson Jobson,* p. 425. The value of this coin varied at different places and different times. From a manuscript in the Bodleian Library (Rawlinson Manuscript 841, fol. 1) it appears that the weight of a Kaveripak pagoda (or hon) was 2 dw. 5 gr. 8 m. ½ atts and its value in Madras currency (in 1679-80) was 18 fanams 1 cash. 'Accounts at Madras down to 1818 were kept in *pagodas, fanams* and *Kas*; and 8 *Kas* = 1 fanam, 42 fanams = 1 pagoda. In the year named the rupee was made the standard coin. The pagoda was then reckoned as equivalent to 3½ rupees.' *Hobson Jobson,* p. 653.

Houdah—Seat carried by an elephant.

Howda—See *Houdah.*

Inam—'Arabic. *in'am,* "a gift" (from a superior), "a favour" but specially in India a gift of rent free land; also land so held.' *Hobson Jobson,* p. 433.

Jahgir—(from *Jah,* a place, and *giriftan,* to take.) 'An assignment of the land revenue of a certain number of villages or of a sub-division.' Irvine, *The Army of The Indian Moghuls,* p. 14.

Jamadar—Petty officer.

Jamadar—Treasurer.

Jari Patka—'The Banner, "Zari-patta" which was always carried before Ragobah, was small and swallow-tailed of crimson and gold tissue with gold fringes and tassels.' Egerton of Tatton, *Indian and Oriental Armour,* p. 114.

Jasud—Scout.

Jejala—(*Jajail or Gingall*). 'A wall-piece or swivel gun.' Irvine, *The Army of the Indian Moghuls,* pp. 109-11. 'They use large heavy wall pieces called gingalls, which send a ball of two or more ounces to a very considerable distance.' Fitzclarence, *Journal of a Route across India,* p. 246.

Jinsa—Grand park of artillery. See p. 149. Irvine interprets *Jinsi* as 'the artillery attached to the emperor's person.' *The Army of the Indian Moghuls,* p. 133.

Karbhari—'A manager or Major domo.' Molesworth, *A Dictionary—Marathi and English,* p. 159. 'An agent, a manager.' *Hobson Jobson,* p. 475.

Karkonnas—More correctly, *korkhono,* a workshop, a manufactory. The word, when applied to a state department, means a royal establishment. See Sen, *Administrative system of the Marathas,* p. 668.

Kaul—Writing of assurance, agreement or engagements as granted by Government.

Kaveripak Hon—See *Hon.*

Khalasi—Seaman, chainman, tentpitcher, gunner or artillery man.

Khandi—Measure of weight equivalent to twenty maunds.

Khasnis—Private scribe of king or grandee.

Khijmatgar—More correctly *khidmatgar* (from Arabic *khidmat,* service), a servant.

Kuran—Ground preserved for growing grass.

Laskar—Army or camp; also, soldier or gunner as well as a sailor.

Mahmudi—Silver coin current in Gujarat and the west coast of India. According to Herbert, a Mahmudi was worth eight pence in English money. Fryer says, 'Mamodies are current only in Surat. and Parts adjacent; they are worth somewhat less than an English Shilling.' Mahmudi chaparis carried a higher exchange value than Mahmudi chalanis. See Dalgado, *Glossario Luso-Asiatico,* Vol. II, pp. 18-19.

Mansab—'The word *Mansab* is literally the place where anything is put or erected; and then, as a secondary meaning the state or condition of holding a place, dignity or office.' Irvine, *The Army of the Indian Moghuls,* p. 3.

Mukkadam—Village headman.

Mulukgiri—(From *mulk,* a country, and *giriftan,* to take.) Foreign expedition; generally a plundering raid.

Musand—'The large cushion, etc., used by native Princes in India, in place of a throne.' *Hobson Jobson,* p. 600.

Nakhoda—(From Persian *no-khude,* lord of the boat.) Skipper or captain of a ship.

Nalbandi—Literally the price of shoeing a horse. 'A small advance of pay made to horse-soldiers on engaging them, or on dispatching them upon any service.' Molesworth. *A Dictionary—Marathi and English,* pp. 460.

Nishan—Letter written by an imperial prince.

Nujeebs—(from Ar. Najib 'noble.') 'A kind of half-disciplined infantry soldiers under some of the native Government.' *Hobson Jobson,* p. 631. Also see Irvine, *The Army of the Indian Moghuls,* pp. 164-65.

Ol—Hostage.

Pal—Frigate, *see* p. 180. Also 'a cloth or a large blanket, etc. stretched across a pole, forming a sort of tent with two sloping sides and two open ends.' Molesworth, *A Dictionary—Marathi and English,* p. 512.

Parangue—(Probably derived from Tamil *padagu.*) Small boat, used for transporting provision on the Malabar coast. See Dalgado, *Glossario Luso-Asiatico,* Vol. II, p. 169.

Parasnis—Persian secretary.

Pataxo—'A pinnace. It is generally used for any tender that waits upon fleets and men of war.' Lacerds, *A New Dictionary of the Portuguese and English Languages,* p. 681.

Peshkash—'Persian *Pesh-kash.* Wilson interprets this as literally 'first fruits'. It is used as an offering or tribute but with many specific and technical senses which will be found in Wilson, *e.g.,* a fine on appointment, renewal, or investiture; a quit-rent, a payment exacted on lands formerly rent-free, or in substitution for service no longer exacted; sometimes a present to a great man or (loosely) for the ordinary Government demand on land.' *Hobson Jobson,* p. 701.

Potdar—Officer whose duty was to assay all money paid into the treasury.

Pradhan—Minister.

Purvia—One belonging to the eastern provinces. The Marathas applied this term generally to recruits from Oudh.

Rahdari—Transit dues, originally meant for paying travelling guards. See Moreland, *From Akbar to Aurangzib,* p. 286.

Rajmura—Wages.

Ramoshi—'They claim descent from Ram, who they say created them when he passed through the Deccan to Ceylon. Their rites, ceremonies, and home speech seem to show a Telegu origin. They are divided into Chavans and Jadhavs. Like Kunbis they eat fish, fowls, and the flesh of goats and deer, and differ little from them in house, dress, or customs. They have a bad name for committing thefts, burglaries and gang and highway robberies, and stealing cattle and crops. Their children are petty thieves and robbers. They act as village watchmen and in return for their services hold rent-free lands and receive grain allowances. Some are labourers and others husbandmen. Their favourite god is Khandoba, but they worship the usual Brahmanic gods and goddesses. Their priests are ordinary village Brahmans. They practise bigamy and have to pay for their wives. They bury their dead.' *Gazetteer of the Bombay Presidency,* Vol. XXIV, p. 107.

Saranjam—'Lands held in surinjam involve the condition of military service; the term is of Persian origin, meaning "furniture", "apparatus"; implying that the lands are to defray the expense of equipment : in fact Surinjam is synonymous with military Jagheer.' Sykes, *Special Report on the Statistics of the Four Collectorates of Dukhan under the British Government,* p. 286.

Sartandel—Officer superior to Tandel.

Serang—'A native boatswain, or chief of a lascar crew; the skipper of a small native vessel.' *Hobson Jobson,* p. 812.

Shikkdari—A *shikkdar* is a revenue collector of a small subdivision. *Shikkdari* is an *abwab* levied by a *Shikkdar.*

Shutarnal—'*Shutarnal, Zamburak, Shahin.* These words seem all three to refer to the same weapon, what we should call a swivel-gun or wall-piece. *Shutarnal* is literally "camel-gun barrel", and denotes the fact that they were sometimes carried on and fired from camels' backs. *Zamburak* is derived from *Zambur,* a bee or wasp, with a diminutive added, and thus means 'a little wasp', probably in allusion to its sound when fired, or its power of stinging or wounding. *Shahin* literally "falcon", seems a later name for the same thing; a name which was brought into India by Nadir Shah.' Irvine, *The Army of the Indian Moghuls,* pp. 135-36.

Tandel—'Malayal. *Tandal.* Telugu, *Tandelu.* The head or commander of a body of men; but in ordinary specific application a native petty officer of lascars, whether on board ship (boatswain) or in the ordinance department, and sometimes the head of a gang of labourers on public works.' *Hobson Jobson,* p. 923.

Tindal—See *Tandel.*

Varat—Assignments either on a person or on a treasury.

Zamburak—See *Shutarnal.*

Ziyafat—Literally means an invitation or a dinner, hence an *abwab* levied to meet the expenses of a dinner; an entertainment or dinner-tax.

Index